W9-CHC-342

PREHISTORY

The World of Early Man

PREHISTORY

The World of Early Man

Edited by Jean Guilaine
Translated by Stephen Bunson

Facts On File®
New York · Oxford

Prehistory: The World of Early Man

Copyright © 1986 by Librairie Larousse
English translation copyright © 1991 by Facts On File

Facts On File, Inc.   Facts On File Limited
460 Park Avenue South   Collins Street
New York NY 10016   Oxford OX4 1XJ
USA   United Kingdom

Library of Congress Cataloging-in-Publication Data

Préhistoire. English.
    Prehistory: the world of early man / edited by Jean Guilaine.
        p.   cm.
    Translation of: La Préhistoire.
    Includes bibliographical references and index.
    ISBN 0-8160-2432-4
    1. Man, Prehistoric. 2. Anthropology, Prehistoric.   I. Guilaine,
Jean. II. Title.
GN740.P7213 1991
930.1—dc20   90-22931

A British CIP catalogue record for this book is available from the British Library.

Cartography by Michèle Bézille
Text design by Jacqueline Pajovesh, Pierre Aristide, Dominique Sablons
Jacket design by Catherine Hyman
Composition by Facts On File, Inc.
Manufactured by Mandarin Offset
Printed in Hong Kong

10 9 8 7 6 5 4 3 2 1

This book is printed on acid-free paper.

Contents

Note

The chronologies proposed in this work are generally those furnished by the processes of absolute dating, more precisely by radiocarbon dating. The dates obtained by this last method are called "conventional," which means that they followed the carbon 14 calendar, which for certain eras does not correspond to that of calendar years. The refinement of ^{14}C dates in calendar years (or "calibration") by the use of dendrochronological correction is only possible in the present state of research to the last eight millennia. The real dates are about a century older for the first millennium B.C., 500 years toward 2000 B.C., 700 to 850 years for the period dated to the fifth millennium, etc. The discrepancy has a tendency to increase for more distant eras.

In order to avoid repetition in this work, for periods beyond 6000 B.C., two dating systems are used in the conventional chronology: B.C. and B.P. The reader,
however, should know that from the sixth millennium B.C. forward it is possible to obtain a more precise date and to establish a chronology based on calendar years that more accurately reflects the duration of civilization (especially valuable for the second or third European millennia). Thus, one must never lose sight of the fact that there is a risk of error in comparing ^{14}C dates and historic dates for events for which an authentic absolute chronological order based on texts is available.

ABBREVIATIONS:
B.C.: *Before Christ (radiocarbon calendar)*
B.P.: *Before Present (before 1950)*

PREFACE

Prehistory fascinates us, but to what can we attribute our infatuation? International symposia, museum exhibitions and articles about prehistoric archaelogy in the general media contribute; the recent success of J. J. Annaud's film *Quest for Fire* and the novels of Jean Auel bear witness to this interest. The general reader, however, often has difficulty mastering the prehistoric chronology. The very immensity of the span of prehistoric times—about 3 million years—is much more disconcerting than the 2,000 years of European history. Yet the images of humanity emerging from the animal world, the true art of the deer hunters and the imposing megalithic tombs cast a shadow into our own times even if they and their milieu are sometimes interpreted narrowly. Nevertheless, escape and wonder is to be found in their contemplation.

For those who wish to go beyond these vague impressions, this work can bring great illumination. Written exclusively by specialists engaged in modern research, it documents two fronts: that of the objectives of and approaches to study of the past and what we have learned by employing them.

First, objectives and approaches. What are the fields of research in prehistory and on what aspects of the first civilizations can this discipline enlighten us? One can measure the scope of the prehistorian's ambitions, shared by sister disciplines, which frame the research and, on occasion, guide it: Humanity and its cultural traditions, its tools, its domestic order, its economic, social and religious behavior, the world of the dead, the climate, soil, geography—in brief, all the cultural and ecological factors that marked the steps of human progress. Everything that can aid in the most complete reconstruction of a material or biological past is of concern to the prehistorian.

These areas defined, the goal here is not a book on methodology. Some choices being essential, two areas are emphasized: absolute dating and experimentation. Dating methods, always in the process of being refined, remain the most revolutionary tools that researchers possess. They have allowed a greater precision to replace subjective judgment. Experimental archaeology, for its part, allows for a more intimate study of prehistory. To cut flint, to model earth or to rebuild the farms of the first agriculturalists, sharpens our interest. It allows us to reaccomplish the deeds of an already distant world, to understand more profoundly its constraints and motives.

As for what we have learned, prehistory has been far too long conceived of in a linear and Eurocentric manner. This book opposes this view, and its authors consider the questions of prehistory on a global scale. There is not a single prehistory but many prehistories, diverse in their origins, the physical environments in which they developed and in the variety of their expression, totally disharmonious in their rhythms, in their progress and even in their decline, when a means of communication—writing—blurs their differences. Our quest for a better chronological approach allowed us to position these prehistories more accurately in their respective temporal fields and conveys better understanding of their differences. These times, more fully grasped, become representative of the diversity of human cultures. The authors who here discuŝs the richness of this experience prove how much this profusion of past experiments is irreducible to a single unifying thread.

It was necessary to limit our view, always a difficult task, to that which concerns the later stages of prehistory. Regarding the Old World, best represented are the problems linked to the origins of metallurgy. Europe of the Middle Ages shares a similarly rich history. In Asia, the essential stage that led to the implementation of writing and the rise of cities seemed to merit substantial development. From Africa one has retained, aside from the Nile and the Maghreb, the long sweep of eras and prehistoric manifestations, the Iron Age, in particular. The central and southern areas of the American continent are surveyed until the first agricultural developments and the evolutionary phase of religious architecture. It is by design that the pre-Colombian populations, complex societies with elaborate structures, well covered in other works, have not been treated here. By contrast, the long duration of the hunting economy in a large part of North America represents significant development over the earlier cultures. The same desire to represent the recent prehistory in Oceania has prevailed. Here, as elsewhere, the attempt at European hegemony during the era of the great discoverers, 300 to 400 years ago, define the upper limits.

To the reader, discover now the multiple facets of this long history of humanity, begun more than 3 million years ago, ending just before yesterday.

Jean Guilaine

CHAPTER ONE

Jean Guilaine

PREHISTORY: A CHANGING SCIENCE

Solutré.
Early research in the field of prehistory essentially sought the collection of lithic and organic materials. There was little note taken of stratigraphy, the accumulation of deposits, layer by layer over time. Generally attacked with pick or shovel, under the direction of a scholar or a foreman, the sites were often excavated—as seen here—in trenches. The volume of earth excavated was enormous compared to the number of observations made. Ph. J. Campier.

Prehistory is generally defined as the study of the development of the first human societies from the appearance of mankind to the invention and spread of writing. It is defined as both a "science" and a period—the most remote—in the history of mankind. The methodology of the discipline combines research in the field, including the excavation and/or search for the material to be studied, with its typological or statistical classification and with naturalist or physico-chemical analyses that have become increasingly common. In addition, many interpretations are made about economic, social and religious behavior. In terms of dating and chronology, the very definition of prehistory must inevitably be flexible, adapting to the circumstances and geographical area under consideration.

Definitions and Limitations

Prehistory begins in Africa where the most ancient remains of hominids have been found (some 3 to 4 million years for the Australopithecs and perhaps more for the *Aus-tralopithecus afarensis*) as well as the oldest known tools. In relation to the other areas of the world, prehistory ends relatively early in certain regions of Africa (in Egypt, for example, where hieroglyphic writing appears around 3000 B.C.), nevertheless many African populations have remained in a prehistoric state (without writing and characterized by an oral tradition) until relatively recently, despite Roman, Moslem and European colonization. Several groups of hunter-gatherers that remained in the Kalahari Desert are now undergoing the process of acculturation (the adaptation to newly introduced culture). The appearance of prehistoric man in Asia and in Europe took place between 2 million and 700,000 years ago in the southern half, while the northern regions, which were colder and less inviting, were not populated until later. On these continents, the appearance of writing, which marks the end of prehistoric times, varied greatly: as early as 3300 B.C. Mesopotamia enters history; writing (undeciphered) is present in the Indus Valley as early as the third millennium; in China and in the Aegean, writing appears in the second millennium; in Italy around 800 B.C.; in Gaul, in the course of the last centuries before Christ; and after the year A.D. 1000 in the northern regions of Europe.

9

Humankind is believed to have made a later appearance in the Americas, some 30,000 years ago, perhaps less, in parts of North America, while recent research indicates the presence of humans in Brazil around the same period. No doubt these estimates will someday be revised to an earlier date. On this continent, the end of prehistoric times can be correlated with the European explorations: the discovery of North America by the Vikings around A.D. 1000, the Hispanic conquests beginning at the end of the 15th century. However, the emergence in Mesoamerica of evolved cultures, possessing a system of hieroglyphic writing as early as the first millennium B.C., and the political and social structures of pre-Colombian civilizations may also be viewed as bridges to history.

Oceania, too, figures among the recently populated regions—humans have been present in Australia and New Guinea for approximately 40,000 years. Greater Australia (which includes New Guinea and Tasmania), however, may have been populated as early as 50,000 years ago, while remnants found in the islands of eastern Polynesia date only from the first centuries of the Christian era. New Zealand appears to have become populated around A.D. 800. The European intrusions of the 17th and 18th centuries put an end to a prehistory in full flower, which, to some extent, still survives among several marginal populations.

The examples above demonstrate the chronological disparity from one continent to another or even within the same continent. Add to this the fact that civilizations developed in varying ecological environments, which conditioned their ways of life and that cultural expansions are duplicated in various regions and at various times, and the complexity and ambiguity of the term *prehistory* comes to light. To avoid confusion, it is perhaps wiser to speak of *prehistories*.

Despite these limitations, it is possible to outline in very general terms certain basic stages that mark the development of prehistoric human societies. These stages, however, are not unilinear. For hunter-gatherers, the carving of archaic tools came first (as in Hadar in Ethiopia, where some artifacts are about 2.5 million years old), followed by the mastery of fire by the *Pithecanthropus* (*Homo erectus*), the appearance of the first sculptures in the Mousterian civilizations (traditionally associated with Neandertal man in the early Fourth [Würm] Glacial Period, c. 40,000 B.C.) and finally the beginnings of an artistic flowing in Europe of 30,000 years ago.

Humanity next reached the stage of food production with the domestication of plants and animals. Simultaneously, various cultures adapted to the potential of specific ecological areas in the Near and Middle East, in New Guinea, in Africa, China, Mexico and the Andes. The specialization of individuals, the emergence of social units, the rise of political powers within communities organized into a hierarchy ultimately laid the foundation for urbanization, and, secondarily, for the advent of writing: in Sumer (in modern southern Iraq) starting in 4000 B.C.; in the Indus Valley, around 3000 B.C.; in China and in the Aegean, starting in 2000 B.C.; and in the Mexican lowlands in the first millennium B.C. These societies may have trod parallel paths of development, although the inevitable chronological gaps cannot be ignored.

Another ambiguous concept is that of *protohistory*, meaning the existence of populations (ignorant of writing) but about which authors belonging to other cultures have left written texts. The information on these populations is thus determined by outside sources, from different cultures. Pre-

Roman Gaul, described by the Greeks or the Romans, is a good example. Some researchers confer a wider meaning on the term *protohistory*; in their understanding, this period begins with the first civilizations practicing metallurgy. Others give an even wider definition, including within its perimeters any culture with the knowledge of ceramics or pottery making. Following this last definition, prehistory becomes limited to the study of hunter-gatherer peoples.

Geological Perspective, Classifications and Typology: Time and Industries

Prehistory is a young science: It emerged in Western Europe in the 19th century, when the accumulation of data about the existence of prehistoric peoples, the contemporaries of animal and plant species that had vanished, put an end to the traditional teachings based on the biblical theory of the great flood. The breakthroughs of this science are attributable to the quality of observations recorded by the first researchers in France, England and Belgium, those who worked in the rock strata that had accumulated over time in buried sites and in the open air. The names of Boucher de

Perthes (1788–1868) and Edouard Lartet (1801–1871) remain linked to this activity concerning the recognition of fossil man. Once this was achieved, the succession of prehistoric cultures was established by determining the tools characteristic of each period and by associating them with human remains and contemporary fauna, while further exploring their climatic environment. Such classification began around the middle of the 19th century in Europe.

As early as 1865, the British naturalist John Lubbock (1834–1913) distinguished the Paleolithic (Old Stone Age), or the age of flaked stone and now extinct animal species, and the Neolithic (New Stone Age), or the age of polished stone and of current fauna. These classifications were based primarily on the methods used in the science of geology (concerning the origin and formations of the Earth), as well as human and animal paleontology (concerning animal fossils and ancient life forms). The deciphering of stratigraphies (the study of rock strata or layers, especially as to their distribution, deposition and chronological succession) and the analysis of deposits enabled researchers to trace the evolution of the first civilizations, as they do today. At the same time, the typological study (classification) of the stone and bone industries (manufacturing or creative processes) and the more recent phases involving metals, allowed for each recognized culture to establish its identity and its distinctive characteristics through the variety of its artifacts. Thus may be explained the series of classifica-

tions accredited to the French researchers, Gabriel de Mortillet (1821–1898), Abbé Breuil (1877–1961) and especially Denis Peyrony (1869–1954), who devised for Western Europe a chronological framework based on tools from the end of the 19th to the beginning of the 20th centuries.

Research then began to diversify its approaches: Morphology (the study of the anatomy of plants and animals) and technical typology (classification), in selecting precise descriptive criteria, took a decisive step when, in the 1950s, François Bordes (1919–1981) began to use elementary statistics. Standard lists, adapted to the regions and cultures considered, made it possible to compare series of industries in a more reliable manner, in particular, through the use of cumulative curves. In its attempt to take into account all of the information, the so-called analytic typology dismissed no characteristic, such as materials used, the flaking processes, modeling, morphology or measurements, in order to better determine the interaction between these various elements. Today the use of computers enables automatic formal classifications from which subjectivity is, in theory, virtually eliminated.

Classifications based on a functional perspective (the purpose of a tool) present serious drawbacks: the de facto ignorance of the function of the pieces and the possibility of multiple applications. Nevertheless, this field has made remarkable progress, thanks initially to extensive experimental research, such as that of the Russian, S. A. Semenov, and

(Left) **Examples of stratigraphy:** *the shelter of Font Juvenal (Aude, France). Deposits 20 feet (6 meters) deep have been accumulated under the canopy during the Neolithic, protohistoric and historic eras. From the fifth millennium until the present, the Neolithic strata total 16 feet (5 meters). One such sedimentation, which records numerous data, shows in more detail the mutations of the environment (floral, faunal) under the effect of natural evolution or human influence. Ph. J. Guilaine.*

(Right) In recent years, the study of prehistoric deposits has been supplemented with research on the uses of artifacts discovered. Microscopic examination detects traces of wear, and thus the active role of the pieces and also, perhaps, the worked material. Experimental archaeology, which recreates the techniques of prehistoric cultures, has provided much information. Here, the effect of working deer horn with a flint has been magnified 100 times. Ph. S. Beyries.

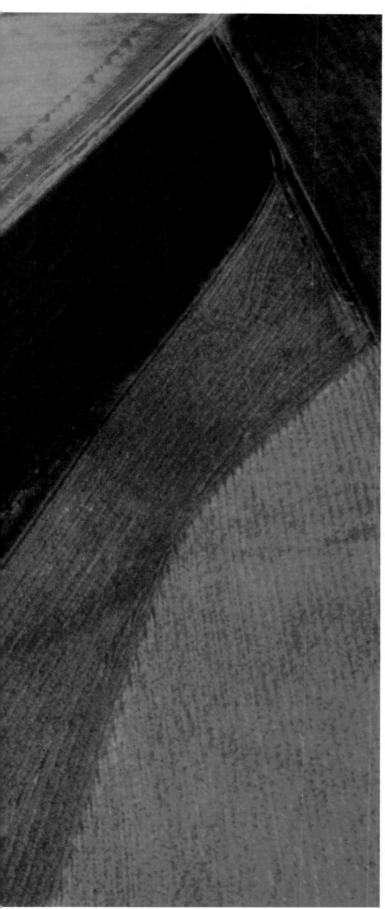

more recently through the microscopic analysis of the traces of wear (evidence of use). Research of this last kind, which is currently very popular, requires tools that have undergone little alteration since their abandonment. It allows for a better approach in determining the use—or indeed the successive functions—of tools (for scraping or sawing) and goes so far as to identify the materials treated (hides, meats, barks, plants, etc.). By better isolating these functions, this method casts some doubts on the all-too-rigid typological approaches. The experimental recourse to the techniques of stone flaking (the process of breaking large stones into smaller pieces) makes it possible not only to determine the successive movements of the artisan but also gives a clearer sense of the life of the tool, from the finding of the flint nodule to its chipping, its shaping, its rejuvenation (to improve edges), sometimes called for by its various functions, and its abandonment.

The Ethnological View

Stratigraphies and typologies stress the importance of the passage of time and the evolution of tools. Ethnology (the study of racial or ethnic groups) has considerably widened the field of prehistoric research by paying close attention to individual sites. It is above all in the field that this development has taken place, due to improved methodology. The first surveying—sometimes supplemented by preliminary approaches, such as cartographic analyses, aerial archaeology, remote detection (use of equipment to establish the presence of a potential site or to map out a known site without disturbing the soil), geophysical methods (study of the Earth as the product of complex physico-chemical forces acting upon it, especially with reference to less accessible regions)—followed by excavations, has contributed to the spectacular progress made in the study of settlements in recent years. The horizontal excavation of settlement sites coupled with the meticulous recording of all of the artifacts abandoned by humans provide the researcher with a more complete representation of domestic spaces. In this search, no artifact is considered to be of secondary importance—obvious structures exist, having been constructed (dwellings, walls, stone piles, wedgings), or dug out (holes for posts, fire ditches, silos, clay extraction sites); similarly, layers of objects or waste (mineral, vegetal or animal scraps, sometimes minute in size) provide information regarding not only craft or refuse sites but also the behavior that resulted in such a dispersal. Finally, chemical analysis has enabled researchers to determine the function of areas that appeared to be unoccupied or unused—areas such as beds (in which waste or objects have been carelessly thrown about) or areas of activity that may have left no visible material evidence. These various observations, both direct and secondary, allow for a better understanding of behavior within family units: highlighting areas for activity, rest, warmth, storage and refuse. This vision cannot remain static, however, to enable one to

For many years aerial photography has been a valuable aid in the location of certain prehistoric and protohistoric sites. These photographs, which highlight the differences in color or density of vegetation, cannot always be clearly interpreted. The use of infra-red photography can help make buried structures appear more clearly. Here, the plan of a Gallic farm at Bray-les-Mareuil (France), is highlighted by the process. Ph. R. Agache.

grasp the relationships between each area. More than the simple occupation of space is involved, actual *existence*, with the various aspects that accompany it, comes to light through this kind of excavation.

On a larger scale, a similar perspective is used in the analysis of settlements viewed in their entirety: the location, protective systems (such as ditches or ramparts), the general layout of buildings, the floor plans of huts or cabins. Only extensive research, which is fortunately becoming widespread, makes it possible to understand the organization or function of the various units of a settlement.

The use of ethnological analogy to living peoples is yet another tool in the attempt to understand better the behavior of past societies. It must be done with care, and there was a time when the excessive use of comparative ethnology—where parallels were drawn that spanned many regions and multiple eras—resulted in the presentation of opinion as fact, which was justly criticized. Today, however, ethnology is once again welcomed by prehistorians, to such a degree that "ethnoarchaeology" has become a promising field of study. Sometimes the prehistorian turns ethnologist when setting out to observe contemporary populations that may provide answers to his questions about the past. Here again, the comparisons may focus on crude facts or materials, such as tools or methods of construction, but may also focus on more complex behaviors, such as economic organization, social relationships or symbols, all of which can be difficult to interpret and transpose reliably. This is why the reconstructions proposed by prehistorians—called "models"—based on ethnological hypotheses, must be rigorously tested whenever possible by experimentation and multiple physical and chemical analyses (archeometry). Beyond a certain threshold of abstraction, uncertainties increase. In the pursuit of veracity, the researcher must constantly employ exacting scientific criteria.

The Environmental Approach

It would be a senseless undertaking to attempt to understand the hunter-gatherer without examining the characteristics of his territory or the first agriculturalists without considering the soil that they cultivated. Indeed, the reconstruction of the landscape is essential, not only to depict human beings in their environment, but also to better grasp

The floor of an ancient Neolithic site with incised pottery (fifth millennium) in Torre Sabea (Gallipoli), southeastern Italy. Horizontal removals allow better evaluation of the plan used by the prehistorics. Here one notes a concentration of hearths, pits encircled and filled with pebbles and limestone blocks, sometimes warmed or cracked by contact with fire. Ph. J. Guilaine.

their economic activities, such as hunting, fishing, food gathering and, in later eras, domestic animal rearing and agriculture. This is why the naturalistic approach has constituted from the beginning a necessary support of prehistoric research.

Today, as a result of intensive specialization, a number of disciplines are involved in any attempt to analyze a vanished community in its natural surroundings. These various analyses, once considered of secondary value, are now viewed as important instruments in working toward a common interdisciplinary goal. A brief description of some of these current approaches follows.

Geological and climatic phenomena greatly conditioned the lives of humans in the past. Over time, and according to geographic locations, climates underwent considerable changes. During cold periods, for example, European glaciers extended well beyond their present limits, and streams and rivers, active agents of erosion, left abundant alluvial deposits every spring; levels of the oceans and seas dropped; coastlines modified; and winds and snow storms decimated the vegetation. Conversely, any rise in temperature brought about a more temperate climate, causing part of the ice sheets to melt, raising sea levels and enabling, with the return of humidity, the formation of river beds, the reconstitution of forests and the regulation of slope deposits. The chronology of geological processes, both general and regional, makes possible the determination of the evolutionary aspects of these natural phenomena in time, and thus provides a better

Example of extensive excavation: *Cuiry-les-Chaudardes (Aisne, France). A preliminary clearing. It is necessary to work in vast areas to understand the general layout of archaeological sites, including the settlement, its borders, its general organization and the arrangement of internal structures. Such extensive digs as shown here require the careful removal of layers of soil, long covered over, to highlight the structure beneath, which had remained undisturbed by human or natural erosion. Ph. A Coudart - U.R.A. 12 C.N.R.S.*

understanding of their effect upon human behavior. Any modification of the natural environment left traces in the form of deposits (periglacial, fluvial, lacustral, desert or karstic), the study of which falls mainly within the scope of the geologist but cannot be ignored by the prehistorian. The same applies to the variations of sea levels, to the rise and fall of continents and to volcanic or seismic phenomena contemporary with vanished peoples.

On a more specific level, the analysis of the sediments of a particular prehistoric site provides the researcher with information regarding climatic and landscape variations, as well as human activities in the local environments. Several kinds of analyses are currently being conducted using this approach, including the morphoscopy (how an organism or one of its parts changes in development) and gelifraction of rocks (how rocks fracture under extreme pressure or cold), the granulometry of rough elements of clay or sandy silt and microscopic analyses (morphology, mineralogy, the study of phytoliths), etc. Geochemical approaches are used to determine behavior or the arrangement of activities on a site, which are otherwise unidentifiable through direct observation. The isotopic composition of carbonates supplies information about paleotemperatures and paleosalinity.

Palynology, the science that identifies pollens and spores emitted into the atmosphere each year by plants, allows the reconstitution of a vanished landscape. It is henceforth combined with the study of charcoal burned by prehistoric man (anthracology) and the study of the grains and plants gathered or cultivated (paleocarpology). The study of fauna once only concerned itself with the determination of species, in order to discern ecological (regarding the environment in which such species existed) and paleoethnographic (regarding hunting or animal-rearing behavior) data. Here, too, approaches have become considerably diversified; highlighting the evolution of the morphological aspects of animals, the quantification of species, slaughtering curves and population structures, meat diet and weight, hunting and butchering techniques, not to mention evident examples of the stocks under study and their metamorphoses from their deaths to fossilization (taphonomy). Continental or marine malecology (the study of mollusks), ichthyology (the study of fish) and the analysis of microfauna (rodents, amphibians, birds), all of which were ignored for a long time, now contribute vital indications concerning the evolution of the species and the effect of humans on the environment. This brief survey already conveys the complexity of research and its manifold facets. Let us emphasize again that although much of the research is conducted in laboratories, its roots are in the field, through the gathering of multiple samples by specialists. These samples often guide or redirect the prehistorian's research, depending upon the problems that they present.

Relative and Absolute Chronologies

Within the laboratory itself, one of the objectives of the researcher has always been the dating of the material evi-

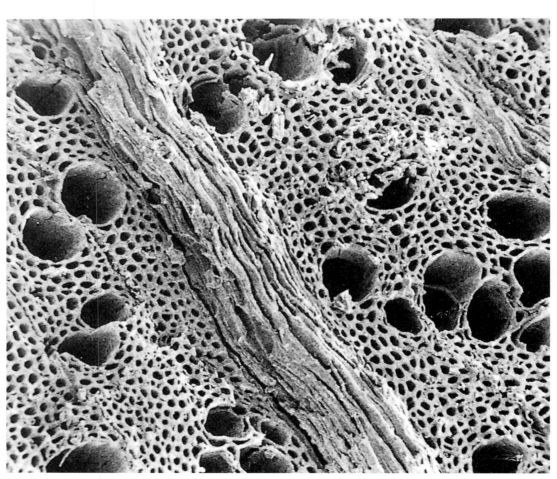

Information about now vanished countryside can be gained through the sciences of polynology (the study of fossil pollen) and anthracology (the study of carbon, or coal). Traces of burned wood, found in archaeological levels or in heating structures, are examined with electron scanning microscopes and magnified many times to determine the structure and species of the sample. Shown here is a detail of a beech taxon from the Copper Age. Ph. J.-L. Vernet U.S.T.L. Montpellier.

dence gathered, assigning such evidence to an approximate or, if possible, to a precise age. However, the only tools available to establish the succession of various civilizations for a long time were stratigraphies including reference pieces, called "guide fossils," and the comparison between the various homogeneous manufacturing (industrial) groups. Approximate or relative scales were thus developed locally. The problem then arose concerning the general view of the phenomena, which required the linking of the various regional or even national systems—a difficult endeavor. Debates took place between the advocates of short, compressed chronologies, and those of longer, (extended) chronologies. General guidelines were devised using selected comparative remains (sometimes considered trade items), which served to place the various archaeological assemblages under consideration in a definite time span, one by one. The cornerstone of this process consisted of a few reference sites or stratigraphies. Although the process did lead to the development of satisfactory systems, it sometimes generated flawed chronologies, which, because they were for a long time considered unalterable, were all the more difficult to eradicate.

In Europe, for example, the traditional theory equated in time the first levels of the city of Troy in Asia Minor and the ancient bronze of the Aegean and the Chalcolithic (Copper Age) horizon of the Balkans. As a result, a general compression of all of the European Neolithic (New Stone Age) and Chalcolithic cultures ensued. Usually, high (or extended) chronologies could not be attributed to Europe, which was considered dependent upon Southeast Asia and on the inventions of the Neolithic Period, because any innovation was automatically linked to its Oriental antecedent.

Absolute chronologies, which have steadily progressed since their appearance in the 1950s, have allowed prehistori-

Pollen diagram.

The expression "Before Present (B.P.)" designates a method of dating, where B.P. refers to a particular date, A.D. 1950.

The expressions AP and NAP designate the relationship tree/herbaceous to explain the whole of the vegetal world.

AP: Arboreal pollen grain/trees;

NAP: Nonarboreal pollen grain/trees. Drawing after Chantal Leroyer.

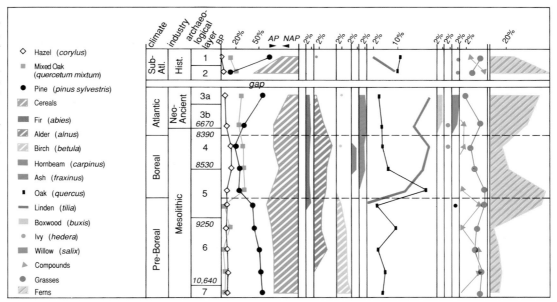

The Jean Cros Shelter (village of Labastide-en-Val, Aude, France) houses an underground chamber of the Corbières massif, frequented during the Old Neolithic Period (fifth millennium). Cachement site analysis, fine-tuned by C. Vita-Finzi and L. Miggs, seeks to determine the natural environment that the prehistoric peoples were able to exploit around their habitats, including possible economic bases (exploitable materials, flora, fauna, soil capacities, etc.). It is thought that hunter-gatherers rarely took advantage of territories more than 10 hours (some 6 miles/10 kilometers) from their base camps in flat terrain. Agriculturalists normally did not exploit a field situated more than one hour (less than one mile/kilometer) away. In the example chosen below, an environment of ordinary mountains, rough and refractory, was used in the fifth millennium for hunting and the breeding of ovicaprins. Design after J. Guilane and D. Geddes.

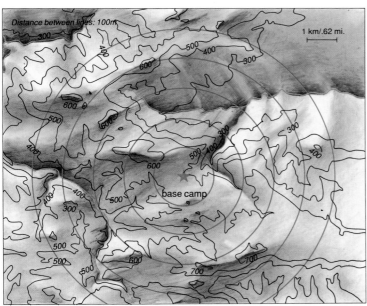

Jean Cros Shelter (Aude, France)

ans to eliminate some of these restrictions and to rethink the time frames involved more realistically and precisely. These new approaches further liberated the researchers, who had previously tended to favor short chronologies (compressed time frames) in their estimate of the duration of a particular phenomena, for fear of error. The use of radiocarbon, potassium-argon and thermoluminescence for dating will be examined in greater detail later, thus we merely mention here some of the breakthroughs that have resulted from them. First, the age of humankind, whose earliest artifacts (at Hadar and Omo, in Ethiopia) are believed to be between 2.3 million and 2.6 million years old; next, a better idea of the early populating of distant lands (in Australia, America), although in this particular area everything must be considered only temporary; also, the true age of the settlement processes, which were probably under way in several areas of the world as early as the recent Pleistocene epoch, has been refined.

Considering the sum of knowledge accumulated by mankind (as demonstrated by intensive gathering processes, adaptation to seasonal or permanent resources, selective hunting, etc.), the relationship of humans to the environment was such that it ultimately rendered irreversible the transition to manufacturing or production. Absolute dating methods (and the quality of both field and laboratory research) demonstrated that the Neolithic "revolution" never took place and that the concept must be replaced by that of a lengthy conditioning of the environment by man, a gradual evolution towards domestication, happening independently at various points of the globe. Absolute dating has also taught the futility of such equations as pottery = agriculture, or the essential role of the Epipaleolithic societies in the march toward a new economic system. Still more is owed, however, to radiometric dating. By demonstrating the ancient roots of many cultures, by not necessarily equating creations of a similar aspect as contemporary, this method freed prehistorians from the yoke of interdependence, pointing toward the multiplicity of the birth of cultures and the burgeoning of inventions and brought to the foreground the numerous facets of mankind's adaptive genius.

populations of virgin lands, although one must still be cautious here. Indeed, images of a one-way progression often cause excessive simplifications, whereas the phenomena often conceal complex situations involving multiple patterns of relationships. However, when a civilization appears in a land already occupied, the exact role of the human substratum must be thoroughly examined. In fact, The stronger the breaks with the earlier substratum, the more passionate the discussions concerning the establishment of the new cultural phase. We need only mention the abundant literature devoted to subjects as varied as the transition of Middle Paleolithic to the Upper Paleolithic, the appearance of the Solutrean (in central France), the Yangshao Neolithic or the cultures using coiled or bell-shaped pottery. The diffusion explanation used in these cases had the advantage of offering an easy alternative, a means of avoiding the problem by assuming that a foreign source is evident; experience demonstrates that the assumed culture of origin is normally quite different from its offspring cultures, which sends the prehistorian back to the beginnings again.

Prehistory has not completely eradicated the old demons of diffusion. A greater number of researchers, however, refuse the temptation of using migratory or other explanations, based on evidence, excessively. In itself, the investigation of local processes of acceleration or adaptive phenomena within a given geographical area implies an analysis of such complexity that it constitutes an experimental field with vast opportunities. In this field, the study of the environment and multiple physico-chemical analyses can provide enlightening data for the determination of the role of internal dynamics, trends or events taking place within the region itself. The more facts are accumulated, the more mutation phenomena appear as the combined result of complex factors (such as production, exchanges, social relationships, etc.), the interaction of which stimulates one another. Following a stage of explanatory generalizing, prehistorians, now of more humble ambitions, have entered a period in which they are fully aware that massive in-depth research must be finished before they can attempt to outline the logistics of human development.

Diffusion vs. Autochthonism: Cultural Change

Prehistory has not been spared the eternal debate about the formation of civilizations. For all periods of human history, sociologists, philosophers and archaeologists speculate about the origins of given cultures: Were these introduced essentially from an external source or are they autochthonous—considered the product of a local dynamic? It could be argued that the problem is an artificial one, inasmuch as all creations are frequently the product of an accumulation of factors, both indigenous and borrowed. Furthermore, the position of the archaeologist is often one in which he can only describe certain characteristics, without being able to explain the interactions that permitted their appearance. Nevertheless, whether stated overtly or not, mechanisms for explanation are present, as a backdrop to the prehistorian's thinking. Thus, for a long time, migration phenomena were believed to involve the consistent or diluted movements of populations over both long and short distances, accounting for the appearance of new cultures. Admittedly, this explanation remains plausible in the case of the

Economic Perspectives

A site is excavated, its layout examined and materials that are extracted from it are dated. What happens then? Is it possible to go further in the study of human behavior? Here, too, prehistory answers in the affirmative. For the community being considered, regardless of its size, is never independent of the environment upon which it acts or from the social milieu of the surrounding region. The study of the production, movement and preservation of goods is also the concern of the archaeologist. Strategies pertaining to the exploitation of the environment and survival, within a given area, are sometimes carefully analyzed to determine seasonal movements linked to hunting and gathering (for example, in the preagricultural phases of Tehuacan in Mexico), the appearance of sedentary life in a hunting environment (as in the case of the Natufians of Palestine in the tenth millennium and perhaps of some of the Mousterians of Aquitaine), the possibility of cyclical habitats in connection with agriculture on burned ground (as in Bylany in Czechoslovakia), the appearance of irrigation for horticulture (as in the swamp of Kuk in New Guinea) or agriculture (as in Bronze Age Mesopotamia).

The availability of materials necessary for the manufacture of tools or objects provides information regarding the dependency of a group on a mastered territory or in relation to neighboring or distant communities that supplied imported materials or finished pieces. Petrographic analyses, infrared spectography, thermoluminescence, X-ray fluorescence and neutron activation, which can lead to identification of trace elements, make it possible to identify the origin of artifacts while also providing information regarding the use of materials, the preparation of tools, peddling, the interpenetration and flexibility of "markets" and the concepts of gifts and exchange. Some applications of this kind of research include the demonstration of the antiquity of navigation in the eastern Mediterranean through the propagation on the continent of obsidian from Milo as early as the 12th millennium, the export in the Neolithic of Aegean spondyles (mussels) throughout the Balkan and Danubian area and the use of hard Alpine or Armorican rocks in the manufacture of polished axes or ceremonial pieces.

The study of survival strategies resulted in a more extensive analysis of the space dominated or endured by human beings. The territory of the groups of hunter-gatherers, the land of prehistoric agriculturalists, in other words the maximum range of action by communities, are presently the subject of greater study concerning the potential of soils and kinds of vegetation, fauna and its behavior and the implantation of a habitat in relation to various biotopes (limited ecological regions). The questions that prehistorians ask of animal and plant documentation (the recovery methods of such evidence having been greatly improved by the method of flotation sifting) have led to a history of food and of the techniques used to acquire it. Assuredly, economic perspectives, in order to be credible, must be supported by precise statistical studies. Thus, this kind of research has had a positive effect on excavation methods by requiring that samples be gathered in large quantities and be more reliable.

These approaches, finally, have made possible the better understanding of the various concepts of domestication. Indeed, they have often shown the arbitrariness of the supposed break between the Paleolithic and the Neolithic cultures, now replaced by the concept of a gradual evolution. Thus a clearer view of the first attempts at animal rearing and agriculture has emerged and, particularly concerning the latter, has underscored the dynamic role of several regions in the conquest of cultivated plants: wheat and barley in Southeast Asia, corn in Mesoamerica and the Andes and millet in Africa.

Social and Ideological Factors

Is prehistory of necessity destined to consider only material vestiges and their biological environment? This assumption overlooks the fact that as a science belonging to the humanities, prehistory must also encompass the aim of determining social and ideological behaviors. The "sociological" dimension of prehistory, first claimed by the British archaeologist Vere Gordon Childe (1892–1957), has since expanded greatly, judging by the abundant literature in "social" archaeology (English language for the most part) published in recent years. Compared to the archaeologist of the historical period, who is able to cross check his information with that found in contemporary texts, the prehistorian encounters more difficulty verifying his hypotheses. Therefore,

although probing the workings of societies and their laws is fascinating, this field remains speculative and its limits must be kept in mind. Nevertheless, the meticulous excavation of habitats can yield data regarding the function of certain buildings, the specialization of quarters devoted to a specific craft, the spatialization of activities within family units, sectors allotted to husband, wife or children and, also, where recent periods are concerned, hierarchy, etc. The analysis of necropolises also makes it possible to sketch out a rough outline of social status. In this kind of inquiry, the structure of a tomb and the objects placed there for the deceased are important evidence. Still other information emerges from certain groupings of graves, the recourse to individual or collective burial and the topographical arrangement of the body. These observations, together with the determination of sex and age at the time of death, contribute to the understanding of social relationships: the place of men and women in the community, the division of labor, the role of each individual within the subsistence economy, the influence of certain age groups, the social causes of death (war, illness, poisoning, old age).

This is a difficult field and particularly where questions of social status are concerned, the researcher sometimes remains in the dark. Indeed, apart from the exceptional case where he is confronted with the tombs of important figures, such as the kings of Alaca Hüyük or Mycenae or the Vix "princess," the prehistorian generally deals with anonymous subjects, whose social position is unclear, commoners or dignitaries of lesser importance. The researcher must examine the slightest clue and question the data in his possession relentlessly. Fortunately, anthropologists, who presently lend a hand in the field, no longer limit themselves to morphological or metric classification of bones. Their work is now also guided by a broad approach to vanished societies: the study of funeral rites, of nutrition, of all kinds of illnesses, and, recently, the study of paleoserology (fossilized traces of blood), which may some day make possible the better understanding of population phenomena.

Other information can be gleaned from deposits of both everyday and valuable objects. These constitute a form of capitalization, the accumulation of wealth according to class, which calls for an explanation. Safe storage areas, offerings, voluntary abandonment of goods, the hoards of the powerful in a given region, the burial of the elite in tombs are all examples of such deposits. Tombs, in fact, are the primary sites for the conservation of exceptional objects of value. At the highest level, the prehistorian examines the structure of societies and their evolution in a given period. In this field, neoevolutionist ethnology has made considerable contributions that suggest several stages of development in communities: groups of hunter-gatherers in the Paleolithic; egalitarian tribes in the era of the beginning of agriculture; potentates and small states in the era of the birth of metallurgy; nations of historical times. However, this outline clearly simplifies and standardizes a phenomenon—that of human societies—that tends from the onset toward complexities and variations. Here again, anthropology, by providing evidence of the role of root stock peoples or the presence of inequalities in a community before production processes or industrialization takes place, compels the prehistorian to be cautious in his conclusions.

Mankind also expresses itself through symbols, which the prehistorian studies to further his social inquiry. Generally, art works, figurative or abstract, are the objects closely analyzed. Rock (cave or shelter) paintings and etchings, pictograms, decorations found on ceramics are all considered prewritings, which must be decoded to deepen understanding of the peoples or communities on several levels, both pragmatic and ideological. Such levels include accounting systems, calendars, mythology and magic or religious concepts. From Paleolithic or Neolithic figures to the statues of divinities and heros of the prehistoric period, all works of art may be regarded as the reflection of specific social ideas.

From the preceding pages one may already developed a broader understanding of the multifaceted field of prehistoric research—the subject's immense chronology (at least 3 million years) and the vast geographic areas involved (land masses around the globe, to which must be added the vestiges immersed in oceans, lakes and rivers). Within such a time frame, historical civilizations, limited to a maximum of 2,000 or 3,000 years of existence, often appear as epiphenomena, secondary developments accompanying and resulting from others. Today, however, the methods used by prehistorians are expanding considerably. A new prehistory is taking shape, the methods of which are so diversified that specialization is taking over in research. Emerging fields are the prehistory of technical gestures, the prehistory of landscapes, the prehistory of food, the prehistory of mentalities and rites, the prehistory of illness or disease, etc. In this search, the influence of the physico-chemical and naturalist sciences, supported by the refinement of dating methods, has become considerable. It is possible to imagine that new related disciplines, as yet unknown, will arise from this expansion. The results, which can only be more rigorous and more precise, will allow people of the 21st century to be more familiar with the lifestyles and behavior of their prehistoric ancestors, to whom they may feel more closely related as a result of their knowledge. The global expansion of prehistoric research cannot obstruct the fact, however, that the number of actual excavations remains low in many regions, permitting no generalizations for such areas as yet. In other parts of the world, where research is more advanced, as in Europe, several millennia of cultivation and the intense mechanization of our times have ruined forever the sources of information. There, indeed, lies one of the dramas of the work of the prehistorian, who as he considerably refines his methods measures more acutely the bias of his data and the limits of his knowledge. A prehistorian also knows that laboratory studies are not as good as field samples. Thus the field, starting with excavation, is the mother to theories. In such a science, in which the interdisciplinary character is rapidly evolving, everything first depends upon the reading of the site, a unique phase of the scientific process that cannot be done. Thus the excavator remains, ultimately, the master of the game.

Excavation of a dwelling floor from the end of the Upper Paleolithic: Pincevant, Seine-et-Marne (France). With the help of very fine tools, dental instruments, for example, diggers remove layers of soil, starting from a raised platform a few inches above the archaeological strata. The uncovering of structures, activity areas, layers of debris etc. help us understand the arrangement of domestic space. Ph. R. Burri/Magnum.

DATING METHODS

Part of the preparation of a bank of samples for radiocarbon dating, in the laboratory of the Claude-Bernard University in Lyon. (Photo Lab 14-C U.C.B.)

The detection of radiocarbon radioactivity requires a long chemical preparation of the sample because the levels of radioactivity are very low. On the counter are some of the samples to be dated. The operator purifies carbonic gas, obtained by combustion, that will be transformed into benzine for its measurement in a liquid scintillation counter.

Above all, archaeology is a field science—it is in the layers of the ground that researchers collect the evidence of the past left by our ancestors. However, it is no longer paradoxical to say that archaeology is also a laboratory science. Indeed, while excavating remains, the first act of archaeological research, the analysis of what has been gathered is now done in research laboratories rather than in the field or in the vicinity of the site.

The growing importance of laboratories with various specialties influences the way in which field studies are conducted. Thus, modern excavations are designed and operated to provide laboratories with the most useful samples while, at the same time, requiring a great deal from laboratory specialists. Archaeological excavations are unique in that, unlike geological studies, for example, they irreparably destroy the pattern of objects—yet, in some cases, the pattern is more significant than the objects themselves. Furthermore, the collected material is always gathered in limited quantities and usually can be analyzed only once. Because of the irreversible character of laboratory analyses, a dialogue must be maintained between the archaeologist and the laboratory specialists of the various scientific disciplines working toward archaeological interpretation.

This interdisciplinary dialogue in archaeological research has been further developed by the introduction of more and more sophisticated investigation techniques. Collaboration deepens the value of field research by exploiting to the utmost its possibilities and is also fundamental for the laboratories involved, because it forces researchers to take into account the practical application of their techniques. It is sometimes even the origin of new techniques.

Different Dating Methods

Relative chronology and absolute chronology

As soon as archaeology went beyond the stage of simply collecting objects, one of its essential goals became the establishment of chronologies. Superimposition was the first basic principal of such chronology: *Any object located beneath another antedates the latter; all objects located on the same level are contemporary.* A great deal may be said regarding the practical application of these maxims, which assume, for instance, that nothing has happened to modify the levels since their formation. It is important, however, to note that the goal of the study of relative positions is to pinpoint a relative chronology of the collected items, in other words, to differentiate the time between the moments of their deposit or formation. In order to express the evolution of this time span in numbers, a timing method is required, a means to measure duration within a precise time unit.

Archaeologists and geologists saw that the objects present in the strata had different shapes, markings or colors; they detected evolutionary processes. Consequently, for a long time this made it possible to "date" a site according to the "position" of the samples gathered in a general evolutionary pattern. This dating method, using relative chronology, was the only one available for some time. Essential at the beginning of any study, the method makes it possible to establish the stratigraphy of a site, without which no orderly excavation is possible, and assumes that this evolution is related to time, without further clarifying the relationship. With this method, one can only divide the study of the objects found in a site into approximate "chronological brackets," without determining the length of these brackets or their "absolute" age. (In other words, placing these periods along a fixed time scale and establishing dates for the beginning and the end of each of period.) Before examining the means at our disposal to address this last question, it is necessary to understand the methods used to establish a relative chronology or stratigraphy.

Relative dating methods

Among these methods the first is the study of the general aspect of the sediment: alternation of light or dark layers, of carbonated or noncarbonated levels, of the different size of grains of sediment. These alternations demonstrate variations in the environment and are obviously time-related, although the relationship remains unknown. The thickness

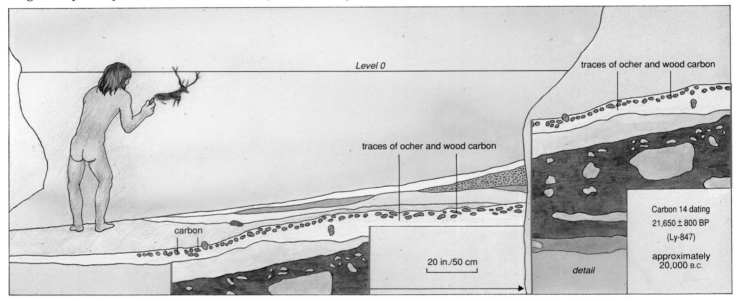

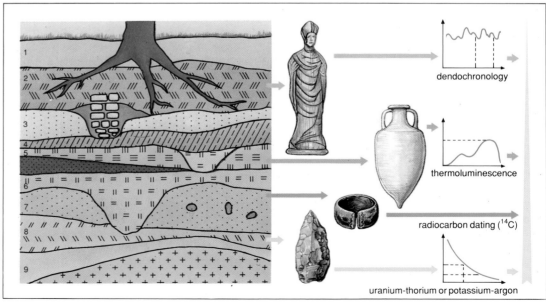

Example of dating an archaeological site:** The Grotto of the Cow. **Choice of dating methods for various eras and sample types.

The evidence of diverse human occupations is accumulated in levels, according to age. Below the superficial layer (1), in layers (2) and (3), wood can be dated by dendrochronology and fragments of brick (T) by paleomagnetism. Below, in layers (4) and (5), pottery is datable by thermoluminescence. In the center (F) and below, at levels (6) and (7), the carbonized elements, bones or charcoal, are analyzed by radiocarbon dating. Finally, the deepest layers (8) and (9) can be dated by uranium-thorium or potassium-argon.

of each layer, a function of the rate at which the sediment was deposited, varies according to many factors and cannot provide precise chronological information. Other than the thickness and texture of layers, local variations of the conditions of deposit can result in modifications of the chemical compositions of the sediments. The percentage of variations of this or that element can be detected through refined analyses. Allowing for some exceptions, these analyses do not help in establishing whether these variations are continuous or regular.

The variations of fauna and flora provide more general indications. These are more easily linked with climatic changes spread out over long time spans, but the same environment, for a given site, can be present several times. Thus, this succession cannot serve as a reference point. It is possible to compare levels of neighboring sites through the study of all of the pollens or gastropod shells present, but this will not allow absolute dating because of the reversible character of fauna-flora evolutions, which are dependent upon the climate. Finally, in order to study the layers of human occupation, one of the principal methods in archaeology is the comparison of industries between them, which vary according to the evolution of techniques. But human progress is essentially discontinuous, and the appearance of this or that cultural clue can only constitute a reference point.

A number of means are available to compare one site with another or the levels between them. Correlations must be established, but the only possible results are what are called "floating" chronologies, approximations, which then must be linked to an absolute age.

Absolute dating methods
All of the dating methods that make it possible to evaluate exactly the age and, thus, the duration of events of archaeol-

ogy have one thing in common: the measured variable is in relation to time and independent of the environment.

Thus the rate of this variation must be known. The variables linked to time are numerous, but for some the relationship is not regularly continuous. Consequently, there are two main clusters of dating methods: those using global or regional fluctuations of phenomena affecting the biosphere (climates or variations in the magnetic field of the Earth, for example) and those using the natural radioactivity of certain elements that constitute organic or mineral matter.

Methods Not Using Radioactivity

The inclination of the axis of the Earth in relation to the sun determines the seasons, which are the function not only of latitude but also of annual variations in solar activity. Furthermore, the flux of cosmic particles varies according to periods and, for a given period, is linked to the magnetic field, which, in turn, fluctuates with time. These variations may be reflected by certain elements present in the archaeological strata: the effect of the climate on the thickness of age-rings in trees and the modification of the terrestrial magnetic field visible in the ferromagnetic parts of certain objects.

Dendrochronology
The growth rate of trees varies with the climate. Each year adds a ring of growth to the trunk, referred to as a "tree-ring," the thickness of which depends upon the humidity and the temperature during that year. This growth is comparable within the same species of trees of a region, in the same year, providing the basis for dendrochronology. The counting of tree-rings gives the number of years a tree

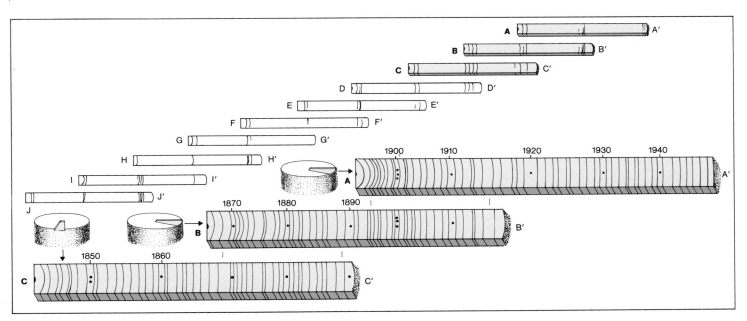

Dating by dendrochronology.

Examining small sections of wood extracted from fossil trunks, one can see that the differences in thickness of growth rings from year to year are well marked and can be compared in sections of wood of identical age, A, B, C (fragments of AA', BB', CC'). One can thus date wood, by successive alignments, to relatively distant periods (sections D to J).

has grown, the successive widths of tree-rings permit the elaboration of variation "profiles" or "sequences," characteristic of a given moment in the history of vegetation. Long sequence curves have been established for some species in certain regions. They present maxima and minima, which serve as reference points. By comparing a curve obtained from wood to be dated to a standard curve, one deduces the age of the tree in question at the moment that it was cut.

In order for the method to be used widely, a large number of standard curves are needed. Furthermore, it is more reliable if the sapwood of the tree has been preserved, which is not always the case. Finally, it is necessary to have a large number of well-preserved tree-rings, which is rare in many samples found at ancient nonimmersed archaeological sites.

Currently, reference profiles for various regions exist only for the historical period, extending no further than 9,000 years into the past. The only long profile that permits dating over several millennia was drawn from Swiss and southern German oak trees used in the dating of lacustrian (lake) archaeological sites of those regions. For the moment, then, it is fair to say that the range of the method is small and geographically limited.

Archaeomagnetism

In contrast with the preceding method, which is sensitive to regional climatic fluctuations, archaeomagnetism is based on the planetary variation of the terrestrial magnetic field, which affects objects uniformly, independent of their location. It is completely defined by three measurements: the inclination (angle between the magnetic meridian plane [magnetic north] and the horizontal plane of the place of measurement), the declination (the angle between true north and magnetic north) and the intensity of the terrestrial magnetic field.

All clay contains a small percentage of iron oxide. At relatively high temperatures, the thermic agitation in the crystal lattice (the arrangement of atoms and ions) allows for the orientation of the ferrous elements, according to the direction of the Earth's magnetic field. For the clay, this results in a magnetization lined up with the local terrestrial magnetic field. In the course of the cooling period, the magnetization remains locked in the acquired direction, whatever the variations subsequent to the baking of the clay may be. To determine magnetic orientation, clay samples for archeomagnetic dating from both fixed structures (hearths, kilns) and, in some cases, from moveable objects (pottery, tiles) can be used.

These fluctuations of the measurements of the terrestrial magnetic field, like those of the climates, are more or less cyclical over time. If, then, these fossil orientations can be measured in well-dated locations, it is possible to establish a sort of year-by-year calendar that is valid for the entire region.

In the present state of the technique, we have good standards for the two or three last millennia in Western Europe, so that edifices made of brick fired in place can be dated to the very year. However, the use of this method still only applies to isolated areas.

Obsidian hydration

Every buried site or object undergoes an alteration that, even for the hardest materials, is greater the longer the submersion. Nevertheless, the measurement of the layer of alteration generally cannot be used as a precise dating method, primarily because of the physico-chemical conditions of the soil, which vary greatly according to deposits.

There is, however, one exception: the alteration of obsidian or, more precisely, its hydration. This rock, which is a volcanic glass, has often been used as a raw material for tools in many regions of the globe. Furthermore, on any breaks or cracks of these obsidian objects, a sort of patina layer forms, which is thicker the older the break. Hydration, the joining of water with the chemical elements of the object, is relatively uniform wherever the site may be, since water is present everywhere in sufficient quantities. A break therefore can conceivably be dated by measuring the thickness of the hydrated layer. It remains only to standardize the method for various types of obsidian. The application of the method is relatively simple and one can obtain dates of several tens of thousands of years with a precision comparable to that of radiocarbon dating. With this technique, the reuse of objects or materials in subsequent periods can also be detected. However, while many sites in America and Oceania were dated in this manner, in Europe the rarity of obsidian objects renders this method less useful.

Methods Using Radioactivity

A few definitions

The structure of the atoms of various elements were studied in the first half of the 20th century. We know that the arrangement of electrons revolving around the nucleus differentiates the elements present in nature and defines their

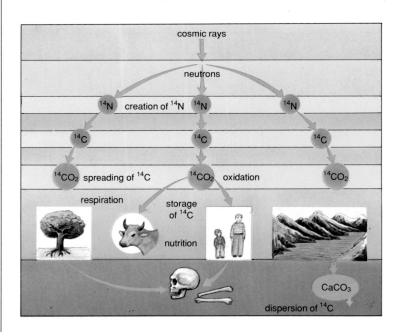

cosmic rays

neutrons

^{14}N creation of ^{14}N ^{14}N ^{14}N

^{14}C ^{14}C ^{14}C

$^{14}CO_2$ spreading of ^{14}C $^{14}CO_2$ oxidation $^{14}CO_2$

respiration   storage of ^{14}C

nutrition

dispersion of ^{14}C

CaCO$_3$

The disintegration of radioactive isotopes.
The original quantities in radioactive isotopes are halved during each time interval corresponding to one period. The limit of detection is gen- *erally 8 to 10 periods. The curve above is approximately 5,500 years, which serves as a base of dating the various prehistoric industries indicated.*

chemical properties. Some elements are composed of atoms with different nuclei, even though the electronic arrangement is the same. These are isotopes; they differ only in the number of neutrons present in their nucleus.

In nature, some unstable nuclei, the internal cohesion of which is weak, undergo violent reorganizations with particle emissions (disintegration). These nuclei are said to be radioactive, and the isotope is called a radioisotope. They turn into other elements, which can be either stable or radioactive. Thus a radioactive decay (sequence) occurs until a stable element is obtained.

The "half-life" characterizes the duration of the transformation of a radioactive nucleus. It is the time required for half of the original quantity of the element to be transformed into a stable element and is expressed in seconds, minutes, hours or even years.

Because the particles emitted in the course of disintegration contain a certain amount of energy, they are detectable and thus measureable, either directly or through their effects in an appropriate environment. The quantity of radioactive elements of a compound can therefore be determined through the analysis of its radioactivity.

Principle of a dating method based on radioactivity

Based on the process described above, the principle of any dating method using radioactive isotopes may easily be deduced: *Any object found in the archaeological strata is "datable" if it contains a radioactive element of which the original ratio can be determined, that is, the ratio at the moment the object was formed, as well as that remaining, or that of the isotope formed by the disintegrations.* The time span between the present and the period in which the object was formed is

Number of disintegrations
per minute and per gram of carbon

Disintegration
of radiocarbon
in conjunction with
prehistoric industries

PRESENT

NEOLITHIC

MAGDALENIAN

SOLUTREAN

harpoon

hunting pole

MOUSTERIAN

age B P

The ^{14}C method of dating.
Radiocarbon, formed by the action of cosmic rays, is returned into the atmosphere. When plants and animals die (symbolized by the small vertical arrows), radioactive carbon decreases at a constant rate whose measurement permits the dating of all carbonized samples.

calculated based on the ratio between the two contents, original and present, according to the half-life of the isotope.

The precise half-life of an element or isotope must be known for dating purposes. This, however, is not a problem because physicists have been able to measure the half-life of all radioisotopes. Above all, the radioactivities of chemical elements, which are sometimes very diffuse in the objects to be dated, must be measured or calculated with the greatest care. To this end, various measuring instruments are used: chemical analyzers, photometers that measure radiation, mass spectrometers (that accelerate streams of atoms and use magnets to sort them out according to their mass and electric charge), radioactivity meters. They must be very precise as they are expected to detect very small variations in ratios that are themselves minute.

Sampling is a strategic problem in terms of dating. Indeed, the natural environment is continually changing because of the interaction of chemical elements that come into contact with one another. If the radioactive phenomenon is one of the rare transformations that can precisely reveal time, all of the other modifications may more or less disrupt its measurement. The difficulty in sampling, therefore, rests in the discovery of a specimen containing the adequate radioisotope or its product, preserved in a state that will allow a meaningful analysis. Each method has its own rules concerning the collection and selection of samples, although it is more difficult to find the "good" sample than it is to analyze the sample in a laboratory, so numerous are the causes of modification of the original structures.

Whereas many other methods of investigation in archaeology can furnish abundant results, which are often easily verified by the repetition of certain measurements that can then be treated statistically, dating remains the exception in many studies: Usable radioisotopes are few and samples are rare. This explains why fewer than 10 dating methods have been developed, among which three are frequently applied.

The three principal methods

RADIOCARBON—General considerations regarding dating methods are particularly illustrated by the radiocarbon dating method, which at present is unquestionably the most widely used in prehistoric archaeology. Indeed, this method, developed 40 years ago, has the most general scope, both in terms of the time span it covers and the abundance, although relative, of samples to which it can be applied.

Radiocarbon, or carbon-14 (^{14}C) is a carbon isotope that is present in most fossil matter, as are ^{12}C and ^{13}C. It is constantly produced, as it has been for millennia, in the upper atmosphere by the neutronic reaction of nitrogen nuclei to cosmic radiation. It is then rapidly oxidized into $^{14}CO_2$ (carbon dioxide) that, diluted in the air or dissolved in sea water, is absorbed by plants, plankton and the living creatures who eat them. All living organisms thus absorb a certain number of ^{14}C atoms, but also lose some through disintegration. A balance is reached, allowing for the formulation of a basic principle concerning the method: *All living carbonated matter maintains a certain level of constant radioactivity, regardless of the place or period considered, as though one assumes that the production of radiocarbon has not noticeably varied over the course of time.*

As soon as death or chemical deposition takes place, the radiocarbon, ^{14}C is no longer recharged and the ^{14}C ratio diminishes with time at the rate of a half-life of about 5,700 years. By measuring the residual ratio of radiocarbon, the age of the death of the sample can be deduced.

Because of the half-life of this isotope and the small amounts involved at the start (13.6 disintegrations per minute per gram of carbon), the practical range of the method is limited by the detectable residual ratio in fossil samples. In fact, one cannot go much further back than five or six half-lives—30,000 to 40,000 years. Note, however, that 40 millennia encompass the entire history of the *Homo sapiens sapiens* and that if ^{14}C dates are less precise for the last two millennia, historical data compensates for this shortcoming.

Two kinds of devices measure ^{14}C age. The first, which is most common and used at present (1986) in almost all laboratories, consists in measuring the B (beta) radiation emitted in the course of disintegration. This detection is carried out by using devices called proportional counters or liquid scintillation spectrometers. The second, currently in the process of development, consists in the counting of the ^{14}C atoms present after the different elements are separated according to their mass in the sample. This kind of analysis requires heavy and sophisticated machinery (a particle accelerator and high precision mass spectrometers). This second method makes it possible to work on a sample of only a few milligrams. At the present state of the art, only three or four laboratories in the world are capable of routinely conducting these analyses.

The number of dating laboratories in each country varies considerably. While in the United States there are about 20 capable of processing many samples per year, elsewhere there are only a few per country.

As is the case with other dating methods, all of the samples discovered in the archaeological strata cannot be used for measuring purposes. Even if they are carbonated, their carbon content must be sufficient to allow the transformation necessary for the analysis. Moreover, because carbon is present everywhere and particularly in the first few feet of any ground where bacterial activity is intense, there appears a mixture of carbon of both ancient and recent origin in organic or mineral matter; the purification of either sometimes proves difficult, if not impossible. This greatly reduces the number of carbonated materials suitable for the dating process. In archaeology, the only ultimately reliable dating is that of the organic matter of bones and of large charcoals. In some sites, wood or grain is found, which can also be used. Only rarely in archaeology are shells, paleosoils or hearth soils dated.

In the past 25 years, thousands of dates have been obtained, and it can be asserted that most prehistoric civilizations since the beginning of the Upper Paleolithic (Old Stone Age) Period are roughly placed within a time frame defined by radiocarbon. For some civilizations, known only through a very small number of excavations, the few dates that have been obtained do not allow rigorous comparisons from region to region. On the other hand, for other cultural phases, the beginning and end of each subperiod can be precisely determined, and useful interregional comparisons can be made using the many results obtained with the help of a precise statistical analysis in the various regions.

An important point remains concerning the absolute chronology established by radiocarbon. Indeed, if the con-

currence of the results obtained from the data of stratigraphy is certain, it must be said that for the last eight millennia B.C., there is a discrepancy between ^{14}C dates and the calendar defined by the rotation of the Earth, i.e., in actual years. This discrepancy, which globally increases as one goes back in time, is about 800 years, around the seventh millennium B.C. It is probably that beyond this date the deviation maintains itself or even worsens, reaching 1,000 years in the Upper Paleolithic Period. In a study conducted by the Lamont-Doherty Geological Laboratory of Columbia University in 1990, the discrepancy was as much as 3,500 years for samples 20,000 years old.

The Omo Valley.
In the heart of these sloping volcanic beds numerous hominid remains were found that increased our knowledge about man's origin.

These discoveries were particularly valuable because these rocks correlate well with very precise datings made by the potassium-argon method, allowing each human fossil

The measuring of ^{14}C activity in the tree-rings of very old trees accurately, through dendrochronology, has made it possible to establish a correction table for ^{14}C dates, to bring them more into line with real years, but this diminishes precision. On the other hand, the discrepancies are identical when it comes to contemporary samples, regardless of their geographical origin. The archaeologist thus is faced with the choice between "corrected" dating, with a certain amount of imprecision, which can be expressed in time intervals, or with a more precise "absolute" chronology, on a time scale different from real time, the relative position of the various cultural phases remaining perfectly established. For exam-ple, a sample dated 5,000 years ± 150 B.P. (Before Present, that is, before A.D. 1950) will be placed when corrected within the time span of 3940/3640 B.C., that is, at the beginning of the fourth millennium. For the moment, the chronology in radio-carbon years is still widely used, because the calibration tables do not proceed beyond 7,200 B.P., in other words beyond the end of the European Mesolithic Period.

This last reservation regarding the exact meaning of radiocarbon dates does not limit the use of the method that remains, the main source of chronological information in archaeological studies. Any study aiming at synthesizing a cultural phase or a succession of such phases of necessity

to be dated within a few dozen years—between three and one million years. Ph. G. Gerster.

relies on radiocarbon dates. This is not without danger, as it often entails neglecting the possibilities offered by other methods, which may lead to the overlooking of clues that could provide supplementary data.

POTASSIUM ARGON—This method is highly perfected and is the basis of any chronology concerning prehistory of the most ancient periods. It differs from the preceding method in that it utilizes the measurement of the isotope produced through disintegration. Potassium is one of the elements present in the magma (molten rock) beneath the Earth's crust. One isotope of potassium is radioactive (potassium ^{40}K). Its half-life is approximately 1.5-billion years, and it disintegrates to produce argon 40 (^{40}Ar), or radiogenic argon. The potassium-argon method is used to date volcanic rocks, since the solidification of the rock traps the radiogenic argon, which accumulates inside the solid material. The quantity of argon is directly linked then to the length of time elapsed since the solidification of the rock. The measurement is made by extracting the gas from the rock, purifying it, and determining its concentration through mass spectrometry.

It is theoretically possible to date all of the minerals containing potassium found in volcanic rocks. Materials "datable" in this method are either included in the volcanic rocks proper (mica, sanidine feldspath), or indirectly contained in sedimentary rocks (glauconite or argillous minerals) in these same formations. The method is more appropriate for ancient periods than for the archaeological periods because of the very long half-life of potassium 40. It is relatively easier for this reason to date lunar rocks than volcanic lava of the Quaternary (the most recent geological period). For more recent times, the difficulty resides in the fact that the argon content is very weak, and the nonradiogenic argon in the atmosphere becomes a non-negligible "pollutant." Precise dating of recent minerals is exceptional.

For archaeological purposes, measurements have been carried out on acid volcanic rocks, associated with the most ancient sites. As a result of the employment of this method on African sites, the time of the origination of mankind has been placed at 2 to 3 million years ago, as opposed to the date of one-million years previously arrived at through stratigraphy. The potassium-argon method is seldom used on European sites, where the association with volcanic rocks is rare.

THERMOLUMINESCENCE—This method uses another consequence of radioactive phenomena: the discharge of alpha, beta or gamma particles, which brings about disruptions in the surrounding crystal lattice, in particular, the release of electrons from certain elements. The elements are then said to be in a "metastable" (capable of being transferred or altered) state. To return to their fundamental state, they must receive energy (thermal, for example), and this return is accompanied by an emission of light.

Clay and minerals used in pottery contain traces of natural radioactive isotopes (uranium 238, uranium 235, thorium 232) that emit particles that re-create, in pottery buried in the ground, metastable states that will become fundamental again only through a new increase in temperature. This is performed in the laboratory and the intensity of light emitted in the course of the return to a stable state is measured to determine the length of time the piece was buried. The overall energy received since the first firing and that received over the years must be determined. The first is measured by luminous intensity, the second by chemical absorption, or with the help of a radioactivity dosimeter, placed on the site itself.

This method is very widely used because it can be applied to a single fragment and can be repeated several times on the pieces contained in a single group. It can be used for relatively recent ages and has sometimes made it possible to test the authenticity of objects that were presumed to be ancient. It is used for ceramics and construction materials, ovens, molds, etc. Used on burnt flints, this technique can almost bridge the gap between the radiocarbon method (40,000 years) and the potassium-argon technique.

There are several laboratories around the world, some of which perform routine measurements. The notation of dates is similar to radiocarbon dates (including B.P. or B 1980 = before 1980, the statistical margin, and laboratory reference).

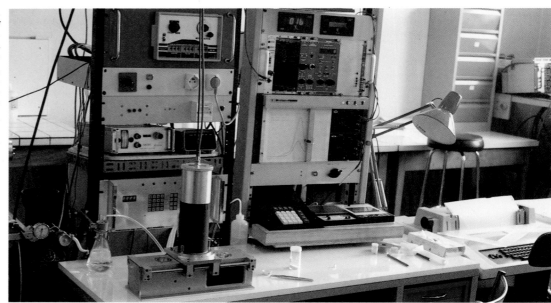

Laboratory for dating by thermoluminescence at the University of Clermont-Ferrand. The equipment in the foreground is a stove used for controlled heating and an optical photomultiplier reader which captures the light emitted by the sample as the temperature rises. The signal is processed in an amplifier, located at mid-height beside the chart recorder, which reproduces the results of the TL as a function of the temperature of the stove. Ph. D. Miallier.

Other Dating Methods

There are other dating methods that we will not explain in detail here. Their importance is relatively small where prehistory is concerned. These methods use isotopes with long half-lives, such as rubidium, uranium or thorium, particularly for marine series, calcareous rocks or cave concretions. However, new dating possibilities for archaeology appear with the use of amino acids or that of the electronic spin resonance.

Racemization of amino acids
The amino acids are present in live organisms only in the L-form or levorotatory form (orienting polarized light to the left as it passes through them). When an organism dies, part of the L-form will become "racemized" or combined with the D-form, or dextrorotatory form, orienting polarized light to the right. Racemization increases with time, depending upon the temperature and according to the nature of the amino acid.

The electronic spin resonance
This method, like thermoluminscence, is based on the creation of metastable states in crystals found near radioactive isotopes. It has been demonstrated that the total quantity of radiation sustained can be measured by the intensity with which the crystals are able to absorb certain waves if they are placed in a strong magnetic field. If the dose received annually can also be measured, their age can be calculated, and very small objects a few years or one billion years old can thus be dated. This dating process, however, is still in the developmental stage.

An Assessment, and Future Prospects

General characteristics of the absolute chronology of prehistory
The relative importance given above to the various dating methods was dictated by the real impact of each of the methods discussed on the present sum of knowledge of the absolute chronology of the various cultural phases of prehistoric archaeology.

The last 30 millennia are distinctly those for which the largest amount of data is available, not only because of the decisive contribution of radiocarbon methods, but also to the more limited contribution of one or the other of the less-developed methods and by the marked evolution of the humanities.

For the remotest past, to about 1 million years, the essential contribution has been provided by potassium-argon, which is fortunately usable precisely where the oldest human remains are found in the greatest number.

Between the two extreme limits posed by ^{14}C and potassium-argon, there is a long period for which an absolute chronology is admittedly rarely established. The recourse to the simultaneous use of multiple methods, as for the Arago cave near Tatauvel (in the French Pyrénées), has sometimes made it possible to approach the absolute age of some layers of the site, while revealing curious diachronisms. Of course, paleomagnetism provides some points of reference, and the method using uranium-thorium permits the dating of a few calcareous rocks. Finally, the evolution of fauna and of large and small mammals contributes clues that can be decisive. However, evidence of human activity is rare, dispersed or disrupted by more than 10 advances and retreats of glaciers, so that the chronological limits attributed to the industries in many regions are not precise or, in some instances, completely imaginary.

Possible development of methods
The greatest efforts have been made to attempt to bridge the significant gap mentioned above and particularly to determine a somewhat precise chronological framework for the Middle Paleolithic Period. Undoubtedly, much is to be expected from a greater precision in radiocarbon dating, which can be applied to small samples because of the new technique of accelerators. On the other hand, great hopes lie in the application of thermoluminescence and the paramagnetic spin resonance. The study of deep continental peat bog series, or of volcanic lakes, of long loess profiles (thought to have been deposited during the Pleistocene Age) or of cores taken from the deep ocean floors, will lead to a system of keys to the absolute chronology of the various climatic fluctuations of glacial periods. Only then will it be possible to examine their relationship to the evidence studied in prehistory, which will thus be fixed in time, despite the slow evolution of the industries or the scarcity of human fossils.

The importance of laboratory techniques will undoubtedly be confirmed, while the continually growing cooperation between archaeological or geological researchers working in the field and laboratory specialists will be reinforced. Indeed, the advancement of dating techniques has only been possible precisely through the trials and errors of analysts confronted with the rigorous field data—the privileged site where all the hypotheses elaborated upon in the laboratory are verified.

Suggested Reading

Graslund, Bo. *The Birth of Prehistoric Chronology*. Cambridge: Cambridge University Press, 1987.

Renfrew, Colin. *Before Civilization: The Radiocarbon Revolution and Prehistoric Europe*. London: Jonathan Cape, 1973.

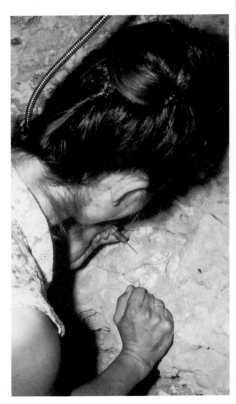

The Arago Grotto: *the porch of the grotto, with an archaeologist who is freeing the skull "Arago XXI," discovered in July 1971.*

The discovery of one of the "first" Europeans at Arago caused great interest and it was essential that this fossil be dated with the greatest precision. Thus, several methods of dating were used simultaneously on various materials from the grotto. The comparison of the results did not, however, permit the determination of the exact age of the human fossils and revealed the limits of the dating methods in environments that have undergone great geochemical changes. Ph. H. de Lumley and P. Starosta.

CHAPTER THREE

Hélène Roche

THE BEGINNINGS OF THE HUMAN ADVENTURE

Pebble chipped on one side from the Kada Gona site, at Hadar (Ethiopian Afar). This very rudimentary tool, dated at more than 2.6 million years, is among the oldest tools now known. Ph. H. Roche.

The origins of humankind are incontestably African. It is necessary, however, to specify what we mean by "origins," "humankind" and "Africa."

For paleontologists the starting point of a history of humankind is identical to that of the appearance of the first primates and began some 65 million years ago, in the early Tertiary, somewhere in the Rocky Mountains, in western North America. At that time the *Purgatorius* appeared, a small primate with 44 teeth and a promising morphology. Some paleoanthropologists pay greater attention to the evolution of primates during the Miocene Period (from approximately 23 to seven million years ago) because they find in that period the separation of the branch of human ancestors from that of the big apes (gorillas, chimpanzees), belonging to the same family of Hominini.

Others believe that this separation may be more recent. According to these scholars the last common ancestor of Man and the chimpanzee, our closest cousin as it were, dates back to no more than 6 or 7 million years ago. They are confirmed in their opinion by biologists who, because of the progress in genetics, are able to analyze the structure of certain characteristic molecules (nucleic acids, proteins), or of chromo-somes themselves, and to date the stages of their evolution. Hence they arrive at identical conclusions: recent separation and very close kinship between Man and the chimpanzee. It is after this separation that the *Austrolopiths* appeared, an extinct branch of the same hominid family, followed by *Homo habilis,* the first of the *Homo* genus.

As for the prehistorians,they may not at present assert with certainty who, of the *Australopithecus* or *Homo habilis,* is the maker of the first flaked tools found in Ethiopia, which date back to more than 2.6 million years. However, once the first limited sets of stone tools were fashioned, the progress was irreversible and as important as the other elements of the evolutionary process whereby Man definitively distinguished himself from the other primates.

If the history of all primates involves three continents, the final stages of the evolution that led to present human beings concerns only Africa. At first, let us confine ourselves to two large regions: East Africa and its vast expanses of arboreous savannah across which, from the Red Sea to the Transvaal, runs the long Rift Valley; and southern Africa, where fossilized remains have accumulated in the many cavities of the Earth.

Exceptional Sites

One may wonder about what led to the discovery of so many fossiliferous and archaeological sites in East and Southern Africa. In our opinion, their number provides evidence that an adequate environment existed that first favored the development of the Australopiths, then of Man. This is not the only reason, of course. If, as a rule, the preservation of stone tools is good, that of bone remains is linked to a fossilization process that must be particularly active, a process in which water plays an important part, combined with an intense sedimentary activity, thus enabling the rapid burial and preservation of the bones.

These conditions were met during the Pliocene Period in the Rift Valley. All of the known sites are located on the edges of lakes that have now disappeared (with the exception of Lake Turkana) or on former river banks. At the end of the period of sedimentary accumulation, erosion uncovered these ancient levels, where fossils and flaked tools may be spotted fairly easily. Hence, over a period extending from 1 to 4 million years, all of the elements that make it possible to follow the evolution of the *Hominidae*, as well as the reconstitution of their environments, are combined in these two regions. The rest is a question of making a lucky discovery. It is thus understandable why in that region geologists, paleontologists and prehistorians have been prospecting, excavating, analyzing and comparing for several decades.

The main sites that will be mentioned for this very first page of the history of mankind are, from north to south: Hadar, Bodo, Melka Kuntouré (all three located along the Awash River) and the Omo Valley in Ethiopia; the Turkana and Baringo Lakes, the sites of Kanam and Kanapoi in Kenya; Olduvai and Laetoli in Tanzania; and Makapansgat, Sterkfonstein, Swart'krans, Taung in the Transvaal in South Africa. In the Rift Valley, tectonic activity (the movement of plates on the Earth's crust) has often upset the accumulation of sedimentary stratas that can be more than 300 feet (100 meters) thick, and almost all the deposits exhibit faults (fractures). Sometimes the layers are tipped upwards, thus presenting a strong incline (up to 45% in the Omo Valley). Volcanic activity has also been intense, as is shown by the numerous flows of basalt and other volcanic substances, but mainly by the important levels of ash (tuffs), which are often excellent level indicators in stratigraphies and allow the setting of absolute datings through various methods (potassium-argon and uranium-thorium, traces of fission, paleomagnetism). Unfortunately, this is not the case for the Transvaal sites, which at present are poorly dated.

The Olduvai Gorge, Tanzania. Ph. Ch. Lenars.

The First Primates

Humans are placental mammals that belong to the order of primates. Primates are divided into two groups: a first collection of primitive primates known as prosimian, of which the lemurs of Madagascar and the Comoros, the tarsiers of the Philippines and Indonesia, a small galagos of tropical Africa, and the lorises of Ceylon are today the main representatives. A second group, more complex, including humans and all of the other primates, is the suborder of the anthropoids. When paleontology discovered them, in the early Oligocene (35 million years), they already appeared in two distinct forms: the Platyrrhinians, or monkeys of the New World, with a long tail and 36 teeth, and the Catarrhinians, or monkeys, apes, humans, and "prehumans" of the Old World, with only 32 teeth. The problem of their common origin, and especially of their separation on two continents (the southern Atlantic was smaller than at the present) has not yet been resolved. Among others, the Oligocene levels (35 to 25 million years) of the famous Faiyum deposit, south of Cairo, have provided numerous fossil remains, among which one may identify the Great Apes of the Old World: the *Propliopithecus* and the *Aegyptopithecus*.

The Hominoid Primates

At the beginning of the Miocene Period, about 24 million years ago, and only in Africa, three groups were subsequent to these first Catarrhine primates: the *Cercopitheci*, the *Pliopitheci* and mainly the *Dryopitheci*, to which the *Proconsul* species belong, considered for a long time by the supporters of an ancient separation to be the common species at the origin of mankind and the Great Apes. In the middle of the Miocene (about 17 million years ago) an important geological event occurred: the Afro-Arabian plate met at Eurasia, closing in what is referred to as the Thetys, the sea that lay between the Mediterranean and the Indian Ocean. The three aforementioned groups continued to evolve in Africa, but also

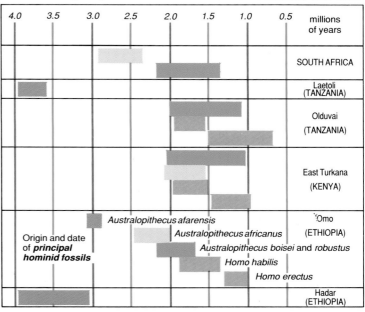

Chronological position of different types of hominids in the principal deposits of eastern Africa and southern Africa

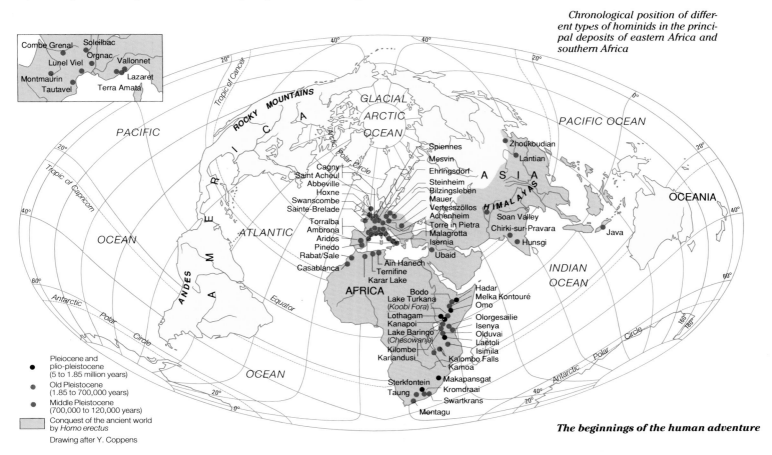

The beginnings of the human adventure

spread to Asia and Europe. We will follow only the *Dryopitheci*, which appear in various forms: the *Gigantopithecus*, a somewhat aberrant Asian type, affected with giantism, as the name implies, and without descendants; the *Sivapithecus* and the *Ramapithecus*, very closely related, representing perhaps the ancestral forms of the Asian Great Apes (the orangutan); lastly, the *Kenyapithecus* classified with the *Ramapitheci*, but which recent discoveries now make possible to constitute as a distinct species, which could also represent the common branch of the Hominidi and the Great Apes, if this separation really took place at the end of the Miocene.

Although the first *Dryopithecines* are quite well known to us because of numerous fossil remains, the period that precedes the emergence of the *Australopithecines* (between 10 and 4 million years ago) is more obscure. Indeed, the last third of the Miocene and the beginning of the Pliocene have left few remains notwithstanding several promising discoveries in Kenya, including a fragment of an upper jaw in which humanoid and simian features are mingled.

The World of the *Australopithecus*

More than 60 years have passed since the paleontologist Raymond Dart announced in 1925 his discovery of an Australopithican skull on the site of Taung (South Africa). The discovery of this fossil, closely related to the monkey and an ancestor of mankind, provoked strong reactions partly because its African origin. Could one believe that Man's origins resided elsewhere than in Europe? Discovery followed discovery, however, thus convincing even the most reluctant scientists, yet each fossil was generally surrounded by numerous taxonomic controversies that have lasted until the present day. They were and are linked to the difficulties of attributing fossil fragments to species that are still poorly defined and for which the observer lacks many important elements; the often incomplete state of the discoveries, the underestimation of factors such as individual and intraspecific variations and sexual dimorphism (in which males and females differ), often very pronounced among primates, are the main causes.

However, paleontologists seem to have come to a consensus and most of them agree today upon the distinction of four main species within the *Australopithecus* genus: *Australopithecus afarensis*, the most recently defined species, yet also the oldest (between 3.7 and 2.7 million years), a very small and lightly shaped being, discovered at Hadar (Ethiopia), at Laetoli (Tanzania) and possibly in the Omo (Ethiopia). A semimandible brought to light at Lothagam (5.5 million years) and a fragment of a thighbone at Kanapoi (4 million years), both of them in Kenya, may be attributed to it. *Australopithecus africanus*, a slender-shaped being as well, more recent (between 3 and 2 million years), was found in Sterkfontein, Makapansgat and Taung in the Transvaal, and in the Omo and East Turkana in East Africa. The robust shape of the *Australopithecines* is doubly represented by *Australopithecus robustus*, on the one hand, found at Kromdraai (the *Paranthropus*) and Swartkrans, but in these two South African sites it is not dated with precision (between 2.5 and 1.5 million years). *Australopithecus boisei*, on the other hand, discovered in the Olduvai Gorge in Tanzania (the famous *Zinjanthropus*), in the Omo and East Turkana, is between 2.3 and 1.5 million years.

The shape of the skull of the *Australopithecus robustus* is most remarkable, with its very pronounced sagittal crest, the bony ridge running along the center back of the skull bearing witness to the insertion of powerful masticatory (chewing) muscles. Likewise, the massiveness of the ascending ramus of the mandible (lower jaw), the large size of the molars opposed to the smaller canine teeth, point to an essentially or totally vegetarian diet. The height was approximately five feet (1.5 meters) with a weight ranging from 90 to 135 pounds (40 to 60 kilograms).

The slender shaped *Australopithecus africanus* is characterized both by its small size and a brain proportionately more developed up to (600 cm³) 37 cubic inches. The chewing muscles are still powerful, combined with a strong prognathism (projecting jaw), yet there is a clear tendency toward the reduction of the jugate (paired) teeth and the growth of the front teeth, which indicates a more omnivorous diet. However, the difference is most perceptible in the shape of the skull: little or no sagittal crest and the appearance of an actual forehead, although modest.

Because of the chance involved in discoveries and the more-or-less good condition of fossils, the oldest ones are also the best known, as concerns the bones of the skeleton (postcranial). The most famous remains are doubtless those of "Lucy," i.e., the 52 bones of the semicomplete skeleton of a young female *Australopithecus*, found at Hadar. *Australopithecus afarensis* is short—3.6 feet (1.1 meters) at the most—with a small head (27 cubic inches, or 450 cm³), a face strongly projecting forward, modest upper teeth and developed jugate teeth covered with a thick enamel. The upper limbs are proportionately quite long, while the lower limbs and the pelvis indicate a biped upright step.

This is corroborated by a most extraordinary discovery made at Laetoli, Tanzania. This is the bed, which contains fossils attributed to *Australopithecus afarensis*, where Mary Leakey brought to light footprints of individuals walking upright, mingled with the footsteps of other animals (elephants, antelopes, etc.). The morphology of the feet (short toes, close together) and the distribution of the body weight in relation to the arch of the foot already announce modern man. However, the study of the articulations (of the feet, hands, elbows and knees) and of the muscular links show that the mode of locomotion of the *Australopithecus afarensis* was as much meant for tree climbing as for walking on two feet. One thus pictures a life very different from that of humans. The last *Australopitheci*, in the robust form, seemed to have died out about one million years ago.

Mary Leakey studying footprints of the Laetoli site (Tanzania). These hominid and animal steps were imprinted in volcanic ash moistened by rain. They dried and hardened before being covered up by other ashy deposits, which preserved them until their discovery in 1976. Ph. Bob Campbell.

The Appearance of *Homo Habilis*

More than 20 years ago, Louis Leakey excavated (at Olduvai) and described the first specimen of *Homo habilis* amid the same pervading scepticism with which the first *Australopithecus* had been met. Many scientists were not ready to accept an age (1.75 million years) for the appearance of the genus *Homo*. Other, subsequent, discoveries confirmed its great age. Between slightly less than 2 and until 1.5 million years ago, *Homo habilis* was present in the Omo, in East Turkana (of which the famous KNMER 1470 skull, believed to be 3 million years old, caused much ink to flow) and also in Sterkfontein and Swartkrans, at an uncertain date however.

Very little is known about the postcranial skeleton of *Homo habilis*, as only a few elements of the lower limbs are available. Therefore, the analysis of cranial remains determined the identity of the new species, the first of the genus *Homo*. Its cranial capacity can reach up to 46 cubic inches (750 cm³), which is still small but greatly superior to that of the slender *Australopitheci*. Its morphology includes the disappearance of the sagittal crest and a reduction of the eye ridge and prognathism of the face. The lower teeth take up more space than the jugate teeth, the thickness of the enamel diminishes, as does the width of the ascending ramus of the lower jaw. All indications point to a more carnivorous diet, or at least one not requiring a masticatory apparatus as specialized as that of the *Australopitheci*. Also, the positioning of the occipital hole (where the skull is joined to the vertebral column), clearly suggests an upright stance.

What Path of Evolution for Man?

Before examining the *Australopitheci*, we mentioned the lack of fossil remains for the period extending from 10 to 4 million years. The separation of Man from the Great Apes cannot be established with certainty, nor can the relationship among the Hominidae, present since the end of the Miocene. Therefore, we are left with a first species, *Australopithecus afarensis*, whose link to man cannot be posited without the risk of error concerning the anterior hominoidal primates. Two others were subsequent to it, a slender one (*africanus*), the other robust (*robustus* and *boisei*), and lastly, *Homo habilis*. How shall this whole be classified? The consensus of opinion among paleoanthropologists ends here, and the suggested theories are numerous. However, they can be reduced to two great hypotheses. The first: *Australopithecus afarensis* evolves to *africanus*, which gave birth, around 2 million years ago, to the robust *Australopitheci* (an evolutionary dead end), then to *Homo habilis*. The second: *Australopithecus afarensis* gives birth directly to two branches, *africanus*, which evolves first into the robust form and into *Homo habilis* somewhat later.

The main stages of the evolution of this group of hominids are now quite well known and it will no doubt be possible to relate them better to that of the hominoidal primates at the end of the Miocene Period when the true age of *afarensis* is known. Some scientists already refer to him as the great pre-*Australopithecus*, and, if he is older than 5 million years, why not imagine that he may be the ultimate ancestral form common to man and the Great Apes? His still imperfect, yet attested, bipedalism, combined with a still arboreal mode of locomotion—and probably a mode of life—supports, among other clues, this hypothesis.

The Role of the Environment

Finding and interpreting fossils does not suffice; a researcher must try to reconstitute the environment in which these ancestors lived because the climatic, plant and animal environment played an important part in the evolution of primates. Poorly known for the early primates, later environments become more and more apparent, especially that of the *Australopitheci*. The Hominoidea that were discovered at Hadar, in the Omo, at Olduvai, etc., lived mainly in an environment of arboreous savannah (acacias) quite similar to the landscape of certain lakes of today's East Africa, amongst abundant and varied fauna, the ancestors of today's varieties: hippopotami, giraffes, warthogs, antelopes, zebras, elephants, carnivorous mammals, apes, rodents, crocodiles, snakes, etc. At Hadar and Olduvai, the old lake shores were covered with reeds, rushes and graminea (grasses).

It appears that in the greatest part of this region, around 3 million years ago, a more humid climate than the present one prevailed, more humid in any case than that subsequent to it in the Omo Valley (between 2.5 and 2 million years), in East Turkana (1.9 million years) and at Olduvai (between 1.8 and 1.6 million years). This relative drying of the climate is measured in the deposits, where signs of the recession of lakes can be detected. In the vegetation, analyzed through pollens, more rarely through wood and on occasion through fossil seeds and fruits, a reduction of the arboreous species to the benefit of open field grasses is evident. In Southern Africa, similar signs tend to prove that, around 2 million years ago, there was a shift from a relatively dense arboreous vegetation indicating a rather high rainfall to a more open and dry savannah. With certain animal species (Bovidae, Equidae, proboscibians [elephants], rodents, etc.), the emergence of forms adapted to a less-wooded environment, in which the grass is also less tender, has been noticed. This transformation is perceptible through its effect on dentition, which is higher and covered with a thicker enamel.

The emergence of the genus *Homo* would thus correspond to that of a drier savannah landscape. However, the studies that have been made to the present day bear more of a local value than a regional one, and it is not yet possible to reach a consensus on the matter. The drying up of the tropical zone was probably less general than was believed for a time. One also has but to reside some time by a lake of the Rift Valley today, where the natural habitat has nevertheless been subject to modification, to be convinced that man and his close ancestors lived in a welcoming environment. Some scientists have sometimes deemed it hostile, because of the presence of carnivores, who nevertheless had other prey on which they fed. This drawback was minor in regard to the hospitality that the habitat could provide to superior primates already very evolved and ready to begin the human adventure.

The Tool and Man

One can wonder at will about what the first tools were really like, whether they were made of wood, bone, horn or stone. If nothing prevents speculation about the use of these materials, nothing proves it either. The occasional use of a rough object, immediately abandoned, does not leave convincing traces. Thus, we shall know nothing of the wooden hunting spear, the bone splinter, the horn fragment, the rough or cracked pebble, used but not improved upon. Yet, the preartisan stage most likely existed with the hominoids just as today are encountered certain monkeys who know how to break a nut between two stones or search for termites with a trimmed tree branch. The object, most often employed as an intermediary between the animal and its food, is rough, slightly or not at all modified, and immediately abandoned. The stone tool, for which the raw material was chosen and which was intentionally made and maintained, is still far off.

Can we nevertheless be satisfied with the statement that *A tool makes man*? Such satisfaction may prove precarious to maintain, if one poses as a possibility that certain *Australopitheci*, who are certainly in the human lineage but not properly belonging to it, may have used some such tools. A more exact statement might be that The technical innovation of an *action upon a certain material*, an *organized, repeated, transmitted action* is a phenomenon proper to humankind, of which *no equivalent* may be found in any other superior primate, not even among the Great Apes with their complex social organization, a kind of language, etc. The stone tool is introduced with the appearance of *Homo habilis* and, during several tens of millions of years, was the main artisanal product of prehistoric mankind. It is sometimes the only witness that has survived.

Technological progress can be compared to biological evolution: thus, for example, in relation to *Homo habilis, Homo erectus* increased his range of tools and perfected his techniques and his last representatives achieved a good mastery of the flaked stone. If the close relationship between the development of the brain, language, social organization and technical activity (of which the tool is the product) is recognized then, one grasps the important part that the technical activity has played in the process of human evolution.

The First Tools

In the beginning tools were quite simple, or at least appeared to be: a rock or a small rounded block was crudely fashioned by the removal of several *flakes* with the help of another pebble, used as a hammer. A first flake is removed from the *core*, the negative scar of which provides a striking angle for the second one, etc. Simple gestures, an elementary operation that enabled the creation of a fashioned tool with sharp edges and also of sharp-edged flakes, made it ready for use. Thus were made the most ancient tools known today, which come from Hadar, in the Ethiopian Afar. Volcanic rock, basalt, trachyte and andesite were flaked on one or two sides, as just described, or further truncated according to their thickness, the cut part forming a convex surface suited for grinding and crushing. This evidence, modest in number and between 2.6 and 2.4 million years of age, is precious for what it tells us about the origins of the flaked stone. Only 20 years ago one barely dared to suggest that the first human industries could be older than 1 million years.

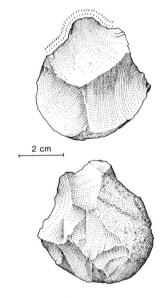

2 cm

Tool from Afar.

A small pebble, flaked on both sides, from the site of Kada Hadar, at Hadar (Ethiopian Afar). The furrowed grooves and polish indicate that this tool was used to scrape wood.

The site of Gomboré I, at Melka Kuntouré (Ethiopia), an Oldowan site covered with bones and tools, in the process of being cleared. Ph. J. Chavaillon.

When hominoids exhausted the better raw material in their close environment, they were content with breaking small stones into more or less sharp flakes. This is the case for industries discovered in several sites of the Omo Valley and that are dated at between 2 and 2.5 million years old. Differing from those found at Hadar, these specimens are flaked from small nodules of quartz and are essentially cores, splinters and flakes. Only one flaked stone has been found, fashioned out of quartz.

Who were the originators of these very first industries? This question cannot be answered with certainty. At Hadar, *Autralopithecus afarensis* is present, however the upper strata where the archaeological horizons were discovered contain no other fossil remains, not even of fauna. In the Omo, both kinds of *Australopithecus*, slender and robust, are found (no one has suggested that the latter may have used flaked stones) and also *Homo habilis*. It is very possible that the slender *Australopithecus* may have both used occasional tools and also have been a stone flaker; nothing, however, has yet proven this assertion. The period of 3 to 2 million years is of utmost importance, yet the archaeological documents are still insufficient, and we know almost nothing of the behavior and way of life of the ancestors of mankind.

The Oldowan, or the First Technical Experiment

From 2 million years onward, the elements, until then very scattered, fall into place more precisely. *Homo habilis*, the "skillful" human, is encountered in several deposits where archaeological remains have been brought to light. *Homo habilis*, as we know, lived alongside the robust *Aus-*

tralopithecus—of which a skill, mingled with industry remains, were found in the Olduvai Gorge in Northern Tanzania. There is agreement however, that *Homo habilis* was the inventor of the Oldowan, the most important and best characterized industrial period of this very ancient Paleolithic era, which is also referred to as the Preacheulian Period.

More than 20 sites were excavated in the 1940s and 1950s by Louis and Mary Leakey at Olduvai, the type site for the Oldowan, thus providing abundant material, dating from 1.9 to 1.7 million years. The typical tool is still the pebble, fashioned by a facial or bifacial (two-sided) flaking, which accounts for up to 80% of the implements discovered. Then come pebbles flaked on their entire surface, which gives them a polyhedral shape or tending toward the sphere form, or the flat disk. There are also some rare "protobifaces," which prefigure the Acheulian bifaces. The scraps of the core yielding the rough flakes differ from one site to another, but can be very abundant. Some of these flakes were further worked or retouched to form scrapers, piercers or planes.

Melka Kuntouré, excavated by Jean Cavaillon in the high Awash Valley, is the second Oldowan type site. It has an equally abundant number of sites as the Olduvai, dated at 1.8 to 1 million years. The industries are similar, primarily flaked pebbles and polyhedrons, but there are as well planes, thick scrapers, nibs, notches and denticles made on stones. The scraps and tools made from flakes, however are only a few.

Koobi Fora, east of Lake Turkana, Kenya yields two groups. Both what is referred to as the industry of KBS, dating back to 1.9 million years, which is scarce and comprised of cut stones, polyhedrons, disks, cores, splinters and angular fragments and the industry known as Chari (around 1.25 million years), which is more abundant and divided among 20 or so sites, are present. In places, chippage forms between

General view of the Hadar site in the Afar (Ethiopia). In the foreground, the riverside forest that lines the Awash River; in the background, the accumulation of stratas of the Hadar formation. Ph. H. Roche

85% and 99% of the overall amount of material; proper tools are made up of flaked stones, disks, polyhedrons and scrapers. Last, Chesowanja, also in Kenya, may be mentioned, near Lake Baringo, whose industry of the same age and very similar to that of the Chari.

The classical lithic (Stone Age) groups of the Oldowan (Olduvai, Melka Kuntouré) and its various facets clearly appear to have a common characteristic: simplicity. Two sorts of products exist: the fragments themselves in the broad sense of the word, rough or retouched, and any piece from which the flakes have been obtained (flaked stones, polyhedrons, disks, cores, etc.), in the same operation. The flaking technique of cutting is most rudimentary, without any special preparation. None of these objects really suggests a particular function. To cut, a rough flake may have been just as useful as the cut edge of a fashioned stone; to grind, a rough stone would have been as efficient as a polyhedron.

Ways of Life Still Poorly Known

The sites of the Preacheulian Period are all found on the edges of lakes, ponds or rivers and archaeologists have attempted to group them within different categories. It seems, indeed, that the distinction can be made between flaking sites where the implements, which are generally few in number, are associated with a skeleton of a large animal or of several small ones; the settlements, in which tools and remains of fauna are laid out on the surface of the ground; and the sites on the edge of a river, where the accumulation of material may be the result of the activity of water rather than of human processes.

Generally speaking, the settlements seem to be precarious, and the techniques of defense against large carnivores must be taken into account. In their most ancient levels (1.8 to 1.6 million years), the Olduvai and the Melka Kuntouré deposits have revealed elementary structures, or at least what have been considered as such. They are round structures, approximately 11 feet (3.50 meters) in diameter, simply raised in the shape of a platform lined with stones, or comprising a single rough circle of stones (a low wall for protection or for wedging branches to serve as a frame for the hut?). The best protection against predators, however, even today in these same regions, is a thick thorny enclosure (fashioned out of acacias) that, once dismantled, leaves no trace.

Some scientists deem that because of their exposed positions, these sites could not have been the permanent dwellings of Homo habilis, but rather the center of daytime activities, such as the making of tools, the cutting up of the dead animals, etc. The permanent dwelling, and especially the shelter for the night, would be located away from water, a place where too many animals dangerous to humans congregated.

The occasional presence of the remains of big animals such as the hippopotamus or the elephant raises the question: Are they the product of a hunt? It is certain that through evolution the Australopitheci and the Homo habilis had lost their defense and attack features such as fangs, claws and speed. Moreover, they were still armed with puny weapons for the hunting of large game. One therefore supposes a quest for food based on the practice of carrion seeking, possibly combined with hunting. It is also certain that meat foods were complemented by vegetal products, berries, roots, tubers, etc.

Homo Erectus Conquers the Old World

One must look outside of Africa for the coming of Homo erectus on the prehistoric scene. It is in the form of Pithecanthropus that was discovered for the first time, as early as 1851, by Eugène Dubois (1858–1941), an obstinate and confident Dutch anatomist, who went in search of the "missing link" on the isle of Java. Under the name Homo erectus are included all of the African and European Homo erecti, the Indonesian Pithecanthropi and the Chinese Sinanthropi. They have many comparable features: a face that is projected only slightly forward, a thick eye ridge, receding forehead, a slight keel on the median line of the frontal bone, prolonged toward the back by a sagittal crest. Yet there are also noticeable differences: first in the cerebral capacity, for the Sinanthropus an average of 65 cubic inches (1,075 cm³), but no more than 53 cubic inches (870 cm³) for the Pithecanthropus. Moreover, in his general appearance, Pithecanthropus seems more primitive than the Chinese form, with lower forehead, more robust jaw, less parobolic tooth row etc. This form appeared in Java (1.8 million years) rather than in China. Nothing is known of the Pithecanthropus culture, while that of the Sinanthropus is better known to us, thanks to the Zhoukoudian (Chou-koutien) site, where the remains were discovered, along with a settlement and signs of industry. Most of the sites where

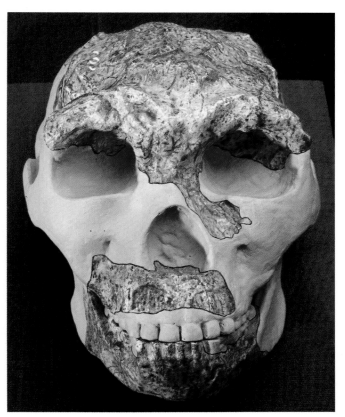

Skull of Homo erectus *from the Chinese site of Lantian (Shaanxi).* Ph. E. Lessing/Magnum.

Australopitheci and *Homo habilis* were discovered in East Africa have revealed remains of *Homo erectus* as well, as if some sort of evolution had continued on the spot: in eastern and now western Turkana, in the Omo, at Melka Kuntouré, Olduvai and Laetoli, to mention a few.

Northern Africa presents its own problems. There industries that seem ancient, but poorly dated, have been brought to light, particularly those in the regions of Rabat and Casablanca in Morocco and on the site of Ain Hanech in Algeria. They are sometimes found with fauna, yet the remains of the most ancient known hominids found there belong to *Homo erectus*. Thus, one cannot presently assert that this part of Africa was peopled before the emergence of *Homo erectus*. Most often, the exhumed remains are in stratigraphic relation with fauna and manufactured tools. Such is the case at Ternifine (now called Tighenif, in Algeria), which has provided three mandibles, a parietal bone (from the roof of the skull) and three isolated teeth. Because these fossils displayed some differences with those of Asia, Camille Arambourg (1885–1969) termed them *Atlanthropes (Atlanthropus mauritanicus,* Man of Atlas), yet there is no doubt that they are related to *Homo erectus*. The mandibles are remarkable for their sturdiness and very similar to those of the Pithecanthropes, but they also present striking differences, possibly because of sexual dimorphism. The parietal bone also seems to indicate a degree of cerebralization equal to that of the Asian *Homo erecti*. Several other fossils have been discovered in northern Africa, in particular at Salé near Rabat and in the Thomas quarries at Casablanca, which are generally similar to those of Ternifine.

In Europe, nothing yet allows us to say that there was human occupation prior to *Homo erectus*. The most ancient remains, which date from the Mindel glaciation and from the Minde-Riss interglacial period, are quite fragmentary. A mandible was discovered in 1907 at Mauer (near Heidelberg, Germany), robust, with a parabolic outline and teeth that have a modern aspect. An adult occipital bone and several children's teeth brought to light in the archaeological site at Vértesszöllös (west of Budapest) display a mixture of archaic and modern features, however, they do belong to *Homo erectus* of Central Europe, as do those of Steinheim and Bilzingsleben in Germany, all of which are approximately 350,000 years old.

In France, the Montmaurin mandible, also dated at 350,000 years, is similar in character to that of Mauer, yet corresponds, for certain specialists, to a more evolved form closer to *Homo sapiens*. The same is true for the human remains of the Arago Cave (near Tautavel, in the French Pyrénées), which comprise a complete mandible with six teeth in their proper place, a half-mandible, with five teeth, and the whole face of a skull with a receding forehead, a thick eye ridge and a large nose—a face that projects only slightly in relation to the cerebral skull and appears to date back 450,000 years.

Varied Environments

Homo erectus had to adapt to environments as diverse as those engendered by a tropical or periglacial climate. In Europe, their development corresponds essentially to the Mindel and Riss glaciations and to the Mindel-Riss and Riss-Würm interglacial stages, according to the terminology of the Alpine glaciations. The harshness of the glacial climate should not be exaggerated, however, considering that the

zones most hostile to man were avoided. During the Ice Ages, and even more so during the interglacial periods, there were variations and increases in the temperature. The establishment of a temperate climate in the northern zones (the southern zones being less frigid, even in times of intense cold) resulted in the development of forests with varied species (hazel, alder, hornbeam, birch, pine, etc.) that required an average temperature of at least 50°F (10°C) in July. Such forests gained ground over prairies. In the regions closer to the glacial zones, where the substratum stayed frozen most of the year, a landscape of steppes and tundra (grass, moss, willow, dwarf birch) prevailed.

Fauna have been subjected periodically to climatic variations and the same region will show a succession of species adapted to harsh climate ("cold fauna") and to a more temperate climate ("warm fauna"). At the very beginning of the Acheulian period, there still existed species originating in the Tertiary—the mastodons, the saber-toothed tiger (*Machairodus*), a giant beaver (*Trongontherium*)—while the Stenon Horse, still very different from today's horses, makes its appearance, as do two proboscidians, *Anancus osiris* and the southern elephant, the Etruscan rhinoceros and primitive bovidae (*Leptobos*). During the Mindel glaciation, three kinds of elephants replaced the southern elephant: an elephant of the steppe (*Elephas trogontheri*), the mammoth (*Elephas primigenius*) during the cold periods and the antique elephant (*Elephas antiquus*) during the warm periods. During the Mindel-Riss interglacial stage, which was quite warm, the Merck rhinoceros, in particular, emerged. Small fauna were abundant and extremely varied. The tropical zone displays no such diversity in fauna adapted to different climates. The aforementioned species for the lower Pleistocene Period evolved toward our present-day species, often with minor modifications, particularly in dentition related to the climate and, therefore, to the diet.

The Acheulian Civilization

In the presence of a history spanning 1,500 millennia, which took place on two vast continents, one can only begin to imagine the cultural diversity that emerged from this large group of *Homo erecti,* whose intraspecific variations we have seen from one continent or even one region to another, as well as the diversity of the numerous environments in which they evolved.

The Acheulian civilization (named for the site at St. Acheul, France, where numerous handaxes from this period were first discovered) has been revealed to us by hundreds of prehistoric sites throughout the Old World. It is not a homogeneous culture but characterized by adaptive behavior, traditions and various technical acquisitions, in relation to the degree of the evolution of the species, which itself was subject to the pressure of the environment. Found as early as 1.3 million years ago in Africa, it appeared a little more than 900,000 years ago in the Near East and then spread to Europe. At the same time appeared cultures that differ slightly from it, in particular by the absence of characteristic tools such as the biface. A certain unity emerges from this very long period of human history that forms the Lower Paleolithic and ends with the disappearance of the last *Homo erecti* around 100,000 years ago.

The Acheulian in Africa

East Africa contains the oldest known Acheulian site, dated to 1.3 million years at Olduvai. In this deposit, with long and complete sequences, as well as in Melka Kuntouré, the transition from the end of the Oldowan to the beginning of the Acheulian seems to have taken place smoothly. Numerous sites have also been found all along the Rift Valley, more just outside of it. Gaps in the chronological sequence often correspond to a lack of excavations. Bearing south from the Olduvai, one finds Isimila (Tanzania), then Kolombo Falls (Zimbabwe), which both belong to the recent Lower Paleolithic and illustrate an evolved Acheulian, while the Zambezi and Vaal Valleys bear evidence of older longer occupation.

Sterkfontein and Makapansgat, in South Africa, often mentioned for their fossils, have revealed several Acheulian levels, ancient and recent, yet unfortunately poorly dated. Northwards, one encounters the Kenyan sites: Olorgesailie, Kariandusi, Kilombe in the Rift, Lewa on the slopes of Mount Kenya, Isenya on the heights overlooking the Rift. The Acheulian is also present in Somalia, in Djibouti, in Egypt and in the Sudan, as well as in several areas of Central and Western Africa, in Saharan and tropical zones, and in equatorial zones (in the deposit of the Kamoa, in Zaire). In Algeria and in Morocco, the Acheulian presence is certainly very ancient, even if it is still poorly dated. At Ternifine (Tighenif), an industry made up essentially of bifaces, small axes and flaked pebbles was found with the remains of the *Atlanthropus*.

The Near East and Asia

In the Near East, the most ancient traces of human occupation were brought to light in the site of 'Ubeidiya ('Ubaydiyya), in Israel, 900,000 years old. The Acheulian population is as old in northern Syria, from whence it spread to Lebanon and Jordan.

In China, some bifaces were exhumed with the human remains at Lantian, yet it is in the mid-lower Paleolithic (700,000 to 300,000 years) that it mostly developed. The site

(Left) General view of the excavation of the Orgnac site (Ardèche, France). The total archaeological stratas reach several feet/meters in height. Some of them are separated by sunken blocks from the former roof of the cave. Ph. J. Combier.

(Above) Isernia la Pineta (Molisa Italy). Deposit of the ancient Acheulian, where a large quantity of bones (bison, rhinoceros, bear, elephant, hippopotamus, cervid) were found, mixed with a sparse industry, composed mostly of flakes and flaked pebbles. Ph. R. Burri/Magnum.

of Zhoukoudian, which is already known for its *Sinanthropus* bones, contains an important industry in rather roughly flaked quartz. The Acheulian is abundant in India and in southeastern Asia, where several facets appear, where the biface is sometimes completely absent (Birmania, in Thailand), and is also found in Japan.

Europe

With the exception of the central and eastern zones, where it is scarcer, the Acheulian is very widespread in Europe.

An archaic period is represented in France by the Vallonnet Cave (near Nice), where abundant and well-preserved fauna, as well as several tools were brought to light, including a filing that was dated at 900,000 years by use of paleomagnetism. In the Massif Central, the site of Solheilac (1,000,000–800,000 years) contains a rough industry of basalt, mingled with the remains of fauna. The terraces of the Rousillon and Catalonia region also contain ancient industries, yet they are poorly dated. From 700,000 years on, the true Acheulian developed everywhere in Western Europe. In France one must first mention Abbeville where several crude biface handaxes were discovered, dated to 700,000 years, then Saint Acheul, somewhat more recent, and finally Cagny-la-Garenne, all three located along the Somme Valley, where, in the last century, the study of French prehistory was born.

In France, Achenheim (Alsace), Lunel-Viel (Hérault), Tautavel (Pyrénées) and Terra Amata (Maritime Alps) represent the Middle Acheulian; finds in Orgnac, Combe-Grenal and Le Lazaret (Martime Alps) date from the Upper Acheulian. The Acheulian is also notably present in discoveries at Belgium (Petit Spiennes, Mesvin); in Great Britain (Hoxne, Swanscombe) and in the Anglo-Norman Isles (the coast of Saint Brelade in Jersey); in Germany (Bilzingsleben and Ehringsdorf), and in Hungary, with the very beautiful site of Vértesszöllös. In southern Europe, finds have been made at the Italian Torre site in Pietra, near Rome; Venosa in the Basilicate; Isernia la Pineta, in Molisa; and finally, in Spain, Aridos, near Madrid, Pinedo near Toledo and above all, Torralba and Ambrona, northeast of Madrid, where the Acheulian resembles the African Acheulian.

Fire

If the preceding stage of human development is essentially characterized by the acquisition of the fashioned tool, Acheulian times are marked by notable technical progress in stone flaking, wood and bone fashioning (even if these materials have rarely survived) and, mainly, by the domestication of fire. It seems quite likely, indeed, that fire was discovered in Europe during the Mindel glaciation. If the evidence was first scarce and sometimes debatable, it is finally convincing:

The DK hearth of Terra Amata (Maritime Alps) in the shape of a small basin, dug into the ground (6 inches/15 centimeters deep), encircled by a few stones and pebbles. Ph. H. de Lumley/Museum of Man.

ashy levels at Zhoukoudian and unbuilt hearths at Vértesszöllös, some of which were filled with fragments of calcined bones (fuel?), and hearths dug in the shape of a basin in the site of Terra Amata, possibly with a small protecting wall. Generally speaking, in the course of this first epoch of the Lower Paleolithic, the hearths are not highly structured, much less built. Only from the Riss glaciation on are the first constructed hearths apparent. Noteworthy also, for the same epochs are the lack of any definite traces of fire in both Africa and in the Near East. For this one must wait until the final Acheulian interpretation (Kalombo Falls, Makapansgot). Whether this lack is due to real absence or the poor preservation of ashes in the soil, is now difficult to tell.

The possession of fire, which was first probably simply "captured" then maintained by percussion or friction, certainly affected the relationship between humans and the environment, and, consequently, brought about behavioral changes. Domestic fire was both a source of heat and light. The possession of fire and the colonization of cold regions have often been linked, but some known sites in periglacial regions have yielded no fossil traces of fire to date. It has also often been suggested that fire strengthened man's defensive capabilities by allowing occupation of the grottos, but there are numerous open air deposits where the presence of fire is evident, while certain occupied caves are devoid of such evidence. In fact, the role of fire is more complex, and if fire illuminates, warms, and protects, it can also be utilized as a tool, as a transformation energy. The introduction of new methods of cooking (on braziers, in cinders, on spits, by heated stones, etc.) is hard to prove. It is not certain that fire was used in the Lower Paleolithic Period, but it is also not impossible to speculate that it may have been used.

Fire also, perhaps, had more technical applications, such as the working of wood. Unfortunately, here as well, direct proof is lacking. In the sites of Kalombo Falls, wooden spikes that were perhaps passed through flames to harden have been found. Another specimen, from Swanscombe (England) has led to a similar interpretation, but recent analysis has cast doubt on this hypothesis. At Zhoukoudian, it has been suggested that humans resorted to using fire to facilitate the

(Above) Scouring of an Acheulian field on the site of Isenya (Kenya). This open-air deposit, from the Middle Pleistocene, is characterized by an abundance of bifacial pieces (small axes, bifaces), cores and flakes, and possibly animal remains. Ph. H. Roche.

(Right) From Isenya (Kenya), a biface, a characteristic tool of the Acheulian. This biface is perfectly regular, rough-hewn with a stone hammer, then finished with a soft hammer. It is made of phonolite, a volcanic rock common in the vicinity of Isenya. Ph. H. Roche.

working of cervidae (deer) antlers, to remove the antlers from the head, and of bone, although there is no final proof that these materials were really worked, rather than used as fuel. After the Acheulian, it is certain that the use of fire became widespread throughout the inhabited world. It remains nonetheless the great discovery of *Homo erectus*.

Other Technological Progress

The stone tool is the main evidence of the artistic activity of prehistoric man. In the course of the Acheulian, the working techniques were remarkably refined. The main tools of the Oldowan were stones or small blocks partially chipped with a stone on one or two sides, if not fashioned completely, the remaining fragments themselves eventually transformed into tools. Such implements continued to exist, sometimes to the exclusion of any other tools, as in certain sites of Europe and Asia.

At the end of the Oldowan appeared an oblong tool with a pointed or a rounded end: the biface. Thick and with an imprecise shape at first, it became quickly more refined and its shape standardized. It is usually described as simply ovoid, but it also appeared spear-shaped, heart-shaped or almond-shaped. This variety of shapes is most likely related to its uses by prehistoric people, which are still unclear. The quality of the finish on many pieces is linked to an important technical innovation that appeared in the mid–Lower Paleolithic, sometime around 500,000 years ago: the retouching of stone. A material softer than stone was used to retouch the piece, such as an antler, wood, bone or horn, which enabled more precise and more delicate work, as well as longer and flatter retouches.

A very common tool in Africa and southern Europe accompanies the biface: the small axe, a robust tool with a transverse cutting edge. Many bifaces and small axes have been found in the Acheulian deposits of the Old World; however, we are still confined to hypotheses and conjectures concerning their use. It is known that certain bifaces were used to prepare meat (in England), yet only experimentation showed the efficacy of the small axe in felling and stripping bark from trees and for the dismemberment and cutting up of small carcasses. Yet, the micropscopic analyses of wear, which is the only way to determine what kind of material a stone tool was used on and why, are very difficult to conduct on these tools. Their raw material, composed of granular rocks (volcanic materials, quartzite, limestone, etc.) does not preserve traces of materials they came into contact with, or the traces have been obliterated by water, wind or chemical erosion.

The biface and the small axe were not the only tools used during the Acheulian. Tools made of fragments, present as early as the Oldowan, had also developed and were diversified: scrapers, notches, denticles, nibs, burins, etc. The cutting of the core was more regular and, as early as the Middle Acheulian, a second major technological innovation emerged—a core of material was especially prepared, or preshaped, for the striking of flakes of a controlled shape and thickness, usually as rectangles, ovals, or as points. The shape of the flake was thus imagined and planned before the actual processing of the material, revealing a significant advance in mental ability. This breakthrough is known as the Levallois method (from the name of the site, the commune of Levallois, where it was determined for the first time). We are now very far removed from the elementary beginnings of tools.

Bone was used, at Olduvai even, yet it was rarely entirely fashioned as it would be later on. It is therefore difficult to identify it as a tool, and, here again, the study of the traces of wear plays an important part. Bifaces made of bone have been discovered recently at Malagrotta, Italy, not far from Rome, but these are exceptional. As for wood, it has an even smaller chance of being preserved through the ages than bone. Wooden pieces found at Kalombo Falls, preserved in a very humid environment, were combined with fragments of bark, which were interpreted as containers.

Habitat

Early hominids lived in one of two ways, open air or under cover, depending both on the climate and on the possibilities offered by the landscape. In Eastern Africa, where arboreous savannahs provided a privileged living environment, the absence of caves and the mildness of the climate favored living in the open air, on the edge of a lake or a river. Olduvai, Melka Kuntouré, Olorgesailie, Isimila or Kariandusi, for instance, are deposits of this type. Water as well as the proximity to good raw materials to manufacture tools, were probably what attracted settlement. However, when the environment provided natural shelters, even in tropical areas, prehistoric people took advantage of them (as in the Makapansgat and Montagu caves in South Africa). In the northern regions harsher climate, a larger proportion of sites were established under shelters, although the lack of open-air sites is probably more related to the absence of interglacial deposits, which were covered by the succeeding glacial deposits, than to a scarceness of Acheulian population at the exact time when the climate was becoming milder.

As during the Oldowan, there were flaking sites and possible slaughtering sites for large animals or for several small ones. Moreover, in caves as well as in the open air, the same accumulations of animal bones and of lithic (stone) material is apparent, but it is impossible to distinguish areas devoted to specific activities. These difficulties in interpretation arise from the fact that the grounds of the analyzed living areas are often the result of seasonal occupation, where from one year to the next the same group of humans, or those from different groups, would return, hence the accumulation and mixing of the traces of human activities. The layout of the inhabited spaces, however, remains very modest. It is most often limited to several blocks of stone, whose particular positions suggest a small protection wall, or wedging elements to secure branches (Lunel-Viel, Terra Amata, Lazaret), in which traces of huts can be discerned. The hearths themselves, as mentioned, were not constructed; It is only with their more systematic appearance at the end of the Lower Paleolithic that dwellings start to become more structured as domestic life became organized around the hearth.

Impressive Hunts

The sometimes sizeable quantities of animal bones found in the prehistoric sites of the Lower Paleolithic Period support the presumption that meat was of great importance in the diet of the Acheulian people. At Zhoukoudian, for instance, where the occupation of the site was prolonged, the variety of animal remains is particularly impressive: elephant, two kinds of rhinos, bison, horse, boar, roebuck, antelope, sheep, carnivores such as the *Machairodus*, leopard, or cave bear and a very large hyena. At Abbeville, mixed with a large number of rough bifaces, were remains of elephant, rhinoceros and horse, as well as *Machairodus* and *Trogontherium* remains. At the site of Ambrona, which is more recent, partial remains of some 50 *Elephas antiquus* were found. At Olorgesailie, in Kenya, which comprises about 10 levels of the Upper Acheulian, remains of large wart hogs, baboons, zebras and hippopotami were brought to light. At "Lake Karar" in Algeria, elephants, rhinoceroses, hippopotami, buffalos, zebras, giraffes, gazelles and wart hogs were associated with a primitive Acheulian. Other examples in Europe, Africa and Asia are numerous and the gathering of dead animals may have been widely practiced. However, the beginning of the large hunts probably started during the Acheulian. It was certainly a collective activity, a relay race to exhaust the game or a group of hunters forcing the animal to head for an artificial or natural trap. Hence, at Ambrona, it is believed that the Acheulian hunters forced elephants into swamps, where they were enmired and were killed.

In addition to large animals, smaller game such as rodents, hares and birds was also hunted. Minute excavations have led to the gathering of fish remains, which support a theory that fishing may have been practiced. Plants were probably also gathered, as they were throughout the Paleolithic Period. Perhaps the pieces of bark found on the site at Kalombo Falls served as containers for this foodstuff.

A Very Long Prehistory

Our brief survey of the order of primates affords an extremely simplified view of a very complex history, interspersed with lingering questions and paleontological gaps, which archaeologists hope to resolve over time. One cannot help, however, being struck by the continuing evolution without, as is often alleged, any hiatus or "missing link" from the small Euramerican *Purgatorius*, to the first East and South African hominoids with a still uncertain biped ability, arriving at first *Homo habilis* and then *Homo erectus*. Even if *Australopithecus* may have been an equal for a time, *Homo habilis* was the first consistent maker of stone tools. For more than 1 million years *Homo habilis* repeated the same elementary flaking gestures, limited by raw material. The territory of this people was confined to eastern and southern Africa, where they led a relatively precarious existence in an environment that was still hospitable. In a later time of a similar length, *Homo erectus* freed himself of the constraint of a found raw material, created forms, multiplied them, comprehended and reproduced symmetry, invented the "soft" hammer, domesticated fire and colonized the Old World. At this stage of human evolution, which precedes the appearance of *Homo sapiens*, it is necessary to imagine one or rather several complex social organizations, and hence, the command of a language. Thus may be summarized some 2.5 million years of our prehistory.

Cagny-l'Epinette, an Acheulian deposit in the Somme Basin. Freeing an antler. Ph. A. Tuffreau.

Suggested Reading

Bishop, Walter W., ed. *Geological Background to Fossil Man.* Chicago: University of Chicago Press, 1977.

Isaac, Glynn L. *Olorgesailie, Archaeological Studies of a Middle Plestocene, Lake Basin in Kenya.* Chicago: University of Chicago Press, 1977.

Johanson, Donald. *Lucy: Beginnings of Humankind.* New York: Simon & Schuster, 1990.

————. *Lucy's Child: The Search for Our Origins* New York: William Morrow & Co., 1989.

Lambert, David, and the Diagram Group. *The Field Guide to Early Man.* New York and Oxford: Facts On File, 1987.

Leakey, Mary D. *Olduvai Gorge.* vol. 3. Cambridge: Cambridge University Press, 1972.

Rukang, W., and Olsen J. W. *Palaeoanthrology and Paleolithic Archaeology in the People's Republic of China.* London: Academic Press, 1985.

Tattersall, Ian; Delson, Eric; and Van Couvering, John, eds. *Encyclopedia of Human Evolution and Prehistory.* New York and London: Garland, 1988.

FROM THE MIDDLE PALEOLITHIC TO THE EPIPALEOLITHIC IN THE OLD WORLD

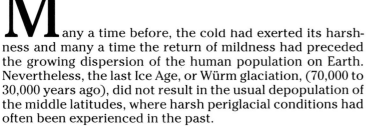

Mousterian lithic industry.
Flaked tools, generally made of flint, comprised numerous scrapers, robust points, denticles and a few small bifaces. Saint-Germain-en-Laye, Museum of National Antiquities. Ph. Lauros-Giraudon.

Many a time before, the cold had exerted its harshness and many a time the return of mildness had preceded the growing dispersion of the human population on Earth. Nevertheless, the last Ice Age, or Würm glaciation, (70,000 to 30,000 years ago), did not result in the usual depopulation of the middle latitudes, where harsh periglacial conditions had often been experienced in the past.

Indeed, through numerous dead ends and failures, but also decisive advances, a new humanity was slowly developing—that of *Homo sapiens*, which overcame each time the constraints of its own initial living conditions through the sheer force of its spirit. Humankind, thanks to numerous and immediate cultural responses,did not suffer disunification in order to increase tenfold and to employ great capacities for adapting to the most diverse situations of nature and environment.

After thousands of millennia of maturation, the last 80,000 years had established the bold, daring intelligence required for the development of the species. The challenge of the last glacial progression contributed greatly to ensuring the definitive passage from the last primitives to modern human beings.

The Würmian Chronology

Like the preceding Ice Age, the last glaciation consisted of relatively numerous cold phases of varying duration. These intense periods were separated from one another by more or less temperate episodes, or oscillations. Because of these breaks, the Würmian period itself can be described as having periods of uneven lengths.

The long earlier interglacial period, characterized by a very sharp increase in temperature, came to an end around 85,000 years ago, when an increase in rainfall and a drop in temperature cause climatic deterioration. This was followed by a series of fluctuations, sometimes rather dry, sometimes humid, combined with a continual decline in temperature. An immense glacier, or *inlandsis*, developed, particularly in Scandinavia, in the northern British Isles and in the various mountain ranges. About 80,000 years ago, ice gradually covered the northern part of the great north European plain and occupied the valleys, sometimes extending beyond their openings onto the plain.

More precisely, it is possible to distinguish four unequal Würmian stages, grouped in pairs, they form the old Würm and the recent Würm, separated by minor temperate oscillations around 35,000 years ago. This episode separates in an approximate manner the Middle Paleolithic and the Upper Paleolithic, the last manifestations of which took place around 10,000 years ago. The two *Homo sapiens* populations—*Homo sapiens neandertalensis* and *Homo sapiens sapiens*—which were for a long time considered systematically antagonistic and exclusive of one another—schematically divide this epoch in two, following patterns that are quite complex.

Steppe, Tundra and Shelter

An obvious consequence of the enveloping harsh climatic conditions was the spread of the glacial domain, which is now confined to the circumpolar regions and to the very high mountain zones. By no means should we characterize as "greenlands" the regions located in middle latitudes, which are, whatever their general climatic atmospheres, conditioned by the sequence of the four seasons. The mosaic of landscapes, therefore, offered greater differences than that of the present bioclimatic environments.

The Würm I is sometimes presented as a period during which, for 20,000 years, the continental harshness of a cold and dry climate prevailed and the steppe extended as far as the oceans of present temperate Europe. Most likely it was an open landscape of dry grass fields, scattered with scarce pines, birches and willows, and giving way during more favorable eras or in fortunate areas, to open woodlands.

The first glacial maximum was reached between 55,000 and 35,000 years ago, in the course of the second Würmian phase (Würm II) and was probably the result of a noticeable rise in precipitation, while temperatures remained low. Henceforth, vast territories of Europe and continental Asia, mainly plateaus and heights, were covered with snow during the winter months; thus only a meager and discontinuous creeping vegetation could subsist. The deep ground, sometimes frozen on a nearly permanent basis, was affected by important cryoturbation (churning) activity caused by the alternations in the superficial strata of frost and thaw. In regions swept by violent winds, important sheets of loess were formed, as well as other eolian (wind-blown) deposits.

Much more favorable conditions were present at southern latitudes, often owing to steep-sided valleys of particularly favorable exposure or mitigating influences. Hence many shelter zones were created for plant and animal species and, of course, for humans. On the southern edges of Europe, the Mediterranean climate, for instance, retained some of its prerogatives, as is attested by the persistence of several heliophilic plant species. This fact led to the assumption that if winters were harsh, summers must have been warm enough for the Mediterranean forms to develop. Thus, beneath skies that are closer to the tropics, only greater or lesser precipitation, which was certainly reduced during specific cold phases, created difficult living conditions.

The return to a temperate climate occured by stages, with brief intervals of sometimes intense cold, ending 10,000 years ago. From then on, during nearly three millennia, temperatures and precipitation rose constantly, until the mild and humid climatic optimum was reached toward the middle of the fourth millennium. The last glacial moments coincided in Africa with a long, arid period, resulting in the progression of the desert, far beyond its present southern limits. In contrast, the postglacial rise in temperature increased the cloud covering and favored precipitation, which created a green Sahara. Abundant life was found on the edges of the lakes and swamps that were formed in the depressions of this immense grassy steppe.

The Development of Domestic Space in Caves and Rock Shelters

The preservation and thriving of human life achieved in the periglacial zone and elsewhere, without any major biological adaptations were made possible by the mastery of the techniques needed to fashion dress, use fire and construct dwellings.

Without the conservation of organic matter, leather or plant fibers, assessing quality of Paleolithic clothing is impossible. Rare, indirect and relatively late evidence, such as the statuettes of Malta in Siberia or the carvings of the Gabillou Cave (Dordogne), representing figures dressed in a kind of anorak, or the eye needles made of bone, which are undoubtedly sewing objects, nevertheless assure us of their existence.

Fortunately, the development of systematic excavations, which expose large areas, has greatly increased the value of the material vestiges as evidence of the daily conditions of prehistoric life. The fact of the isolated object has been replaced by the documentation of it integrated into its environment. The recognition of the links that run through one similar context has made possible at times the reconstruction of strikingly well-preserved dwelling structures. Their analysis contributes to the rejection of the outdated image of scanty, troglodytic dwellings, considered as the only possible shelters in a frozen world.

Nevertheless, relatively deep galleries, modest nooks or small corridors easy to close off were sometimes used, without any other noticeable developments. The Hyena Cave at Arcy-sur-Cure, in which an important accumulation of discarded materials delineate the limits of a living space, constitutes a classic, although not exclusive, example of the Middle Paleolithic as well as the diverse epochs of prehistory.

In many cases, the rock shelter was but one element of protection. Denis Peyrony perceived this as early as 1924, in the rock shelter called *Fourneau du Diable* at Bourdeilles, where a wall of large bond-stones was linked with lined blocks and with the steep-sided cliff, in order to delineate the surface

A refuge in a difficult environment. In addition to being communication crossroads and contact zones between various natural habitats with complementary resources, steep-sided calcarous valleys in the areas around the Massif Central provided, during the cold period, both proximity to vast open spaces or plateaus, exposed to harsh weather, and refuge zones for plant and animals species and for humans. Ph. Studio des Grands-Augustins.

of Solutrean (an upper Paleolithic complex) huts, covering nearly 100 square yards (80 square meters). The nature of the protective superstructure is unknown. Similar arrangements were found, in particular, at the Abri du Facteur at Tursac shelter, at the La Madeleine rock shelter in Dordogne, at Le Blot in Haute-Loire, at the Tagliente shelter near Verona, etc. There, as in the sites where the infrastructure may have been very simple or even nonexistent, it is easy to imagine partitions made of branches and skins.

Quite similar constructions are suggested by holes and wedges for posts, stone alignments or areas cleared of stones, pavings, hearths, and also by the special distribution areas of lithic, bone, coal-like and mineral vestiges, which have sometimes been observed quite deep in the karst (cavernous) networks. Thus they clearly create the outlines of a doubly isolated area, a series of inside spaces.

According to the example of the Lazaret Cave at Nice, groups of this nature already existed near the end of the Lower Paleolithic Period. The following period does not provide such finely coherent evidence, despite the number of known Mousterian (Middle Paleothic) sites, which were often explored in the past. They are nevertheless very plausible, inasmuch as modern excavations point out the great diversity of such establishment types. At Hortus Cave, for example, the large ditch, which is rather similar to a naturally cleared area, may have been used, following the various occupations, as a spot for skinning, as a hunting rest stop, as a simple bivouac or as a camp.

Those of the Upper Paleolithic are better known. A level of the archaic Aurignacian industry at the Cueva Morin (Spain), testifying to an intense and long-term occupation, has revealed an artificial depression with a rectangular shape, corresponding to the likely placement of a hut. An oblong surface with a series of holes for posts was recognized at la Grotte du Renne at Arcy-sur-Cure. Long bones and mammoth tusks may have served as the framework for a sort of tent; the base of the tusk, still set in the ground, would confirm this interpretation.

Open-Air Establishments: Light Tents and Huts of Mammoth Bone

The same architectural principles were used for making open-air shelters. Such shelters obviously took into account the drawbacks and advantages of the environment and the particular needs of each human group.

The Molodova deposit on the Dniestr River in the Ukraine, located close to the latitude 53°N, in an already clearly continental environment, provides evidence of the complete ability of the Neandertals to endure the conditions of a particularly harsh environment. The great accumulation of large mammoth bones delineate an oblong hut of 33 feet

by 23 feet (10 meters by 7 meters)—not a temporary or hasty campsite. The 12 skulls, 34 shoulder blades and pelvises, the five mandibles and 14 tusks, which ensured the preservation of a defense system, testify to a relatively stable settlement. Later on, this principle of construction, carried out as early as the Middle Paleolithic in regions lacking other heavy and compact materials, was very widely used.

In the Upper Paleolithic, most likely to protect a more important group, perhaps a clan, large shelters were erected with multiple hearths, generally stretched out over several tens of feet. The diversity of their shapes could be the expression of ethnic or cultural differences. Particularly remarkable were constructions such as the long Gravettian industry "house" of Kostienki I, on the Don River in the U.S.S.R., which measured 120 feet (36 meters) long and 60 feet (18 meters) wide, lined with large pits, from which the earth had been removed, thus forming a protective mound at the base of the roofing system. Later on, these pits, lined with large bones, were used to store fat destined to fuel hearths. Such groups, of remarkable size, have been revealed, among others, on the Gravettian site of Dolni Vestonice in Czechoslovakia, on the little plateau of Barca, where a group of the evolved Aurignacian fashioned a peculiar shelter in the shape of an H, measuring some 80 feet (25 meters) in its longest dimension, as well as the site of Pouchkari, near Novgorod.

Of the system, inaugurated at Molodova, of simple huts that were well implanted and built to last against the cold, many widely disseminated examples stand out. Later establishments of the arctic peoples have perpetuated and sometimes improved such protection principles. The sites of Malta and Bouriet in Siberia, with numerous establishments, of Pavlov in Czechoslovakia, where at least 13 grouped habitations were found, of Mezhirich in the Ukraine, or the site of Vigne-Brun at Villerest (Loire) are characterized by a slight subcircular depression of quite modest size, surrounded by a significant accumulation of heavy materials, which served to reinforce and support perishable roofing: skins, bark, clods of frozen and wet earth, patches of grass. On the 15,000-year-old Ukrainian site, the protective rampart, which may be the base of a cupola, consisted of 95 mammoth mandibles, neatly fitted into each other, and reinforced by big, long bones and shoulder blades.

The settlements in caves or in the open in regions devoid of natural shelters that were meant to last, could be replaced by much lighter tents, sheltering for a short period the diverse segments or products of more important and complex initial societies. At Corbiac near Bergerac, at Dosmos in Hungary, at Breuil and Cerisier in Dordogne, at Fontgrasse in the Gard, at Etiolles, at Pincevent in the Parisian Basin, at Lassac in Aude, as well as in countless open-air locations, the structures generally occupied surfaces of a few square feet/meters, made recognizable by the area over which the various objects manufactured by the prehistorics are spread out and, in some cases, by the areas that are paved or provided with holes for posts.

The diversity of settlements as early as the Middle Paleolithic is thus clearly perceived, and it did, of course, lengthen and develop into the Upper Paleolithic. To consider this diversity in enclosed space renders possible our gradual perception, of the flexibility with which Paleolithic human groups adapted to varying and often harsh living conditions. On a long-term basis, the indisputable increase in the number of sites occupied during the last Würmian phase bears evidence to the success of the system.

Relatively stable habitations in protected environments, often amidst perennial hunting grounds, were followed by specialized hunting expeditions, which offered opportunities for adventure and exchanges.

The profound renewal of the ecosystems in the postglacial stage put an end for a time to large gatherings in Oceanic Western Europe, and most likely favored the most adaptive social segment: the nuclear family.

Vast Herds of Herbivores

One can easily picture large, free herds of herbivores living on the vast open spaces of cold steppes and tundra in the most exposed plains and plateaus. Thus appear, at random, the compact herds of migrating reindeer, bison, horses and, very occasionally, musk ox or saiga antelope. In smaller and more numerous herds, reindeer inhabited the forests, which were never really thick and followed the course of the valleys. In these same forests, in winter, according to the time and place, hordes of mammoths, wooly rhinoceros, as well as deer and reindeer, which are clearly adapted to a temperate climate, roamed. In the steep areas and down to the lower altitudes, chamois and ibexes thrived. Wolves, foxes, lynxes, wild cats and many other species, sometimes cave bears, were the major predators. As the competitors of humans, they too became prey.

Hunting: The Importance of Technological Improvement

Collective hunting certainly represented one of the most early, active and stimulating forms of prehistoric social life. It may also be reasonable to assume that food requirements influenced hunting practices when, for instance, the group grew, by intensifying and rendering them more efficient through the perfecting of weapons.

The study of animal remains shows that in the Middle Paleolithic Period, in fact as early as the last part of the Lower Paleolithic, men applied the principles of specialized hunting to the prevailing species in their environment. The hunting techniques, which are unknown to us, may have been simple, and expeditions and the range of weapons limited.

During the Upper Paleolithic diversifying and lightening lithic implements,as well as the fashioning of dart points made out of bone, ivory or antler, improved the individual success of the hunters. One finds split-base spear points, lozenge-shaped or biconical, according to the various periods of the Aurignacian, and rare striated spear points of the Upper Perigordian industry, perhaps compensated for, as in the Solutrean, by various stone points.

The slow population growth, which must have resulted from a favorable environment, may have created needs that were satisfied toward the end of the Upper Paleolithic by the combined effect of communal hunts in favorable areas and more specialized individual activities. The spectacular development of bone tools in the Magdalenian industry stage is probably a sign of such progress, with many different types of spear points with simple or double bevels, a forked base, grooves, semicircular sticks,various harpoons—possibly designed for aquatic hunting—bir "forks," hooks, etc. Henceforth, small animals are no longer subject to a mere predation, a sort of random gathering, but to planned hunts, made easier by the significant invention, as is believed, of the bow and arrow.

In the postglacial stage, the disappearance of large herds of herbivores put an end to big hunts; the larger animals were replaced by herds of the much-smaller deer and boar of the vast European temperate forests. These smaller targets made individual skill stand out and of necessity brought the hunter closer to the game—making the prey more difficult to kill. Because of this, the existence of a post-Paleolithic crisis, one that was not necessarily demographic, is more easily asserted. The crisis was of social structures—not of food resources, which were greater and more diversified.

Ultimately, from the completion of this adaptation, which in turn caused a slight population increase, was born in part the dynamic that led to the neolithic changes of Western Europe. It enabled humans to take the place of herds of large herbivores in spaces newly opened by the clearings. The difference is that assuredly these builders were somewhat better able to master periods of uncertainty.

(Left) Reindeer, small-sized cervids well adapted to the climatic conditions of the Würmian glaciation, provided easy and abundant game for Paleolithic hunters. Besides meat and fat, they provided skin, bones, antlers and tendons. The abundance of their remains in numerous prehistoric deposits, as kitchen refuse, hunting weapons and works of art, fully justifies the designation of a "Reindeer Age." Ph. Massart/Jacana.

(Above) Distant descendants of the herds of wild horses of the Pleistocene, this mare and her foal, last remnants of the Equus ferus Prjevalskii, *still gallop freely in the cold steppes of Central Asia. Their carriage and morphology are very close to those of their ancestors, sometimes represented in cave art. Ph. Méro/Jacana.*

The First *Sapiens*

Human fossils are too scarce to allow a retracing in detail of their evolution. They are sometimes compared, despite large chronological and geographic gaps, but they very imperfectly punctuate the history of mankind. Anatomic peculiarities sometimes make it difficult to distinguish between what stems from the morphological variations between individuals from the differences between species and subspecies. Nevertheless, ever since the beginning of the last glaciation, and probably even before, numerous observations converge in indicating that in anatomic and mental composition, human beings had reached the era of modernity.

After the discovery in 1908 of the skeleton of La Chapelle-aux-Saints, in Corrèze, Marcelin Boule exposed in a detailed study *Homo primigenius* (the first human) as a rudimentary being, with a heavy gait, a man still incompletely freed from his recent animal past. Deformations arthritis, which are normal in a relatively aged subject, and also several deep-seated prejudices misled the famous paleontologist. This presentation nevertheless went much further than the judgments issued after the discovery of the Feldhofer Cave skeleton in the Neander Valley, near Dusseldorf (Germany), in 1856. Then, the discovered subject was deemed to be an abnormal or pathological being. Several years later, however, his specific originality was acknowledged, yet in those days *Homo neandertalensis* was considered to be a primitive example of humanity—very clearly distinct from our own species.

At present, a precise portrait can be outlined from the common features recognized in more than 300 fossils, which are, however, very unevenly preserved. His silhouette is totally human; he owes his robustness, his resistance, his strength, the fineness and dexterity of his movements to his often modest height, sometimes close to 5.5 feet (1.60 meters), despite a perfectly straight stance, and to his solidly built and muscular body. His head is more amazing. The skull is quite low, but very large and elongated, which gives it a volume sometimes noticeably superior to ours. The top of the skull develops beyond very strong eyebrow arches,in a rounded yet receding forehead, and ends toward the back in a bony pre-eminence, or occipital knot. The face is surprisingly heavy and poorly expressive. The orbits, sunken under thick arches, are large and circular; the cheekbones, which are not thrown into relief by hollows below, recede in back of a strong and flat nose. The powerful maxilla project forward above a generally receding chin.

These original features were perceived for a long time as so many anachronisms, defining a general, clear cut stage in human evolution. They are, in fact, the sum of a series of adaptations to somewhat poorly defined environmental pressures—among which may be climatic conditions and the demands made on the jaws by the components of their diet. Neandertals are therefore the final and homogeneous result of a long evolution, the origin of which should be sought among the more evolved forms of *Homo erectus* toward the end of the Lower Paleolithic Period.

Neandertal Europe

The strong concentration of Neandertals in western Europe cannot necessarily be attributed entirely to the extensive excavations made there; the region most likely corresponds to their area of flowering and development. Several important marginal locations suggest that the limits of their expansion were situated in the Middle East and in Soviet Central Asia. Elsewhere, in Africa and in the rest of Asia, more or less evolved and original parallel lineages developed from other forms of *Homo erectus*, the representatives of which, sometimes referred to as Neandertaloids, generally differ from their ancestors on the one hand by a clear increase in their cranial capacity and the attenuation of their anatomical archaisms,and, on the other hand, by the total or partial absence of the characteristic features of the classic Neandertals.

The Mousterian Cultural Stage

All Mousterian tool flakers were not Neandertals. The contrast that exists between the anthropological diversity and the relative homogeneity of the Middle Paleolithic indus-

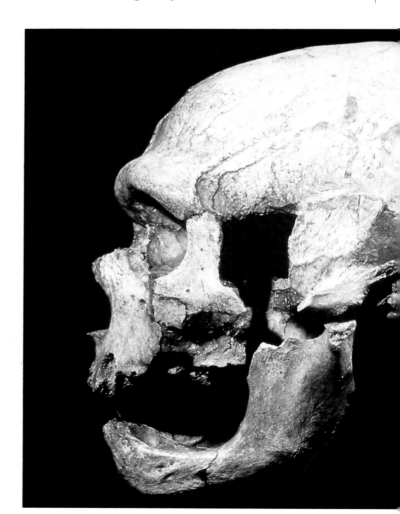

tries seems to indicate that these tools correspond rather to a certain stage of technological perfecting than to the expression of a particular form of intelligence attributable to a precise human type. It is most probably among the fortunate conditions of the environment, amid a favorable economic and social context, that one should look for the causes of the cultural dynamism of Europe and its neighboring regions. It seems to have been the most active center of innovation of the inhabited world, despite the inadequacies in our knowledge regarding vast regions of the Old World.

The Mousterians took on individual characteristics toward the end of the Rissian glaciation, preceding the Würm, according to evidence left by multiple relationships with industries, particularly the flake. In a way, it prolonged the Clactonian and Tayacian industries of tools made on common, generally massive, flakes. Certain of these manufactured items show that they had perfectly mastered the Levallois flaking technique, which permits the creation of flakes of predetermined shapes and dimensions. This already old technique was widely used, but all of the groups did not confer upon it an equal importance.

The Mousterian thus defined appeared with the start of the last glaciation, all the while maintaining two separate cultural traditions, the Micocean, and the impressive Acheulian tradition; the latter joining Mousterian evolution at that time.

The Mousterian: Fifty Millennia of Stability

In reality there is no universal or homogeneous Mousterian tradition, but a series of cultural facets that have in common the same kinds of stone flaked tools—pieces frequently made of energetically retouched flakes with scales arranged along the sides.

The particularly well-represented scrapers appear with multiple and often combined straight, convex or concave, lateral or transverse cutting edges. The Mousterian points display none slender forms and were probably the heads of hunting weapons. More common are the denticled (notched) pieces; the notches may be the result of a particular kind of scraping, such as bark stripping.

The unequal representation of these tools characterizes different lithic series. Sometimes certain objects, according to the context, extend the differences between series apart from statistic criteria. Thus bifaces are objects which continue the Acheulian tradition, in an evolved form in the shape of hearts or triangles. These archaic elements are surprisingly found, side by side, with small and lighter tools of the "Upper Paleolithic type," such as scrapers, borers and especially back knives. The number of back knives increased

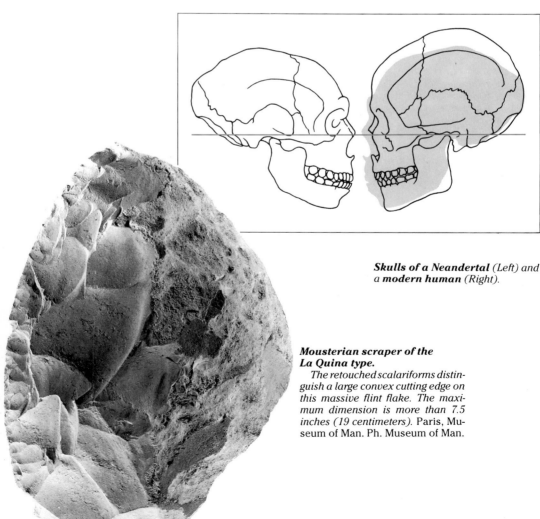

Skulls of a Neandertal (Left) and *a modern human* (Right).

Mousterian scraper of the La Quina type.
   The retouched scalariforms distinguish a large convex cutting edge on this massive flint flake. The maximum dimension is more than 7.5 inches (19 centimeters). Paris, Museum of Man. Ph. Museum of Man.

during the course of the second phase of the Mousterian of the Acheulian tradition. This industry experienced, by far, the most dynamic technological innovations; the others, in contrast, remained extraordinarily static throughout the millennia of the Middle Paleolithic. It is scarcely possible to attribute exclusively to the dated research the fine variety, without equal, of the Mousterian facies (tool kits) from western Europe and particularly from France.

The great French prehistorian François Bordes, identified—in the studies that were to become the basis of a system of tool identification—five main groups. The typical Mousterian, identified from the eponymous shelter of Moustier in Dordogne (France), contains an often important percentage of scrapers. The Denticulate Mousterian is characterized by the large number of notches and denticled objects. The implementation of the Levallois flaking technique or its absence distinguish the Ferrassie-type Mousterian from the Quina type, with its large transversal scrapers. The main features of the Mousterian belonging to the Acheulian tradition have already been described.

These principal divisions are found throughout Europe, with more or less characteristic features, sometimes accented by the presence of original objects that bear a strong local specificity. In Spain and southern Aquitaine, the Mousterian of Acheulian tradition, for example, displays numerous small axes. In Germany, slender foliated (leaf-shaped) pieces with bifacial retouch, the *Blattspitzen,* are part of a perhaps late Mousterian. In Poland, the *Prodniks,* types of biface-backed knives, belong to a Mousterian stemming from the Micoquian industry. Further east, however, the lithic industry of the Molodova site corresponds to the definition of the typical western-style Mousterian. The latter, as most of the other facies, may appear in any location, including southern Europe, where the particular local aspects may be very important. The distribution of the facies—arranged according to a predominant type within relatively contrast-

ing and vast areas—shows that facies style is basically a cultural expression that reflects the exceptional force of each technological tradition which was reinforced for later generations both because the styles fulfilled specific needs and because outer influences were nonexistant—encounters and exchanges were very rare in a world that was essentially "empty."

Birth of Modern Man

The problem of the disappearance of the Neandertals is well-illustrated by the presence of the fossils of one of them in a Chatelperronian level of the Saint-Césaire shelter (Charente-Maritime in France). This 1979 discovery supports the idea of their progressive replacement, perhaps in part through assimilation, by the sporadic penetration by the first representatives of modern humans.

In all probability, the more variable human lines, with the greatest possibilities for evolving, formed first as a group perhaps as early as the end of the Lower Paleolithic, as indicated by the fossil of Mugharet-el-Zuttiyeh fossil in Israel. At this time, this group appears to have been located mainly in the Near East and North Africa. Thus, the fossils of Djebel Qafzeh and Skhùl in Israel, where their coexistence with classic Neandertals—whose material culture of the Mouster-

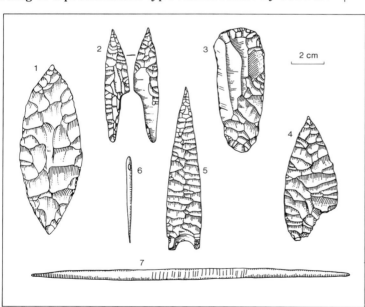

Solutrean industry
1. Laurel leaf
2. Shouldered point
3. Scraper
4. Stepped leaf
5. Leaf with a concave base
6. Eyed needle
7. Sagaie (spear) 3/4 in/2cm

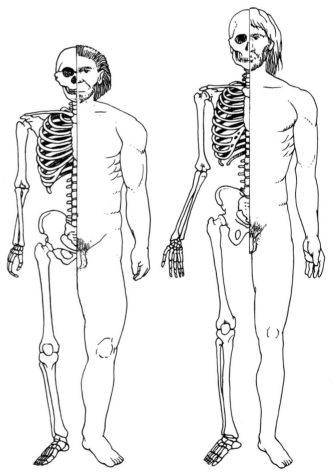

Neandertal man   *Cro-Magnon man*

ian variety they shared—seem likely to show, as those of Jebel Irhoud and Dar-es-Soltane in Morocco, that the appearance of new features was taking place—representing one of the robust early modern populations that still retained some archaic features. It seems reasonable to think that similar processes happened according to different dynamics and chronological rhythms in other human stocks. This phenomenon corresponds to the emergence of another kind of *Homo sapiens*, a second subspecies—*Homo sapiens sapiens*—that survived.

The Combe-Capelle skeleton (Dordogne) was allegedly discovered in the Chatelperronian level in 1909, unfortunately in questionable circumstances. This skeleton represents one of the oldest modern Europeans, who was also identified on the site of Brno in Czechoslovakia. They show a very evolved skull of large dimension, high and narrow with a highly rounded occipital bone and a slender face, that retains, in a very attenuated manner, the archaicism of a somewhat receding forehead, quite prominent eye arches, and a slight projection forward. Their height of 5.25 feet (1.60 meters) is average.

Another human group, identified on the basis of the famous discoveries made in 1868 in the Cro-magnon rock shelter at Les Eyzies in Dordogne is, on the contrary, generally made up of strongly built, tall individuals, sometimes close to six feet (1.80 meters). Archaic features, although strongly attenuated, include a large and low though vertical face and a high forehead with a rear skull where a slight occipital knot is found.

Toward the end of the Upper Paleolithic Period, some regional differentiations clearly appeared. In western Europe the human type represented by the vestiges of the Chancelade shelter in Dordogne and that of Obercassel in Germany, most likely constitutes an evolved and slender form of the Cro Magnon type.

The Technological Change of the Upper Paleolithic: The Leptolithic Tools

Generally considered the product of intrusive cultures, the new tools of the Upper Paleolithic very often seem to have developed from coherent evolutionary processes that were deep-rooted in regional cultural ancestors.

The tools' originality resides less in their novelty, most of them having been, in fact, attempted before, than in the generalization of small, light—leptolithic—and diversified tools, easily fashioned from thin and slender flakes: the blades and bladelettes. Obviously, there was no perfect synchronism in the emergence and development of the phenomenon—and massive flakes were, in many cases, still

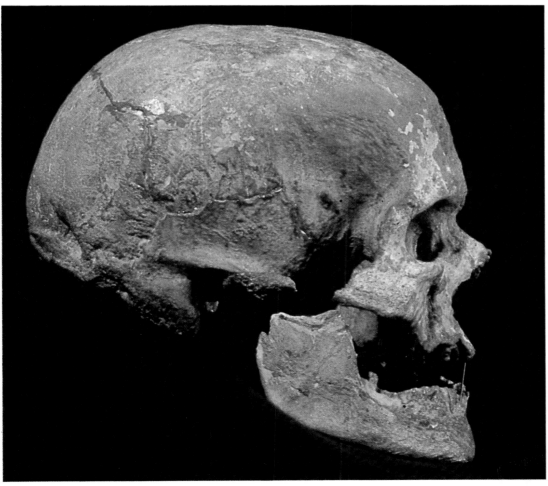

Homo sapiens sapiens.
Skull of the "old man" from the Cro-Magnon shelter at Eyzies-de-Tayac (Dordogne, France). Paris, Museum of Man. Ph. J. Oster/Museum of Man.

Elegant, thin, finely retouched on both faces, this Solutrean "laurel leaf" point was probably used on the end of a hunting weapon. It measures more than 10 inches (25 centimeters). Saint-Germain-en-Lay, Museum of National Antiquities. Ph. Lauros-Giraudon.

used—but a general progressive tendency is apparent. It is indeed this profound renewal of technological requirements, most likely the result of an undeniable general resurgence, which contrasts with the extraordinary stability of the preceding period. It is combined with the sometimes considerable development of fashioning various hard animal materials, such as bone, antler, ivory and, in some striking cases, with the first artistic expressions. Lastly, at the time when the first peopling of America took place, the inhabited world was moving closer to the habitable world.

In detail, the lithic tools often display somewhat stereotyped shapes, such as scrapers characterized by a rounded front at the end of an elongated fragment or blade, burins with a narrow terminal, borers with the bit acting more or less free, as well as retouched blades and bladelets, backed points, denticles and splintered pieces. Yet there are many differences in the proportions of the various types. Their description allows one to isolate the major cultural groups or "civilizations"—Aurignacian, Gravettian, Solutrean, etc.—the characteristics of which are reinforced by the particular style of flaking or manufacture and sometimes by the presence of specific objects. Thus may appear, for example, "Aurignacian blades," "Solutrean laurel leaves," Gravettian "Noailles burins" or Magdalenian "parrot-beak-burins."

The earliness and clarity of the work carried out in France resulted in a classification system that seemed for a time to be a universal one and into which cultural sequences discovered in the rest of Europe, or even outside of Europe, were integrated, sometimes incorrectly. The interest of each of them is nevertheless essentially regional, and the groups that compose them generally bear true original features, despite sometimes misleading convergences in detail.

Numerous models may thus lay claim to serve as a framework for the very diverse expressions of the Upper Paleolithic in the Old World. All have not been identified, much less described, with the same rigor, and it is rare that developments of others have been analyzed with as much precision as the Franco-Cantabrian model, even though it may be one of the most complex.

Southwestern France: A Classic Region

Still close to the Mousterian or Acheulian tradition, in which its origin likely resides, the Châtelperronian, identified for the first time in the Fées grotto at Châtelperron, (Allier), comprises a sufficient number of new artifacts, among which are scrapers, burins, bone tools and pendants, next to Levallois flakes, scrapers and sometimes numerous Mousterian points, for the new technological era to be fully inaugurated around 34,000 B.P. One of the characteristic tools, the Châtelperron knife, is a point on blade fashioned by abrupt retouches. After an evolution of some five millennia, this industry seems to have lost its characteristic features. Nevertheless, the presence of back points in more evolved industries of a rare Middle Perigordian has permitted certain specialists to extend the Chatelperronian, considered as Lower Perigordian, up to the Gravettian rebirth of the Upper Perigordian. For other specialists, however, the Saint-Césaire Neandertal fully confirms the artificiality of such a construction.

The Aurignacian, named after the industry discovered in a small cavity near Aurignac (in the Haute Garonne, France) has a much more obscure, essentially Mousterian origin, possibly residing in central Europe, of which it retains some of the fine flake retouches. Keeled scrapers, Aurignacian retouch blades and Dufour bladettes, with fine semi-abrupt, inverted retouches, developed as early as 35,000 B.P., competing with the preceding tools, as is evident in some cases of interstratification.

From 26,000 B.P. onward, the Gravettian competed with the waning Aurignacian, whose numerous facies mainly include burins and straight-backed points. After 20,000 B.P. the Perigordian VII, sometimes referred to as "Protomagdalenian" because of large numbers of burins and the quality of bone fashioning crowns this magnificent evolution.

The Solutrean, identified near the Roc de Solutré (Saône-et-Loire in eastern France) was an entirely original civilization that started to constitute itself around 19,000 B.P. in the regions bordering the Massif Central, from which it then spread. The Solutrean retouch, fine and all over, displayed on the early points with plane sides, developed remarkably, and subsequently encompassed the two sides of the magnificent and famous "laurel leaves." It is still visible on point heads, which are characteristic of the last phase. The eyed bone needle is considered an invention of this period.

Bone implements developed from 15,500 B.P. onward, during the Magdalenian. The evolution of the various tools—different kinds of *assagais*, long, short or grooved, semi-cir-

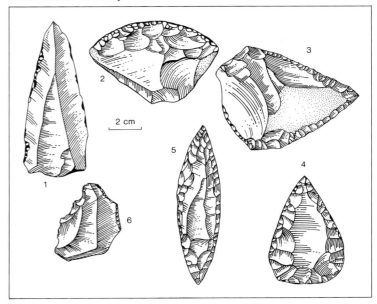

Mousterian Industry

2 cm

1. Levallois point
2. Simple convex scraper
3. Asymmetrical scraper, with spur
4. Mousterian point
5. Limace
6. Denticled piece

Eyed needle, harpoons and Magdalenian spear point with a forked base.
The multiplication and diversification of hunting gear in the course of the Magdalenian most likely reflects an increase and a diversification of man's borrowings from the animal world. Paris, Museum of Man. Ph. J. Oster/Museum of Man.

cular sticks, harpoons with one or two rows of points—served as a basis for Abbé Breuil's traditional classification in six phases, based on the finds at the Picard Cave in Charente and the Madeleine shelter at Tursac (Dordogne). Among the lithic tools, including a strong proportion of burins and back pieces, numerous microlithic points are found. This diversification may be interpreted as the perfecting of hunting techniques, which may have been themselves combined with a strong population growth.

The postglacial increase in temperature—by modifying the basis of the Magdalenian economy—most likely engendered a serious disruption of social structures; the loss of coherence between the different human groups may have been combined with a strong cultural opening, encouraging changes in tools. The Perigordian Azilian, as analyzed in the Villepin shelter at Tursac, developed progressively farther and farther away from its Magdalenian origins, and certain cultures north of the Pyrénées range, also known as Azilian after the site of Mas d'Azil (in Ariège), where a large number of thumbnail scrapers and "Azilian" points were discovered, are a clear break from the preceding civilization and testify to southern influences from the Epigravettian industries of the Mediterranean.

The Mesolithic is divided into two main phases by the development of narrow points at first, such as triangles and Sauveterre points, then toward the beginning of the sixth millennium, by that of large points, such as trapezes. It was on this Mesolithic foundation, a little more than 5,000 years ago, that the Neolithic transformation of implements was founded.

Regional Cultural Diversity of the Upper Paleolithic

The organization of many regional upper Paleolithic cultures have been established throughout Europe as a consequence of the recent development of methodological works. Some of these models only emphasize minor zonal variations, such as the various Magdalenian facies of the English Cresswellien (after finds in the Creswell Crag in Derbyshire), the German Hamburgian (displaying a way of life based on reindeer hunting), the Tjongerian in the low countries and the Bromme culture in Denmark. Others, however, display the originality of the solutions provided within the general leptolithic framework.

The Italian Upper Paleolithic industries are an excellent example, as they produced no Chatelperronian, nor Solutrean, nor Magdalenean tools. Thus, after the ancient period, during which the Ulluzziano, with its abundant scrapers and numerous points, with rounded backs, and the Aurignacian were opposed, a broad Perigordian lineage developed in several phases and after 18,000 B.P., survived the final Gravettian. Successively came the Ancient Epigravettian, including some Solutrean retouch objects and notch points, the Middle Gravettian and the Final Gravettian that abundantly produced scrapers and back points near 12,000 B.P. This polymorphous Gravettian background encompassed the Mediterranean peninsulas; the Iberian peninsula was, however, strongly influenced by the nearby Franco-Cantabrian domain.

In central and eastern Europe, the Mousterian, with foliated (leaf-shaped) points, evolved very progressively toward the Szeletian, named after the Szeleta Cave in Hungary, which is remarkable for its fine bifacial foliated points. Aurignacian groups, sometimes classic, sometimes close to the Middle Eastern Aurignacian, joined with the aforementioned one on the ancient horizon.

The Eastern Gravettian or Pavlovian, from the Pavlov Hills in Czechoslovakia, follows these groups. Its often very abundant industries are sometimes quite similar to the classic Upper Perigordian, as in the various deposits of Dolni Vestonice (Czechoslovakia) where a huge accumulation of mammoth bones, hearths, remains of dwellings and burials were discovered. They become more original as they move toward the Ukraine and Russia.

The amazing vitality of the Magdalenoan is further illustrated by its presence in Czechoslovakia and in Poland, on the site of Masycka. In the U.S.S.R. are found numerous sites of the evolved Upper Paleolithic, their industry organized around the deposits discovered at Molodova V, Mezin, Kostenki-Borchevo, Eliseevichi, in diversified facies with still imprecise chronocultural relationships.

The Paleolithic peopling of the huge Siberian space is likewise poorly known, except for several classic deposits in which maybe included the site of Malta near Kirkoutsk, dating to 22,000 B.P., famous for its dwelling vestiges and its ivory statuettes, or the later one, Afontova Gora at Krasnoiarsk, the tools of which, primarily flakes, clearly exemplify the long Mousterian tradition of Siberian lithic implements.

The Aterian: The Stunning Solution of North Africa

In North Africa, the tradition of the clearly Mousterian flake occupied an important part of the period corresponding to the European Upper Paleolithic. Between 40,000 B.P. and 25,000 B.P., the Aterian industry evolved, identified on the site of Bir el Ater in southern Tunisia. It contains numerous Levallois flakes, some scrapers, a very high percentage of scrapers with a very evolved aspect and, above all, many curious stalks, frequently pointed. Some finely foliated points are included in some places. A clear technological break separates the Aterian from the belatedly asserted real leptolithic industries proper, after what seems to correspond to an interruption in human occupation, of several millennia.

Around 18,000 B.P., the Ibero-Maurusian appeared in North Africa, possibly constituted on a more Oriental tradition, in the form of an industry essentially composed of irregular bladelettes and reduced flakes. It developed three successive phases up to a stage that assimiliated, around the sixth millennium, the new technologies of the Neolithic. The two somewhat synchronous groups, the typical and the Upper Capsian appeared in Southern Tunisia later than the seventh millennium. Characterized by smaller tools, bone awls, ostrich-eggshell beads and polishing stones, they are thus clearly Mesolithic. (They engendered the Neolithic of Capsian tradition.)

The Model of Southwest Asia

The Middle Eastern Paleolithic offers, despite a development in three phases quite similar to the European pace, another fine example of diversity. After ancient and middle phases, characterized by the presence of industries using the Levallois flaking technique and by industries with strong, Aurignacian features, there appeared after 18,000 B.P. industries with a very asserted lamellated (blade-like) flaking, constituting the Kebarian, named for Mugharet el-Kebarah in Israel, in a remarkable geographical development in an important part of southwestern Asia. It includes a classic period, with particularly abundant bladelettes, with a truncated or sharpened back, then a geometric phase, with microlithic frameworks in the shape of rectangles, trapezoids or triangles. Around 12,000 B.P., certain sites in the vicinity of Lake Tiberius have revealed hut bottoms dug on hillsides, provided with small walls, which contain stunning stone objects, such as deep mortars and rammers, millstones and grinders. These artifacts, which undoubtedly testify to progress in settlement and in the processing of edible plant substances, show that profound modifications—which were taken over and developed by the Natufian—had begun in certain areas as early as that period, attributable, in part, to the particularly favorable environment. They determined the dawn of a new cultural, social and economic order.

The Cult of the Dead and the Rise of Symbolic Thought

What a fine diversity and complexity the various material cultures of the Paleolithic offer! They underscore well the intellectual development of their artisans, who acquired at the same time a clear concept of their own existence. Man henceforth grasped the world with this awareness of his life and was endowed with an exceptional destiny among the living creatures.

Behavior that stemmed from this budding spirituality is very imperfectly illuminated by archaeological methods, which only take note of it when fully developed. This, then, was the time of *Homo sapiens*. Among rare vestiges, intentional burial places may testify to a particular attitude toward death, and therefore toward life and its short time span. However, inhumation (human burial) may have been prompted by other than spiritual concerns, and its absence is not necessarily a sign of indifference.

Numerous discoveries allow us to attribute to Neandertal man, *Homo sapiens neandertalensis*, the first sepulchral practices. In 1908, in La Chapelle-aux-Saints Cave, near Brive, the Abbots Bouyssonie and Bardon discovered the skeleton of a man, a Neandertal (that would be the subject of paleontologist Pierre Marcellin Boule's comprehensive study) who had been "intentionally buried." He lay at the bottom of a pit dug into the marly soil of the cave. To establish this discovery firmly, the researchers underscored that "this soil, white-colored and hard to dig, displayed an obvious contrast with the archaeological strata." They also believed that the end of a bovidean hoof, the various bones of which were observed in anatomic connection, provided evidence of a funerary ritual. The setting for practices of this kind, although probably much more complex, was the large Ferrassie shelter, where six Neandertals were discovered by Peyrony from 1906 onward, when two adults resting within the Mousterian strata, were patently linked with a whole system of small depressions and mounds of earth. In this group, a child's skull, without a mandible, was placed beneath a strong flagstone, hollowed with cupules; moreover, the remains of a fetus rested beneath a mound.

The diversity in the treatment of the dead would appear upon examination in the burial place of Regourdou, (Dordogne) where a young adult male was found at one end of a stone-lined pit, with what is thought to be carefully

Reconstruction of an Upper Paleolithic burial place.

Beside burial in a fetal position, such as was found on the Chancelade site in Dordogne, other burial practices, such as the one here in a Grimaldi hollow, were in use. In fact, they underscore the diversity of funerary rites, which may have been used since the Middle Paleolithic. Monaco, Anthropology Museum. Ph. Ch. Lenars.

arranged bones of a brown bear at the other; or of the Shanidar Cave in Iraq, where the body of one of the nine Neandertals discovered was supposedly buried within a pit lined with pine boughs and covered with flowers, according to the interpretation provided by pollen analysis.

Much more definite is the contribution of the Techik-Tach Cave in Uzbekistan, where the skull of an approximately 10-year-old child was surrounded, as if to provide protection, with five pairs of ibex horns, pointing downwards to form a crown. This is similar to the care with which the Guattari Cave Neandertal skull in Monte Circeo, near Rome, was encircled with stones; in this last case a distinct widening of the occipital hole was observed, permitting an easy access to the brain. Ritual consumption is a possibility here, and it is more than likely in the Krapina Cave in Yugoslavia, where the calcinated bone remains, broken and split lengthwise, of more than 20 individuals have prompted speculation about cannibalism, as well as, to a lesser degree about the Hortus Cave.

It seems that the cultural development of the Upper Paleolithic encouraged a multiplication of practices. If, among the different sorts of burials, interment in a position with bent knees recalling the fetal position and suggesting a possible return to Mother Earth, is fully demonstrated as at Chancelade, many other types were practiced. The funerary objects are not often easily distinguished from other archaeological vestiges: canine and other animal teeth, as well as perforated sea shells, probably did not belong especially to the mortuary regalia. Quite similar reservations can be made on the use of red ochre, which permeates even the soil of dwellings, and which may have served as body paint during the life of the deceased. The treatment of corpses by sprinkling them with red ochre—the color of blood and symbol of life—is nevertheless admitted. In the Cavillon Cave, near Menton, a hollow groove in the earth, packed with this coloring material, was reportedly noticed between the mouth of the buried corpse and the open air. The discovery was exceptional!

Complex behaviors undoubtedly existed. Often they involved the skull of the deceased. At Saint-Germain-la-Rivière in Gironde, the head was protected by a box made of slabs. At Mas-d'Azil, two bone plaques sealing the eye sockets may have conferred some semblance of life to the Magdalenian skull.

The Upper Paleolithic Period is thus infinitely rich, its human denizens proving to be so close to us in the working out of their thoughts, and yet so utterly remote by the often mysterious aspects of their behavior. Let us be assured that, armed with their speculations, they recognized the forces of nature and in their own way integrated themselves within it.

Suggested Reading

Clark, John G. *Mesolithic Prelude: The Paleolithic-Neolithic Transition in Old World Prehistory*. New York: Columbia University Press, 1980.

Kirk, R. L., and Thorne, A. G. *The Origin of the Australians*. Canberra, 1976.

MacNeish, R. S., et al. *Early Man in America: Readings from Scientific American*. San Francisco: W. H. Freeman, 1973.

Paleolithic lamp.
Fashioned and hollowed out of a block of sandstone, such as this magnificent sample from Mouthiers in Charente, or by using a concave rock flake, fat lamps provided lighting akin to that of oil lamps, still in use at the turn of this century. After fire was mastered during the Lower Paleolithic, the lamp is the perfect symbol of man's application of the diverse offerings of nature. Paris, Museum of Man. Ph. J. Oster/Museum of Man.

CHAPTER FIVE

Denis Vialou

THE SOURCES OF ART

The large Magdalenian limestone shelter of Angles-sur-l'Anglin (Vienne, France) displays, over several yards (meters), majestic animal low-reliefs, engraved animal silhouettes and deep engravings of human heads, legs and pubic triangles. On this block, a bison head presents all of the figurative characters, extremely well preserved, of the Magdalenian sculptures. Ph. D.R.

Let us imagine for an instant our world without art: no poems, novels, music, dance, statues, trinkets, paintings, or decoration. A truly frightening vision emerges, an alteration of the way we see ourselves and our universe.

And yet there was a period "before" or "without" art, that is to say a period devoid of graphic forms—forms that are fashioned to outlive their creators, conceived to conquer time, representations inscribed on or in stone, caves, bones, teeth, ivory, antlers and horn.

And the Images Peopled the Earth

The period that anticipated the first glimmerings of art is infinitely longer than that which we share with the first artists: 3 million years on one hand and 30,000 to 40,000 years on the other. The "modernesism" of prehistoric representations, in mobile forms, or as monumental efforts on walls, rocks and on slabs, caves and grottoes, is characteristic of humanity, that is the evolution, both technically and culturally of humankind.

The prehistoric creators of art inaugurated a new era by using symbols in addition to making useful and everyday utensils, united in iconographic ethnocultures and, at the same time, participated in a thematic cultural diaspora until the entire world was covered. It is this universality of the artistic phenomenon that shows that everywhere *Homo sapiens sapiens* attained a cerebral "threshold," or a mental, physical, religious or symbolic one, that liberated these images, or the idea of these images, into art in the largest sense.

The universality and moderness of early artistic phenomena characterized the prehistory of man for more than 30,000 years, with certain alterations from one continent to another. Art was not born in one cave or hearth but rather had a multiplicity of independent flowerings.

There exists also a "post-prehistoric art." These are the writings, in their different forms, that slowly but steadily put an end to rupestrian (cave) prehistoric art in several areas.

It is well known that writing accompanies (or is accompanied by) other revolutionary and technological events, such as the appearance of metals, urbanization or the cultural development of mythologies and religious tenets. These are not the only channels for changing forms of expression and communication; by graphically symbolizing ideas or sounds within their linear organizations, artists created substitutes for "ancient forms" to make possible the clear abstracted, conceptual, codified knowledge, such as languages, logic and mathematics.

Art within Nature

The most ancient villages discovered in the western Mediterranean, such as Catal-Hüyük, in Turkey, or Jericho in Palestine come into being near the eighth and seventh millennia B.C. Domestic art, frescoes, murals and incised objects, painted or sculpted, become elements of decoration or art, including the architecture of the places themselves. All of these aspects created a rupture with the original tradition of prehistoric art, executed on natural, immobile, bases, such as the walls of grottoes, shelters and rocky floors. In fact, prehistoric art, which one discovers in the displays of primitive Africa, American and Oceanic art, is located in the heart of nature. An original symbiosis exists between the iconographic images and their landscapes or environments.

A coated mural, for example (sometimes on cloth), relatively flat and smooth on a limestone base, the most frequently used stone of the Paleolithic peoples in Europe, or on sandstone found in numerous shelters almost everywhere in the world, offer some reliefs, some irregularities, some natural forms. Dyes and shades are put to good use by the prehistoric artist to improve their representations: the images are inseparable from their media.

The choice of a grotto or an open-air shelter nearly always involves a relationship to the landscape: sites easily visible from afar, or sites hidden at a distance from the daily activities, sites grouped in a particular geological feature, isolated sites on denuded plateaus, or in covers dense with vegetation.

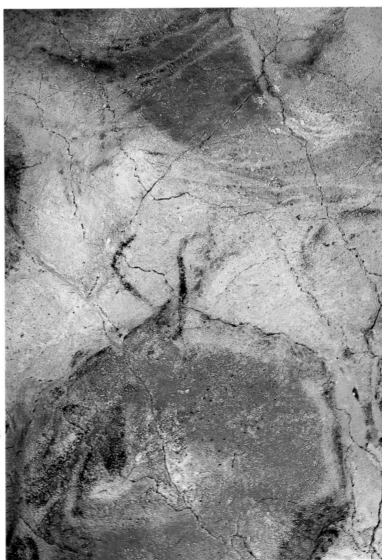

(Above) Large black bull painted in the axial diverticula of the cave of Lascaux (Dordogne) and a black-branched symbol. From the head and neck a pair of ochre horns emerge, belonging to the animals painted earlier. Old Magdalenian. Ph. De Sazo/Rapho.

(Right) Bichrome bisons from the ceiling of the cave of Altamira (Santander, Spain). The spatial composition is remarkable. Middle Magdalenian. Ph. Lauros-Giraudon.

With little exception, the Paleolithic grottoes show no signs of prolonged occupation. Their obscurity and humidity are hostile to humans as they are for animals or vegetation. Certain valleys and alpine mountains,like the Camonica Valley (in Lombardy, Italy), Mount Bego, functioned as sacred places,completely uninhabitable. In all cases, prehistoric art and nature are tightly bound within an elaborate symbolic dimension, outside of the mundane, domestic life of the group. However, numerous decorated shelters, painted caves and grave sites indicate that the idea of wholly separating the sacred from daily activity is a modern concept.

Prehistoric man found his art close at hand, within nature. At the same time he incorporated natural forms into his art, decorating his tools and hunting weapons, cutting into antlers and bone.

Simple Techniques for Elaborate Forms

The discovery of the grotto of Altamira (near Santander, Spain) plunged scientists into doubt at the end of the 19th century. How could these beautiful and elaborate paintings have been done by prehistoric "savages"? Some charged forgery, but the evidence required examination. Altamira was only one of the most beautiful and authentic examples of Paleolithic cave art. Niaux, Lascaux and others came to serve as proof of the extraordinary mastery of Paleolithic painters and engravers (from c. 30,000 to 10,000 years B.P.). The frescoes from Tassili in the Sahara, the "X-ray" paintings from the Arnhemland in Australia, the sometimes gigantic carvings from the Wadi Djerat (Sahara) and those innumerable Alpine displays show that everywhere prehistoric peoples created complex forms possessing an aesthetic power so intense as to transcend time.

And yet the techniques used were most often elementary, of two types: coloring techniques (paintings) and methods to partly or totally decorate or engrave walls, carvings and sculptures.

The colorants used by the prehistoric artists are derived from ferric oxides (reds, browns and yellows), manganese (blacks), and kaolin (whites). Designs were also traced with vegetable carbons, but until recently no other organic elements could be identified in the paintings, or in the coloring compounds (which were mixed with water). The paintings on

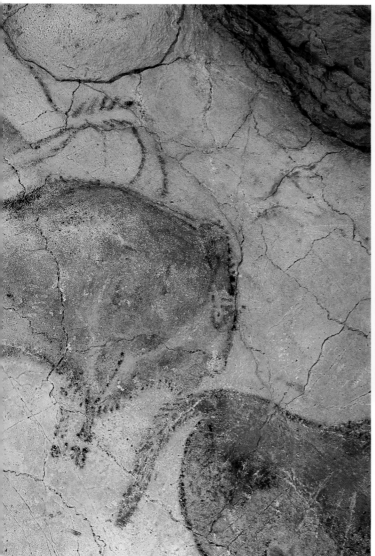

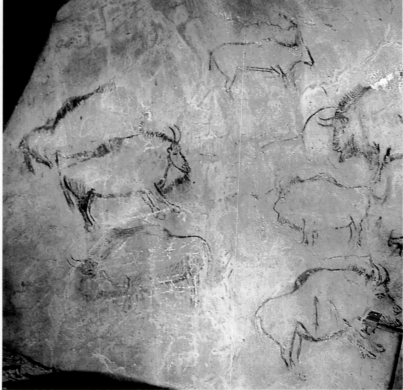

(Above) Black trace designs of bisons, goats and linear signs grouped in panels in the Black Salon of the cave of Niaux (Ariège, France). Middle Magdalenian. Ph. Michel/Explorer.

flat surfaces or filled with shading, hatching or dots, are either monochromes (in one color), bichromes (two colors), or polychromes (three colors or more). In fact, the prehistoric artists often chose the natural coloration of the rocky base to offset a polychrome impression.

The larger designs, with mineral, carbon or vegetable colorings, are silhouettes, with contours fine or thick, blurred or clear, elementary or complex, according to the technostylistic origins. The engravings are similar to designs when there are simple contours, finely incised by flint chisels or strongly dotted with a heavy instrument. When the internal space of the representation is scraped or dotted, the visual effect is similar to the paintings because the rocky foundation resembles a bicolored process.

The figures in paintings and incisings remain superficial. In contrast, a few of the prehistoric artists managed low or raised reliefs. There are high reliefs as well, though rare, and in some cases the art attains three dimensions—the sculpture in the round.

In the following tour of monumental prehistoric art, on grotto walls, in caves, on rocks or on slabs in the open air, including millions of sculpted objects, elegant statuettes, feminine Mediterranean idols, zoomorphic amulets, arms and decorated implements, the creations appear in a spiritual sense humble and beautiful, clearly witnesses to the marvelous and complex symbolic universe of the prehistoric hunters and gatherers.

Cave Art of France and Spain

Times past but already modern

Prehistoric art belongs to the past of modern man, beginning in the 3rd stage of the Würmian glaciation, ending with its fourth and last stage around 10,000 B.P. In its totality, this monumental form of art begins around 20,000 B.P., which was characterized by important climatic fluctuations, warm wet periods alternating with dry and cold ones, with infinite regional variations.

The Paleolithic civilizations that succeeded one another in western Europe, defined by prehistorians as starting with tool making and objects of adornment, lived exclusively by hunting and gathering. Modern excavations, the study of habitats and kill-sites, indicate without doubt that these civilizations—the Aurignacian (35,000 to 25,000 B.P.), Gravettian (27,000 to 20,000 B.P.), Solutrean (20,000 to 19,000 B.P.) and especially the Magdalenian (18,000 to 10,000 B.P.)—had mastered perfectly their means of subsistence. They had oriented themselves, little by little, toward production—toward domestication, breeding and culture, flowering into the Neolithic. The civilizations of these European Upper Paleolithic creators of mobile and cave art, still belonging to the long past of humanity, herald as well the great Neolithic revolution.

An eternity of stone

The great discovery of Aurignacians, who lived near the Vézère, in the surrounding areas of Les Eyzies and Sergeac

Partial view of the frieze sculpted by the Magdalenians, in the Perigordian shelter of Le Cap-Blanc (Dordogne, France). Among the monumental representations of horses, some outlines or rough forms of bison and deer are interspersed. Ph. A. Roussot.

(Dordogne) gave to their images the same strengths as their lithic supports—a sort of eternity. Thus we advance from the dotted incising on thick limestone, found in some underground shelters to animals in stiff and barely identifiable contours, the beginnings of geometric signs, especially representations of female, rarely masculine, genitalia in a display of elaborate sexual symbolism.

The Aurignacian vanguard of sexual representation inaugurates a new kind of Paleolithic figurative symbolism, excluding any contextual reference, any narrative scene, for humans as well as for animals. This "prudery" of Paleolithic hunters is even more remarkable than that of their successors, the pastoral civilization artists, sometimes multiplied human sexual scenes (in Saharan Neolithic art for example), freed from all iconoclast censure.

Underground penetration

The Aurignacians chiseled, marked off, incised and painted their images in their rock shelter habitats by the light of day. So did the Gravettians in the identical region and sometimes in the identical shelters, which had been abandoned by the Aurignacians, as well as in other regions, using the walls of shelters or the foyers of cave. Certain artists among them went underground, to the obscure and separate region of their habitats, giving birth to the unique wall art of the caves about 22,000 years ago.

The techniques used by the Gravettian artists in their caves are already complex, integrating panels of positive images in Bargas (High Pyrenees) and relatively detailed and faithful animal engravings. The majority of some 250 negative red and black hands in the grottoes of Gargas have the mysterious aspect of being "mutilated." The fingers on the wall figures are incomplete, which prompts speculation that the actual digits were either folded (a code equivalent to that of the deaf) or that amputations had been performed because of illnesses or religious rites.

In the small caves of Pair-non-Pair, in Gironde, the Gravettians grouped animals in panels: ibex, mammoths, horses, bovines, megaceros (an extinct species of elk with enlarged antlers)—a testimony to the great diversity of thematic choices in early cave art.

Monumental sculptures

The Solutreans, succeeding the Gravettians, are viewed somewhat as intruders in the west and resorted to wall paintings in caves in Perigord and in Charente. At least two great cave sites are the result of the marvelous chisels of their sculptors: the Roc-de-Sers, not far from Angoulême (Charente) and the Fourneau-du-Diable near Bourdailles (Dordogne). Large quarried limestone blocks, surgically cut, form spectacular low-reliefs animals (cattle, ibex, bison, horses) and humans. Equally extraordinary is a running man with a club on his shoulder, being charged by a bison (Rock of Sers).

The art of sculpture is an art of open spaces, needing both light and shadow to take on its true dimensions. Thus, the Paleolithic sculptures were almost all created in open-air shelters by the Solutreans and the Magdalenians (Angles-sur-l'Anglin, in Vienna, or the Cap-Blanc in Dordogne).

In Ardèche, and in the province of Santander in Spain, Solutreans painted or carved characteristic animal forms according to the figurative norms, realistically and conventionally, in shallow and easy to reach grottoes (Chabot Bidon).

The conquest of the grottoes

Magdalenian art, inaugurated at Lascaux some 17,000 years ago, developed around the 14th or 15th centuries B.C. in the southwest of France and in Spain, especially Cantabria. More than 100 grottoes were occupied by the Magdalenians, who entered the deepest recesses of certain large and com-

Large painted signs in the cave of El Castillo (Santander, Spain). Paired symbols—here parallel alignments and rectangular, divided shapes—to a symbolic codification in the Magdalenian caves of this region. Ph. Held/Artephot.

plex caves, with vast halls and narrow corridors in Castille (Spain). There were long and immense galleries in Cullalvera, Spain, Bedeilhac and Niaux in Ariege, in Labastide in the High Pyrenees, and a dense network of galleries branching out over more than six miles (ten kilometers) at Rouffignac at Dordogne.

Certain overhanging passages, ventilators and shafts, such as those at Fontanet (Ariège) required rather remarkable and adventurous qualities. The obstacles cleared reveal the sculptors' intention to appropriate for themselves all of the underground space, to totally transform the grottoes into "theatrical" sanctuaries, with hidden recesses and spectacular halls, as in the rotunda of the gigantic bulls of Lascaux (16 feet/5 meters long).

Some chosen themes: abstract and figurative

The Magdalenian grottoes enclose three kinds of images, as frequently carved as painted: symbols, the most numerous but also the smallest, animals and human figures. Linked with the Solutreans and the Gravettians, the quantitative differences are very important and the thematic choices much more varied, with more signs and more species of animals.

A horse's head carved from bone then engraved, from the Magdalenian site of Saint-Michel-d'Arudy (Basses-Pyrénées). Museum of National Antiquities in Saint Germain-en-Laye. Ph. Michel/Explorer.

Modeled bison gouged out in the sandy clay of the Grotto Bédeilhac (Ariège, France). Middle Magdalenian. Ph. Michel/Explorer.

Dots of color, isolated, in pairs, or aligned in rows, are very numerous, painted in red and black and most often situated in galleries—the heavily trafficked areas that emphasized the remoteness of the animals. Dashes, lines and composed variations form a second family of signs that are engraved or painted and often integrated into the panels with depictions of animals and humans. Others signs are of geometric shapes, such as rectangles with inner compartments and external appendices, blazons and grids, complex abstract signs, or repeated patterns of more elementary, punctuated or linear signs. The bestiary of Magdalenian art includes a good 20 species, especially mammals like horses, bisons, cervidae (deer, elk, and related animals), but also birds, fish and some reptiles.

The naturalistic tendency of cave expression reaches its height during the Middle Magdalenian, the designs most true to life, with the detailed depictions of the thick coats of bisons and horses. This quasiphotographic art is maintained until the end of the Magdalenian eras (at Teyjat, Dordogne). In post-paleolithic art such iconographic qualities are exceptional (oxen from the bovine phase at Tassili, for example).

Head of male figure engraved by the Magdalenians on a limestone slab that came from the Grotto de La Marche (Vienne, France), along with 1,500 other engravings. The figurative details incorporated in this image are exceptional among all Paleolithic human representations. Paris, Museum of Man. Ph. Museum of Man.

The human figures are more varied than before but relatively infrequent (as on the engraved slabs from the Marche, Vienna). They consist of corporeal silhouettes, isolated heads in full face or profile, which adds to the figurative quality, but are much less realistic than the animals. Sexual representations and perhaps some negative images and handprints are included.

Some coded messages

Comparison of the panels from different grottoes reveal that such depictions both share a coded mode of expression and vary from one grotto to another. In Les Combarelles, horses predominate, bisons and the mammoths are less numerous; at Font-de-Gaume, a neighboring grotto, horses are rare, and the bison and mammoths are numerous. At Les Combarelles, several tectiforms (the shape of roof) form a backdrop to the parade of the animals in the rear of the gallery. At Font-de-Gaume, the tectiforms are more numerous and mingled with mammoths and bisons. At Font-de-Gaume, female figures are exceptional, while at Les Combarelles numerous female silhouettes and visages are distributed throughout the cave.

Such comparisons could be multiplied among sites belonging either in the same chronological and regional phase or in diverse phases. Clearly, the coded messages in the Magdalenian grottoes are a function of individual ethnocultural characteristics.

Paleolithic cave art is the clearest, most precise testimony of the bursting forth of the great cultural currents in multiple regional and local symbols. This regionalization of symbols is highly perceptible in the complex signs that quarter off a well-determined group of sites: tectiforms (roofs or dwellings) in Perigord, claviforms (clubs) in the Pyrénées, partitioned signs in the Cantabrian region. The Paleolithic caves received these symbolic messages, a confidence made in order to escape the mundane and to vanquish the passage of time that makes mortal, finally, all of civilization.

Of New Landscapes and New Ways of Life

The great Würmian glaciation finally ceased in Europe, with deep upheavals affecting the landscapes; the retreat of the polar ice caps from the northern zones, which freed new territories and caused a concomitant reduction of mountainous glaciers, changes in the order of rain and sunshine and the alteration of marine beds with the retreat of the coastline and the elevation of the continental plateau. Vegetation is modified by the new environment but is still undeveloped; forests are sparse.

The Pleistocene megafauna, dependent upon cold climatic and ecological conditions, cannot readily survive the general warming and increase in humidity, and disappear or are displaced. Mammoths, woolly rhinoceroses, megaceros, moose, taiga antelope, wolverines, snowy owls, etc., are wiped out or extend their range, like the reindeer who accompany the receding glaciers near the north. Bison adapt more easily to the forests, which serve as their refuge.

Bison, horses, aurochs (extinct bovines) and especially reindeer had furnished the essentials to the hunter people of the Pleistocene, with skins and tendons used for clothing, the bones and antlers as tools or weapons. Only the horse will, like the aurochs and some livestock, be progressively and in greater numbers domesticated.

Stags, boars and wolves favor the climate and the extension of the vegetatal cover, multiplying and constituting the most important game, although still a predator of man. Antlers, teeth and bones are used in some industries. Bears, ibex and wild sheep, chamois and lynx seek refuge in the mountains and progress into higher altitudes to escape human predation, intensified by the population increases of the last millennium and the dawn of history.

In the cooking debris of Postpaleolithic habitats are found not reindeer but stags and boars. A new phenomenon has arisen, however, throughout the entire world—the extensive consumption of terrestrial and aquatic mollusks. Mountains of empty shells often form along riverbanks, the coastline, or lakesides, such as the Brazilian *sambakis*, the North African *rammadyats* or the Danish *kjökkenmödings*.

In the new prehistoric way of life, there is more harvesting of mollusks and less hunting of large Pleistocene mammals, corresponding to other new technologies; miniaturization of lithic tools and certainly the use of the bow for hunting and defense are confirmed in the first postglacial millennia by rupestrian pictoral scenes.

Paintings from Spanish Levantine Shelters

A mountainous, mediterranean rupestrian art
On its natural border, the Meseta Centrale (Spain) indents deeply and sometimes drops steeply to the Mediterranean between the mouth of the Ebro below Catalonia and Almeria in the south. It is here that most of the 120 painted shelters belonging to "the art of the Levant" are situated. Certain of these shelters are rather near the coastline, such as those from El Polvorìn (Ulldecona) or Sarga (Alcoy), but many are in mountainous regions and some are located more than 75 miles (120 kilometers) from the sea.

In the Albarracin region, prehistoric man painted his frescoes in small open shelters along thick limestone banks. Besides these are openings in the limestone, but of modest dimensions, six to ten feet (two to three meters) in height and three to six feet (one to two meters) in depth, so small that they were not inhabited.

A painted art
Several thousand figures have been found in the shelters of the Spanish Levant. Nearly all were painted or decorated. The poor conservation of the limestone walls, exposure to many temperature changes and climatic variations and contamination by water (which results in the formation of an opaque film), has altered the figures from the principal discovered sites at the beginning of the century, including the splendid painted series from Minateda (Hellin), revealed in detail by Abbé Breuil.

The colors red and brown, with all of the mixed tones derived from organic materials, were most frequently used. Black was used as well. White is rare but brilliantly used in the limestone shelters of Las Taricas (Raco de Molero-Aresde Maestre-Fuente del Cabrerzio-Albarracin); in some paintings the contours are slightly raised (Valcharco del Agua Amarga-Alcanez).

Toward miniaturization
Everywhere, animals are bigger than the human figures. Generally the paintings are in flat tints, naturalistic, and larger than the traced designs. The largest animal, a bull, from the shelter at La Arana, is 43 inches (1.10 meters). Certain human figures, in crude outline, are only less than an inch (two-to-three centimeters) in height, like the figure seen in the shelter at El Polvorìn (La Cenia).

Still an animal art
All of the painted shelters in the Levant display animal figures, though not all of them possess human forms. The art of the Levant is the most ancient European art to depict wild animals still in existence. These images are principally of cerfs (stags or does), more males than females, goats and wild sheep, as well as ibex and some izards (chamois). Bovines are equally numerous. Stags and bovines are often hieratic and naturalistic in the most ancient period, while goats and stags from the more recent eras, like boars, are, at times, schematicized or inserted into cynegetic (hunting) scenes. Horses are much more numerous and more often schematicized.

Enter man
Dressed figures, from the Levant, adorned with ornaments, are resolutely distinguished from the nude Paleolithic forms. A sexual distinction is scarcely made for the dressed figures. The art of the Levant is dicreet in this matter, except perhaps for some notoriously sexual warriors.

A second novelty of human forms of the Levant is their explicit participation in activities of daily life. Shown are hunting scenes and ceremonial dances executed by personages wearing long robes or tunics. The warrior stance is rare (Albrigo de Las Trepadores), as are pastoral or agricultural scenes. The depiction of humans makes narrative the essential part of the Levantine art in this naturalist phase of large animals. The key personages of these figurative mythologies is the archer: always isolated in procession, tirelessly leaping or running. The hunting cult is thus depicted, part of the economy and mythology of these prehistoric societies.

For the first time in Europe, the processes of socialization of human groups toward the acquisition of nature resources and the organization of production, breeding and agriculture, are clearly illustrated. The adornment and clothing of the figures allows one to distinguish their functions or to imagine the hierarchies prevailing (warriors, hunters, dancers, medicine men, etc.). Humans are depicted in groups, and in action, as if the social act was becoming primary for some societies that were confronted by new economic necessities.

From the Paleolithic to the Neolithic

The lack of direct evidence of datable prehistoric occupations and the absence of a mobile figurative art make it very difficult to determine ancient eras, their duration, and the evolutions of the art of the Spanish Levant. It is possible, however, to trace roughly a boundary between the iconographic evidence of some Neolithic or nearly Neolithic cultures from the start of the fifth millennium until the appearance of metals and the symbolic art of the post-Paleolithic and pre-Neolithic, between the ninth and fifth millennia.

Lofty Carvings

The glacial periods forgotten, the European ruperstrian art extends over an area newly freed by the climatic upheavals, in mountains accessible on good days when the sunlight is strongest. The first dimensions of mountainous rupestrian art is solar, and the second, complementary, type is geologic.

Paleolithic art and a good part of European shelter art was executed on walls of sedimentary rocks, limestone, in eroded landscapes dominated by water. Most of these walls are vertical, and thus spatial extensions in height and width were limited.

The mountains are formed of crystalline or metamorphic rocks that supplied vast bone surfaces, often polished by the glaciers, but lacking the cavities or concave formations favorable to the execution of cave art. On the other hand, these rocky surfaces, smoother and flatter than limestone, exposed their horizontal extensions or inclines to the chisel or pick of the cave dweller. In addition, the patterns traced or picked are thus turned toward the light, which plays over it with the passing hours, animating the patterns and enlivening the figures.

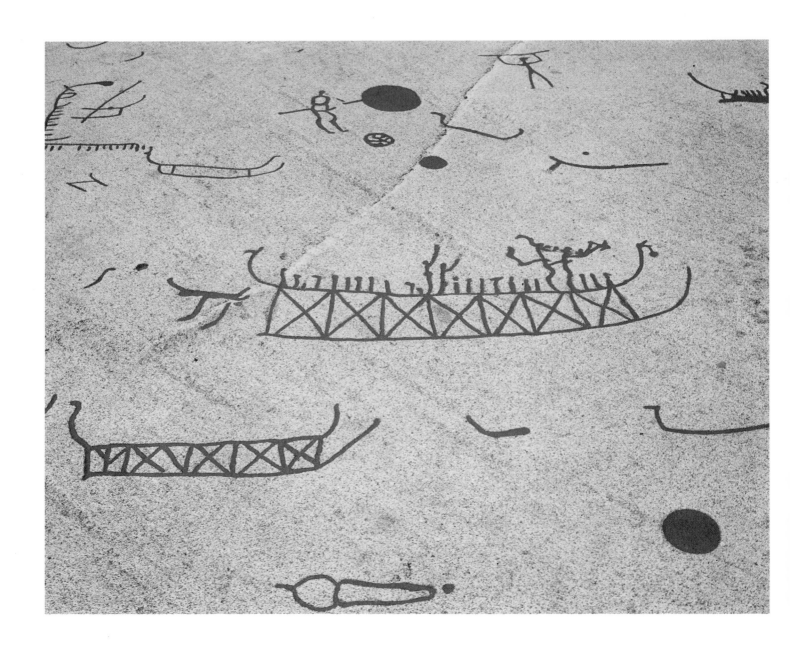

From shepherds to Romans

In the year 16 B.C. the conquering Romans installed themselves in a beautiful Lombard valley, the Camonica Valley, between Lake Iseo and Tonale Pass. They added their own rock inscriptions to the nearly 130,000 carvings in the area, between 1,300 and 3,200 feet (400 and 1,000 meters) in altitude, over eight millennia, according to the chronological data established by researchers.

In this archaic period are found about 10 naturalistic animal figures, of which four are moose. This animal, also carved in the Austrian Alps (Totes Gebirge), recalls glacier climates, still close by.

The most ancient harnessing of these Camonican populations appears during the following phase, which one must consider Neolithic. Husbandry and agriculture would thus endure some eight millennia in the Camonica Valley. The cervidae figures, which dominate all Camonican art are schematicized, as are the human silhouettes, often reduced to two circular arcs, one at the bottom, one at the top, representing the limbs, with a vertical trunk, a head, and indications of the male sex.

In the following stylistic phases, these themes are maintained and schematicized. Harnesses with swing ploughs are more numerous. In the course of the third millennium, four-wheeled carts appear, and there is a diversification of weapons, with daggers and halberds abounding. The most noticeable thematic variations concern geometric signs or symbols, going from the circular motifs in the most ancient period to motifs with stalks to rectangles in the Bronze and Iron cultures.

Several millennia of recent prehistory among Alpine agricultural and warrior populations are thus recounted, with a profusion of intriguing detail.

The cult of the bull

Around Mount Bego, some 50 miles (80 kilometers) from Nice, near 8,200 feet (2,500 meters) in altitude, more than 100,000 engravings from the Bronze Age (c. 1800 to 1600 B.C.) transform these frozen wastes into an astonishing sacred site.

Near the center some carvings are dedicated to a kind of bull cult, giving evidence of an ancient Mediterranean belief. These engravings are very schematicized, with harnesses and animal motifs. The U-shaped horns of the animals are disproportionate to the filiform (slender) body, with or without stick-like limbs, and viewed from above, not in profile.

Human figures are rather rare (about one in 100), often schematic kneeling figures with raised arms, an important aspect. Weapons and tools are frequently depicted, including chisels, halbards, axes and especially daggers, whose precise designs often allow chronological attribution to the Bronze Age. Some geometric shapes, reticulated, circles, elementary signs, lines and cup-shaped forms encompass the symbolic group from the Valley of the Merveilles, lacking an epic narrative or domestic scenes.

On land and sea

While the Alps were being peopled with images, on the frozen shores of Lake Onega on the White Sea, in the Ansevich region in Norway, and as far as Siberia, tens of thousands of engravings were made on the rocks during the last prehistoric millennia.

The two animals most represented during the Mesolithic Period belong to the frozen horizons of the Nordic steppes: elk and reindeer. During the course of the Bronze Age, designs of small boats and canoes became more and more frequent, witnesses to the constant movement of populations within these hard climatic zones. Shown also was hunting on skis or on snowshoes, ancient images of the most adaptive modes of transportation in these unforgiving lands.

Representation of human figure and boats. Rupestrian engravings from Vitlycke (Tanum, Sweden). Bronze Age. Ph. Lauros-Giraudon.

Paleolithic sculpture of a woman, found at Sireuil (Dordogne, France). Saint-Germain-en-Laye, Museum of National Antiquities. Ph. Faillet/Artephot.

Prehistoric Art in Africa

From the past to the present

The multitude of rupestrian forms distributed throughout the African continent reveals the constant fundamental character of the art in the great zones separated by the equator. Northern Africa, between the Nile and the Atlantic, the Mediterranean and the South Sahara, and Southern Africa, from the Cape to Zimbabwe, are characterized equally, as attested in the sites of the eastern zone, the turning point between the Horn of Africa and the central regions, formed by the axis of the Rift Valley and parallel to the east coast. The continuity, uniting the vanished ages to a Neolithic past became an "historic present" in multiple places, with continuity the most pertinent and original characteristic.

The essence of the artistic phenomenon is Neolithic and corresponds to domestication of animals and to the modern peopling of the region. The first element of continuity concerns the human groups living by hunting and gathering; some, such as the Pygmies and the Bushmen survive today.

Figures painted in white and brown ochre in a shelter of Sefar (Tassili-n-Ajjer, Algeria). Note their posture, as well as an ornament around the neck of one of them. "Round-head" Period. Ph. F. de Keroualin.

Graphic art of certain prehistoric hunting peoples, excluding pastoral scenes or the technological innovations of the metallurgic periods of protohistory, is certainly the most ancient known. It reaches as far back as 10,000 B.P., indeed, even further, as in Namibia at the Apollo II, where the oldest art forms in Africa, fragments of pointed slabs, were found. The Neolithic technological revolution was absent or delayed in this area, which only possessed the advances of one or two millennia, or even less. The durability of such cultures, founded on a nonproductive economy, still engenders uniform rupestrian art.

A second phenomenon of continuity characterizes the passages of cultures in the course of several millennia within the same sites and regions. At Tassili, for example, there are no measurable iconographic disruptions between the art of the hunting peoples and that of the pastoralists, between the pastoralists and the horsemen. People belonging to these ethnic groups and to different cultures did not cease painting or carving throughout several millennia in the same sites.

Divergence of views

Two great forms of expression share the rupestrian art of the hunters and livestock herders in Africa. One is naturalistic, the other is schematic, or stylized. Schematic African rupestrian art is prior to the Neolithic and is contemporary with great protohistoric and historic movements. Abbé Breuil united in the same "great naturalist art" the paintings of the South Africans and those of the western style in Europe and compared them to earlier decadent forms. This point of view, excessive and baseless in relation to chronology, provided a valuable view of the aesthetic qualities of painted animal representations to which it is necessary to join some remarkable engravings (often polished) in numerous regions in shelters or on laterite (a ferrous, reddish soil) slabs.

The hunters and their art

On the techno-stylistic level, the art of the hunters is very elaborate, like European Paleolithic art. It is not, or very slightly, narrative. The animals, placed in an uncertain manner, may be symbolically grouped.

The African megafauna are largely represented. From the Atlas to Fezzan and Tassili, the antelope and eland were used to symbolize the most ancient artistic "stage" in the northern Sahara and the Sahara. On the entire continent, local variations correspond to different biotypes; naturalistic depictions of elephants, giraffes, hippopotami, rhinos, antelopes, deer and goats are found in abundance. Some of these figures are immense, such as the giraffe engraved at Wadi Djerat (Tassili), which is 28 ft. (8.5 m.) high. Depicted in great numbers are felines, wild horses (primitive form), ostriches and other birds, such as owls and pelicans, as well as fish, monkeys (at Tassili) and cattle (at Wadi Djerat). The single domestic animal is the dog, which accompanies human figures in some hunting scenes at Tassili. In the northern and Saharan zone, hunting scenes are rather rare, but the bow is well-documented toward the south (Zambia), and again archers are found in multiple cynergetic narrations.

In North Africa, blacks and whites, depending upon the region and the often tenuous interpretations from faint images, are depicted as hunters—many times simply drawn next to animals, particularly bulls and rams. Sexual scenes are rather common (Tassili), some with predominant phalluses. When human representations are dressed or adorned, the distinction between sexes is obvious in a number of cases, for example, short loin cloths denote men and long tunics women (Tassili).

A few symbols are associated with animals and humans from these ancient naturalist phases. Moreover, the numerous spirals, simple or complex, from Fezzan and Tassili, as well as circular motifs are notable. In Tassili, and sporadically in the Tibesti mountain area and Ennedi, disks and circles and geometric shapes served as heads in human representations. In this region there developed, at the beginning of the 6th millennium, a very stylized iconography of "round heads," small and monochrome figures, then large (more than six feet, or several meters) and polychrome, among some of the wild fauna characteristic of the epoch: hippopatami, giraffes, elephants, etc.

The pastoralists and their flocks

The importance of animal domestication is strongly underlined in the African naturalist art, more here perhaps than anywhere, during the Middle and Late Neolithic in Europe (from the beginning of the fifth millennium). Pastoral art showing domesticated herds of many cattle (two types), sheep, asses, goats and dogs inaugurates the rupestrian art of some regions in East Africa (Somalia, Ethiopia). It is sometimes later (as in Cape Province) or even small compared to the art of the hunters (carvings in Wadi Djerat). Elsewhere, it dominates, in particular in the painted forms at Tassili, the center of bovine paintings, with Acacus, Tibesti and Ennedi. In Jabbaren, Tamrit, there are mighty herds of steers accompanied by people black and white with elaborate hairdos, elegant, animated and often armed with bows or javelins. The art of the pastoralists is scenic, narrative and interspersed with many wild animals, which shows the ecological and climatic stability of these Neolithic millennia.

The engraved or picked art of the pastoralists is very different. Few narrative scenes are depicted, nor have large frescoes been attempted; the animals are less animated and the human form is rare. Morocco, Mauritania the Hoggar and Tibesti Mountains and the Fezzan desert region account for the bulk of these images, much less spectacular than the contemporary paintings or earlier naturalist engravings.

The flying gallop

With the representation of the horse (several species), artists entered into historic times. Two-wheeled carts drawn by horses in a "flying gallop," found in the Tassili, Hoggar, Tanezruft and Fezzan sites, demarcate the routes of invasion, ancient but no longer prehistoric. In general, the era of the horse marks an aesthetic change and a thematic turning point. In mode of expression, both carved and painted, the tendency towards schematicism is strengthened, demonstrated by triangular figures, faces sometimes transformed into an abstract designs (bifid stems). Thematically, the bridle, or the image of the harnessed animal, and rider with armed shields, lances, javelins, swords, and daggers are shown outside of the usual war or hunting scenes. There is a noticeable decrease in the depiction of oxen and the disappearance of hippopotami from the Saharan regions—attesting to important climatic changes, desertification, and economic changes. Other larger, wild mammals are still represented, especially giraffes; dogs, goats and sheep, also present, confirm the pastoral occupation of these people at the gates of history. The appearance of camels marks a new Saharan rupestrian period called "camelid," entirely historic and already modern.

In Southern Africa, the chronology of paintings and carvings seems shorter and less divisible into distinct stages. The Bushmen hunters and the Bantu stockbreeders form a sort of continuity, expressed in a rather realistic esthetic fashion, in particular in human representations like the famous personages of Philip Cave in the Brandberg, so admired by Abbé Breuil. Like the Saharan and Northern African examples, the chronology of Southern African cave art is marked by the gradual change from wild fauna to domesticated fauna, corresponding to the adoption of Neolithic practices, through space and time, until the modern conquest of the African continent by the West in the last century.

Art of the Great Spaces

It is still too early to present a synthesis on the prehistoric cave art of the vast Asiatic and American expanses. Numerous lands remain unsurveyed or are only now beginning to be examined: cave paintings in central India, near Bhopal, engravings of wagons harnessed to protohistoric horses in the Gobi Desert in Mongolia; abstract and decorative engravings in the regions of Lake Baikal (Siberia) and the Amur River; and, more to the north, the area of Ankara, the Lena River (Russia) and Senissei with naturalistic paintings of animals, especially ibex.

At the crossroads of Africa and Asia, in Anatolia, in the Negev Desert in eastern Arabia, cave art is well known, recalling aspects of Saharan, African and North-Saharan cave art. Once again is established a progression from the ancient series (fifth and sixth millennium B.C.) of spare and naturalistic depictions of wild animals (ibex, oryx, big cats) only through plentiful scenes of domestication and breeding (dogs, cattle and goats), depictions of industry, weaponry and war. At the beginning of the last millennium B.C., the horse and then the camel appear, as in Africa.

The "Lagoa Santa man" (in the state of Minas Gerais, Brazil), was one of the first prehistoric fossils of *Homo sapiens* discovered and one of the first to be described in 1836. It was found in the vicinity of some of the most beautiful cave art on the South American continent. Several dozen limestone caves harbor thousands of paintings and engravings, executed by various groups for around 12,000 years (Lapa Vermelha). Elsewhere in Brazil, large rupestrian centers are under study: paintings from São Raimundo Nonato de Piaui, perhaps the most ancient site now known in America, more than 15,000

years old; paintings and engravings in sandy shelters of the central plateau in the states of Goiás and Mato Grosso, etc.

Themes and styles vary greatly from one region to another, but the animals are generally "naturalistic," and humans most often are presented in a schematic fashion—animated by movements, gathered into scenes of

The "crying cows," incised in a sandstone shelter of Djanet (Tassili-n-Ajjer, Algeria). Certain deep incisions in asymmetric borders tend to bring the representations into relief, taking advantage of the unevenness of the surface. Ph. F. de Keroualin.

daily life, with depictions of sexuality, warriors and cynegetic (hunting) scenes. Except for small figures with globular heads, which are common, the Brazilian shelters contain humans so completely stylized that they are difficult to recognize. They are placed in innumerable rows of small figures, with stick-like appendages to represent the legs or flowered headdresses. There are also large geometric figures, facing forward, whose bodies are similarly patterned with geometric shapes. The same style is used for animals, notably the cervids (deer and related animals), seen in profile.

Stags and does are the mammals most frequently depicted in the Brazilian shelters. Capibaras, (the largest rodent

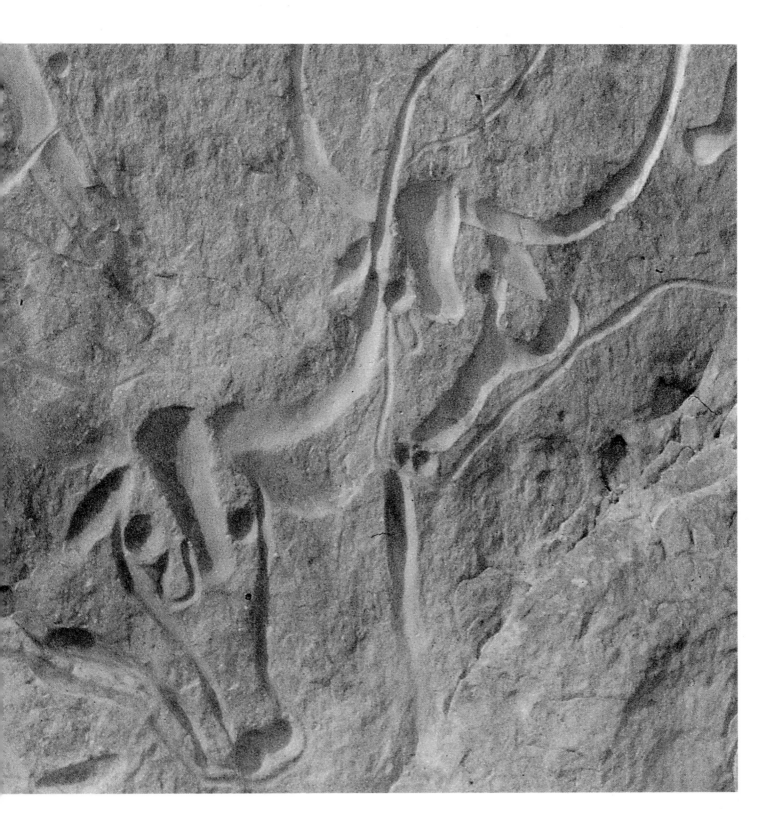

in the world), pecarries (wild pigs), panthers, various monkeys, armadillos, wading birds and birds with spread wings are present, as well as snakes, lizards, crocodiles, frogs, all prominent, as are fish depicted in placid water.

Brazilian cave art, in the manner of rupestrian styles around the world, also displays a significant number of geometric signs, and certain shelters (Mato Grosso) display only panels of symbols as complex as those from Paleolithic European grottoes. Circles, rectangles, spirals and three-fingered imprints abound almost everywhere, along with other, more regional, kinds.

To the west and south of the Parana-Rio de la Plata, toward Patagonia, the cave art of shelters and rocks is distributed within the mountainous zones abutting the Andes. In the Argentine regions of Catamarca, Neuguén, and Cordoba are gathered together painted or engraved figures by the tens of thousands. In certain sites both positive and negative handprints are found and others are marked by conventional animal images, notably nandus (similar to the ostrich). In the more recent periods, "divine" figures, warrior-gods, appear—as do certain deified animals, especially wild cats.

Elsewhere on the South American continent (in northern Chile, Peru, Bolivia, Colombia and Venezuela) in Mesoamerica, especially Mexico, and North America, sites with paintings from a prepastoral (preceramic) epoch and innumerable sites with petroglyphs attributed to more recent ceramic cultures have been discovered. Significant finds have been made at Chaco Canyon, Indian Petroglyph State Park and Three Rivers Petroglyph Site in New Mexico, Canyon de Chelly in Arizona and elsewhere in the southwest, California, Nevada and the Columbia River Plateau. Rectangular or triangular-shaped humanlike figures are common, as are handprints, and images of deer, wild cats, coyotes, birds and other animals. Geometric designs—circles, spirals, zig-zag lines—and symbols of the sun, moon, stars, clouds and lightening are also used.

The engravings testify to a progression toward figurative schematicization of animals and men, resulting sometimes in a nearly abstract geometric design (in certain Mexican sites). Geometric signs and motifs form decorative patterns on the walls of the shelters, which evoke the decorated walls of Pre-Columbian monuments.

The Long Tradition of the Australian Aborigines

Today, a majestic gathering of great mythical figures can be seen at the base of a shelter in the Kakadu National Park, in the Arnhem region. In this northern part of Australia, the tradition of cave art is several millennia old and of Pleistocene origin (shelter of early man, Laura region). In many ways, time stands still for today's Aborigines.

The exceptional continuity of prehistoric cave art into the present in the Aborigine world is manifested as well by the renovation and reutilization of paintings and engravings through time, reflecting cultural modifications, the evolution of myths and the changes in figurative or abstract themes.

In the course of 20,000 years, but essentially during the last millennia, cave art expanded over the entire continent, including Tasmania, before the formation of the strait. Several million engravings and paintings were executed in the shelters, but also in open-air sites, like rocks, sometimes mountains of rocks, each one displaying one or several figures. The sandy shelters, toward the north of the continent, favored the conservation of the paintings, while the large granite and basalt slabs (toward the central and southern regions), have encouraged the multiplicity of engravings using varied techniques from incising to picking.

Symbols and animals

Geometric motifs, circles, cupules, sticks, etc., engraved or painted; the depictions of arms like the bow and arrow; the boomerang; etchings of emus and engraved kangaroos; and positive and negative handprints are abundant in these sites, some with cultural variations, such as the schematicized symbols of the Panaramitee style from southern Australia.

Kangaroos, oppossums, emus (including the now extinct giant emu, as well as the extinct thylacine "wolf"), birds crocodiles, tortoises, snakes, fish and marine mammals form the core of the Aborigine's bestiary. Engravings and painting are normally done in naturalistic style, but the process of repeating the same animal in thousands of representations in a limited space, during short periods, resulted inevitably in schematic models in a less figurative style.

In the area of Arnhem, a particular style developed for the representations of humans and animals in polychrome fluroscopic paintings, with the body viewed as in an X-ray,

Human forms painted in the Fetcani Glen shelter (Berkley East, Cape Province, Australia). Ornaments and clothes are particularly well marked. Ph. Gerster/Rapho.

that is with the internal organs and the skeleton represented in a more synthetic fashion, as opposed to the figurative style.

Of humans and spirits

The great originality of Aboriginal art comes from its fantastic mythological representations of beings that are half human and half spirit: the Mimi of Arnhem or the Wonajinas of Kimberley (western Australia). These stick figures haunt the shelters or are multiplied on the rocks in the open air, in extremely variable forms, from the true polychrome radioscope figures of large dimensions to small dynamic linear silhouettes to figures gathered into scenes.

The prehistoric, and modern art of the Australian Aborigines is striking in its intensity of life, which frees the figures, and for the light interweaving of the spiritual and the mythic into concrete forms.

Conservation of Ancient Sites

The prehistoric arts, linked to nature by symbolic and complex functional relationships, are abundant on the five continents. A small portion are already under study while a multitude of sites are threatened, indeed even condemned, by pollution, deterioration resulting for the most part from lucrative and rampant tourism, and by the natural evolution of the regions, irreparable on the geological scale.

A recent inventory sponsored by UNESCO has put at more than 20 million the number of preserved rupestrian figures at tens of thousands of sites. In certain regions hundreds of thousands of figures are concentrated in a naturally limited space: 400,000 to 500,000 in the Tassili of Ajjer in the Sahara; 150,000 in the Camonica Valley in northern Italy; 100,000 engravings in a six-mile (ten-kilometer) radius in the region of Dampier, in western Australia. The conservation of the many images that have survived from prehistoric times depends on the awareness of the immense value of this universal inheritance—a respect for these most humble and fragile forms.

Prehistoric art, whether objects on walls or in caves, expresses symbolically the ideas, beliefs and myths of these ancient peoples forever silenced. Prehistoric art has survived around the world for a quarter of a million years, the mirror of the soul of prehistoric man, made beautiful in order to carry into the future the thoughts and dreams of a people.

Suggested Reading

Bahn, Paul G., and Jean Vertut. *Images of the Ice Age*. New York: Facts On File, 1988.

Leroi-Gourhan, Andre. *Treasure of Prehistoric Art*. New York: Harry N. Abrams, Inc., 1971.

Lhote, H. *The Later Prehistory of Eastern and Southern Africa*. London: Heinemann, 1977.

A picked image from the Bronze Age in the Vallée des Merveilles (Maritime Alps): A swing plow and oxen stylized in horn-shaped motifs. Ph. J. Bottet.

CHAPTER SIX

Jean Guilaine

THE FIRST FARMERS OF THE OLD WORLD

Neolithic stone vase *(of andesite) from preceramic Cyprus, the site of Khirokitia (sixth millennium).*

In the course of the first stages of the agricultural economy in Asia Minor, some communities did not fashion terra-cotta containers, pottery arriving there later with agriculture and breeding. In contrast, the use of sculpted stone vessels was earlier there and characterized the first phases of the world of the producers, called "preceramic" or "aceramic" Neolithic. Museum of Nicosia. Ph. Held/Artephot.

The term Neolithic, New Stone Age, has been synonymous for a long time among prehistorians with a particular stage of development, with the persistence of stone tools and with the growing universality of the various stages of agricultural life. The new era contrasts to the Old Stone Age, the Paleolithic, the very long period during which human beings had derived their food supplies from hunting, fishing and gathering.

While this division between the two economic and social systems has been heavily debated since the beginnings of prehistoric research, recent investigations have confirmed the artificiality that is characteristic of such divisions. The formation of farming communities, totally different from earlier social organization, is the final stage of a long conditioning of the environment, of a rapport with the landscape that began well before the New Stone Age. From this fact, the criteria that are used to define the Neolithic (certain settings and techniques, the formation of villages, the rise of agriculture and breeding, the use of ceramics) are most often, in the areas of emergence, the cumulative result of the modification of human behavior in relation to nature. This process is progressive and diversified and in no way resembles the abrupt transformation implied in the expression "Neolithic revolution."

Was the evolution toward agriculture inescapable? More than a successful "invention," food production, within this perspective, appears to be something written into the destiny of Man. However, was this the only possible way? Today we are scarcely equipped to appreciate, beyond a certain level, generalizations advanced by certain technical systems to explain the "success" of agricultural societies.

At the beginning of the Neolithic development in agriculture, diversity, largely confirmed by the variety of cultural expressions, ruled. The following pages will show, within the geographic scope of the Old World (Africa excepted), some very widespread examples of these tendencies toward new ways of life. From these examples let us note: the appearance in Syria-Palestine, within a preagricultural context, of stable locales; the emergence of an agricultural stage in the eastern Mediterranean and in Pakistan, well before the knowledge of terra-cotta while pottery production techniques were already known in Japan and on its periphery very early in any production economy; diverse attempts to domesticate animal species. At the same time, an attempt with indigenous plants, such as wheat and barley in Anatolia, in Palestine, rice in southeastern Asia and millet in China are evidence of the expanding possibilities of agricultural experimentation. They are the effects of these evolutions, rapid or slow, punctual or scattered, which in their higher definition, were supposed to designate the durable implementation of a farming world.

The Settling Process and Architecture in Asia

The settling of human beings in one place is generally deemed a phenomenon proper to the world of the agriculturalists. The farmer lives and stays near his fields, thus forced to relinquish mobility. Now it is one of the accepted facts of research conducted during the last two decades that the settling process was not the *result* of agriculture, but that it well *preceded* it. From the epoch of the last hunter-gatherers, humans frequently established themselves on living sites with environments that could support them through the seasons with an adequate food supply. In general, the settle-

ments were near water courses, lakes or ocean shores. In addition to water itself at these sites the bodies of water provided fish and game (large animals came to drink) and various wild plants. It has not been shown that the supposed displacements of the Paleolithic people from their incessant tracking of game were a very strong force in favor of agricultural settlements and some cases of sedentarism, relatively certain, can be shown from earlier stages.

As early as the Epipaleolithic times, however, settlement in places graced by nature takes another turn. The investment manifested in building allows these settlements to be called villages (or protovillages), whose populations subsisted in part on hunting and gathering. Thus it was with the Natufian, an Epipaleolithic civilization in southwestern Asia. At Mallaha (Eynan) in Palestine, in the 10th millennium, a cluster of round cabins—10 to 13 feet (three to four meters) in diameter on the average and sometimes up to 30 feet (9 meters)—was planned. These houses were dug in pits, and their periphery was surrounded by stone walls. At Mureybet (Syria), in the 10th millennium, circular habitations dug into the ground were constructed, limited by low walls of argil and wood, and covered by a thick coating. The preference for circular houses would be maintained even in the beginning of the Neolithic. In the course of the ninth millennium, Jericho (in Jordan), already occupied by the Natufian, enlarged the

(Above) **The town of Catal Hüyük,** near Konya (Turkey) is the classic example of these Neolithic towns (with more than 30 acres/12 hectares in this case), grouping an active population who lived by agriculture and breeding ovines. The houses of Catal Hüyük were constructed of crude bricks, their floors made of various kinds of platforms. The common walls were decorated by polychrome paintings and sculptures. Catal Hüyük was occupied for almost a millennium (6500 to 5700 B.C., uncalibrated). Ph. J. Mellaart.

(Right) **Jericho** (Jordan). Neolithic Preceramic A. High wall and tower.
Surpassing the Epipaleolithic Natufian construction, the first Neolithic phase is amazing because of its extension (around seven to ten acres/three to four hectares) and the monumental structures that characterize it: a tall protective and imposing tower, 30 feet (9 meters) in height and 33 feet (10 meters) in diameter at the base, with an internal staircase. Perhaps the budding agricultural economy was the source of this appreciable demographic advance and collective works. Ph. Ch. Lenars.

town in association with a development beyond that which was customary for stone architecture. A high wall, 10 feet (3 meters) thick and 13 feet (4 meters) high, could extend out to 26 feet (8 meters), while an imposing tower (33 feet/10 meters wide at its base and 30 feet/9 meters high) contained an interior staircase.

It is at this point that agriculture develops. Some centuries later the spread of quadrangular houses begins, succeeding the round domiciles, as is documented by the examples at Jericho, Munhata and Beidha in Palestine, and, a short time later, at Abu Hureyra, Bongras, Tell Assouad on the middle Euphrates, as well as in Ramad in the area of Damascus, Ras Shamra on the Syrian littoral, etc. Agriculture and breeding appear to have been mastered by that time. It is certain that at Catal Hüyük, in Turkey, the settling process was linked to an evolution into the Neolithic at its most brilliant. A cluster was constructed there on 30 acres (12 hectares) toward the middle of the seventh millennium and perhaps before. The construction is rectangular, one story in height, built in crude brick, sometimes with a vertical or horizontal framework of beams; the roofs, which were flat and formed a series of terraces, provided access. The interiors were abundantly decorated with mural paintings or reliefs, depicting the heads of bovids (cattle, sheep, goats). Those are a few examples of the long march from the early settling process to the architectural evolution that is linked to it.

Emergence of the New Economy in Southwestern Asia

These progressions in the art of building, the act of constructing inhabited villages could not have taken place, one assumes, without a social infrastructure and economic transformations of some scope. Of these, agriculture is foremost. Dedicated over a long period to the gathering of plants and wild fruits, humans from that point on were to interrelate to the vegetation, to sow and harvest grains and leguminous plants. During the eighth millennium, this threshold appears to have been crossed in the Near East. At Mureybet, around 7500 B.C., a form of wild wheat, possibly engrain (*Triticum boeoticum*) was collected there, with barley probably cultivated next and then lentils. Around the same time, further south, in Jericho, the starch (*Triticum dicoccum*), resulting from an indigenous form (*Triticum dicoccaides*), was planted with barley and lentils. The phenomenon spread very fast in the seventh millennium B.C. Thus, the area comprised of Anatolia to Djezireh and to Palestine appears to have played a pioneering role in the domestication of wheat and barley.

The domestication of animals could be scarcely more recent than that of cereals. The time of the dog's domestica-

Possible areas of plant and animal domestication

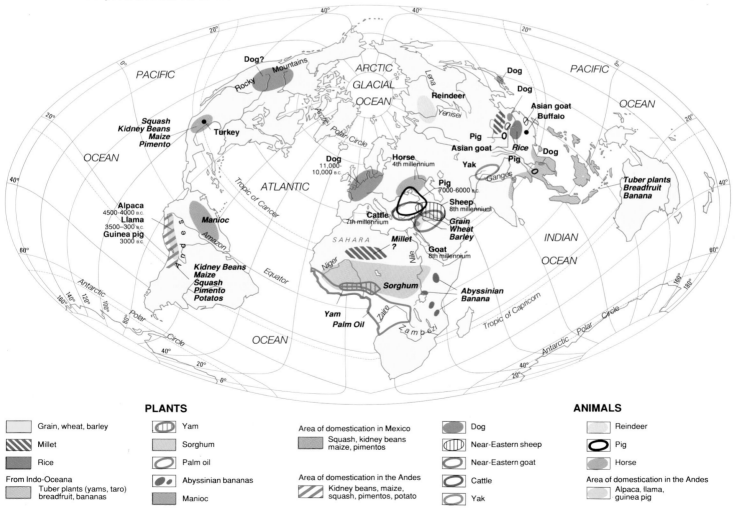

PLANTS				ANIMALS	
Grain, wheat, barley	Yam	Area of domestication in Mexico	Dog	Reindeer	
Millet	Sorghum	Squash, kidney beans maize, pimentos	Near-Eastern sheep	Pig	
Rice	Palm oil		Near-Eastern goat	Horse	
From Indo-Oceana	Abyssinian bananas	Area of domestication in the Andes	Cattle	Area of domestication in the Andes	
Tuber plants (yams, taro) breadfruit, bananas	Manioc	Kidney beans, maize, squash, pimentos, potato	Yak	Alpaca, llama, guinea pig	

tion is not precise. Apparently polygenic, the dog is probably found as early as the Natufian and, at the same time, as early as the Epipaleolithic in northwestern Europe. Sheep and goats, whose role would become essential in the peopling of the middle Mediterranean area, were domesticated in the Near East. The sheep is, at first, a victim of a selective hunting process, for example, at Zawi Chemi at the foot of the Zagros, where a possible domestication as early as 9000 B.C. is postulated. Around 7000 B.C. its domesticated presence appears certain at Ali Kosh in western Iran, at Cayonu in eastern Turkey, and, around 6500 B.C. at Jarmo in Mesopotamia. The goat, which in the aegagre wild form today roams from the coasts of Asia Minor to the mountains of Pakistan, was domesticated around 7000 B.C. at Cayonu, in the preceramic Neolithic B of Jericho and El-Khiam, in Ganj Dareh (Iran). A still more ancient appearance of the goat on the Iranian plateau (Tepe Asiab), remains unconfirmed. The domestication of pigs is more difficult to determine; the distinction of osteological (bone) remains from those of the root stock, the wild boar, is still difficult and has given rise to a variety of paleontological views.

Between 7000 and 6000 B.C., indications of the presence of domesticated *suidae* (pigs) are evident in eastern Anatolia, in Mesopotamia, in the Crimea and in southeastern Europe. Other areas of domestication for this species are possible. The appearance of domestic bovids in the eastern Mediterranean seems both early and late in regard to the species mentioned earlier, as local centers of domestication can only be surmised. Near 6000 B.C., supposedly domesticated bovids are present in the region of the Levant (Ramad), in the Euphrates (Bouqras) and in Anatolia (Catal Hüyük). More to the west, domesticated bovids are noted in Thessaly and in Crete, as early as the preceramic Neolithic, especially around 6000 B.C. Thus, they are present in an area originally rather loosely defined and perhaps extensive (Iran, Pakistan, the Crimea); it is possible that a center of African domestication existed of indigenous species (*Bos primigenius africanus, Bos brachyceros ibericus*) in the Saharan zone and its borders (Maghreb, the Nile region), at the beginning of the sixth millennium.

Pottery, a Multiform Invention

Pottery, long considered one of the principal material elements of the Neolithic period, served very well as a recognizable threshold, authenticating the first agricultural civili-

zations in diverse places in the Old World. It is in the predator's environment that the oldest manifestations of ceramics are found. It was only necessary to possess a knowledge of the properties of argil, an easily malleable clay, and fire, which produced the final cohesion. Thus, in Japan, between 11,000 and 10,000 B.C., a ceramic with figurative or stamped decoration was decorated by groups of hunters (Fukui cave in Kyushu; the Kamikuroiwa site in Shikoku), which was followed by a long tradition of pottery during the Jomon culture.

Similarly in Africa, the emergence of terra-cotta is very early and, here again, in a prepastoral and preagricultural context. The Saharan massifs and their environs have left signs of terra-cotta as early as the eighth and seventh millennia in the Epipaleolithic environments: Montes Bazzanes, Air; Launey site, Ahaggar; Tin Torha, Acacus, Tagra (Sudan), Nabta Playa (Egypt). In western Asia, the definitive mastery of terra-cotta, used for some culinary purposes, is only widespread from 6000 B.C., while agriculture and breeding are already well established. It must be noted, however, that attempts to bake clay are dated much earlier here. At Mureybet (Syria), around 8000 B.C., small pots from terra-cotta were fashioned, in an open and narrow style, whose function was without doubt not utilitarian. However, these inventions, completely "cultural," were without a future. This ceramic disappears from the more recent levels, and the clay, modeled and baked, will serve only for a time in the manufacture of figurines. It is necessary to wait for the end of the seventh millennium, more than 500 years later, to see new attempts in western Asia and the successful production of pottery. This eventually becomes a learned process that spreads widely throughout Syria, Lebanon and in Anatolia.

First Villages of Iran on the Indian Continent

The appearance of a production economy (agricultural) in the Levant, in Anatolia and Djezireh stimulated populations living to the east and to the northeast. Elsewhere, however, the vast, frequently mountainous area—the region between the Zagros and the Indian continent—developed in conjunction with largely autonomous cultural traditions had evolved semi-independently toward a breeding and agricultural econ-

Western Asia and Europe

Cereals
- Grain
- Wheat starch
- Barley

Extension of
sedentary agriculture
- until 8000 B.C.
- until 7000 B.C.
- until 6000 B.C.
- until 5000 B.C.

0   1000 km

omy, just as attempts were made to bake clay (Ganj Dareh). From the mountains of Taurus to the Zagros, the settling of agricultural communities greatly increased in the sixth millennium. The introduction of methods of irrigation allowed communities to develop in dry regions, along the mountainous massifs. The settlements passed rapidly to the use of painted ceramics and to the early practice of metallurgy, hammered copper. Thus the true Neolithic is of short duration in this area, limited to the preceramic stages and quickly replaced by a flourishing "age of copper" (Chalcolithic). In western Iran, some preceramic sites (Ali Kosh in Khuzistan, Ganj Dareh in Luristan) develop, as early as the seventh millennium, an economy of production founded on wheat and barley and the raising of sheep and goats. In the sixth millennium some sedentary communities are known on the Iranian plateau (Tepe Sialk), but also on its southern border, on its northern flank, up to the Caspian Sea and finally in the Caucasus (Kultepe, Shoulaveri), where local grains could be domesticated.

In the north of Afghanistan, a preceramic Neolithic site with remains of domesticated sheep and goats has been found at Aq Kupruk. On this site, pottery made its appearance in the fifth millennium. The oldest Neolithic sites of Baluchistan, Anjira, Gumla, Kili Ghul Mohammad, and especially Mehrgarh, represent perhaps a partly original agricultural center in the border provinces of the Indus Valley. The mound of Mehrgarh, in particular, in the Kachi plain, shows a long preceramic sequence, the course of which illustrates the progressive appearance of a productive economy. The richness in the grasses of the mountainous areas of Afghanistan and Baluchistan would have engendered local agricultural processes, in particular for barley. A long cultural tradition established in the region could constitute the root

of the brilliant civilization of the Indus, which will develop in the third millennium. At the same time, in other parts of the Indian continent, Neolithic groups were subsisting (as in Burzahom in the Kashmir) or developing metallurgy (south of Razasthan). In the valley of Krishna, communities that cultivated a variety of millet and raised ovines (sheep) and bovids developed in the third millennium.

The Oldest Farmers of Europe

In the immediate range of the Levant and of Anatolia, the Aegean lands have all been the first to adopt, probably because of contact with others, new economic systems. The Neolithic Aegean is not, however, a simple replica of other cultures of southwest Asia. A maturation of local populations certainly favored access to new forms of economy, which perfected certain technical institutions. Thus, around 6000 B.C., Thessaly, Crete and Peloponnesia adopted the culture of cereals and the breeding of sheep and goats, bovids and pigs, but ceramics are still absent. Permanent agricultural villages, with houses set in stone and walls of crude brick, were soon being raised in this part of Europe. Diverse styles of painted ceramics (Sesklo, Dimini) characterize the fifth and fourth millennia. On the northern flank, the entire Balkan area, from Macedonia to southeastern Hungary, from Serbia to the Black Sea, displayed the first manifestations of the farmer's life in the Starcevo civilization and, for Bulgaria, one of its variants, the Karanovo civilization. Oxen and swine frequently compete in numbers with goats and sheep, more numerous in the Aegean lands. Some important sedentary villages, regularly rebuilt and thus progressively raised (tells) exploited rich

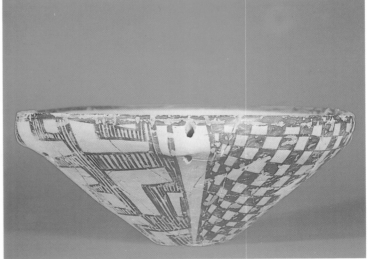

Ceramic from the Danubian Neolithic (eastern France).
The first Neolithic communities that settled during the fifth millennium (uncalibrated) along the Danubian axis, particularly from Czechoslovakia to the mouth of the Rhine, were characterized by a ce- *ramic with chevrons or spiral decorations ("striped ceramic"). This Neolithic phase played a major role in the establishment of farming economies in most of temperate Europe. Saint-Germain-en-Laye, Museum of National Antiquities. Ph. Lauros-Giraudon.*

Sesklo, Thessaly, Middle Neolithic *(fifth millennium, uncalibrated).*
A flattened ceramic with geometric decorations (checkerboards, ladders, meanders). Ceramics rapidly became, in the Neolithic, one of the *essential signs of the originality of certain cultures. Painted pottery is the feature of some Mediterranean cultures, from Mesopotamia to southern Italy. Athens, National Museum. Ph. Ekdotike Athenon-Artephot.*

soils in the cultivation of wheat, barley, peas and lentils (Thrace). The habitations were quadrangular, made of wood and cob (clay and straw). Pottery in simple forms (jars, bowls with feet) was decorated by impressions, castings of clay and, sometimes, painted in an admirable fashion (as at Karanovo).

Within the entire cultural area called "Danubian," that is within the band of lands running from Moldavia and central Poland up to the mouth of the Rhine and to the Parisian Basin, with Hungary and Czechoslovakia constituting the southern limit, a Neolithic civilization was established in the fifth millennium, both original and typical. Some large rectangular houses, with posts and lintels in wood, were grouped in villages constructed on terraces and devoted to the exploitation of loess lands (Bylany, Czechoslovakia). The most ancient phase is called "ribboned," after the ribbons, spirals or meanderings that decorate the ceramics.

In the central and western Mediterranean (Dalmatia, Italy, southern France and the Iberian peninsula), the Neolithic is characterized by groups of pottery decorated by impressions (often of shellfish). The breeding of sheep and goats predominated; such breeding is associated with a well-developed agriculture as early as the sixth millennium in southeastern Italy, combined with activities of hunting, fishing and gathering in France and in Spain. In southeastern Italy, the sites were soon surrounded by ditches (Passo di Corvo); more to the north and the west, habitats in grottoes (Arene Candide, Italy; La Sarsa in Spain) existed for a time with the first villages.

In northern Europe (Poland, the Netherlands, Denmark, Sweden and northern Germany), poor soils and the absence of loess were unfavorable to the development of agriculture. By contrast, the development of the coasts, rivers and lakes assured local populations of varied resources in fish and wild animals. The cultivation of grains becomes established more belatedly in the fourth millennium by the intermediary civilization called "the funnel-shaped beakers." Swine breeding was particularly advanced. Houses were rectangular and elongated.

More to the north, in the area of coniferous forests, the populations did not adapt to the production economy. Hunting and fishing remained the basis of food supplies. They might, however, have been familiar with the art of terra-cotta, borrowed from the more southerly groups.

The Neolithic in the U.S.S.R.

The vast territory of the U.S.S.R. (more than 8.5 million square miles/22 million square km) and the many ecological areas and different climates that characterize it, explain the chronological gaps that mark the settling process. The most ancient traces of agricultural populations appeared on the southern lands because the conditions there were more favorable to the cultivation of grains and to animal husbandry. In addition, these regions were in direct contact with the civilizations of the Near East and Middle East and with Balkan Europe and participated in the same phenomena of economic and cultural innovations.

In the northwest of the Black Sea region, between the Dniester and Bug Rivers, the first sedentary villages succeeding local Mesolithic groups may date to the sixth millennium (Soroki). If pottery is at first absent, and if hunting and fishing still played certain roles, from the moment domestic animals

Terra-cotta statuettes from Altyn Tepe (*U.S.S.R.*). *End of the third millennium.*

From the Near East to western Europe and Central Asia, the civilizations of the Neolithic and the Copper Age produced numerous statuettes in stone, terra-cotta or bone. Each culture displays its originality through certain characterizations or particular styles, most often, but not exclusively, through female figures on which the hips and breasts are well developed, as if to emphasize reproductive or nourishing aspects and the concept of fertility. These statuettes are sometimes viewed as idols, linked to a fecundity cult. Certain researchers, however, believe that they are toys or miniature representations of ordinary people. Leningrad, the Hermitage. Ph. by the museum.

(swine, oxen, dogs) appear, tools will soon arrive for the cultivation of grains.

In the Steppes area, composed of the region between the Black Sea and the Caspian Sea, the raising of oxen and swine is attested to as early as a preceramic phase, characterized by stone vases with pointed bottoms, in the basin of the Dnieper. In the Crimea, swine are perhaps domesticated by the end of the Mesolithic (Fatma-Koba, Tach-Air). The breeding of bovids and ovines (sheep) appeared in the fifth millennium, along with ceramics with conical bottoms and a rudimentary agriculture.

In central Asia, near the Iranian civilizations, and more particularly in Turkemenia, one witnesses, as early as the sixth millennium, the appearance of sedentary communities and the development of an agricultural economy, aided by irrigation. Villages were constructed of crude brick and adobe. The tool kit was built on a previous Mesolithic tradition (Djeitun).

In contrast to these southern lands, where the settlement process was established without difficulty on an Epipaleolithic foundation, the northern U.S.S.R. followed a totally different path into the Neolithic. In the European and Asiatic lands, at the fringe of the Arctic Ocean, covered by tundra, a vast forested expanse without interruption from the Baltic Sea to eastern Siberia, the inhabitants lived traditionally by hunting (elk, boar, brown bear), fishing and gathering. The population showed some unequal densities and was, in general sparse. Also, while the southern lands already possessed stable villages, the north remained impervious to the penetration of the new economies. However, Neolithic techniques were slowly borrowed: mines and galleries for obtaining quality stone, the perfection of hunting weapons and fishing tools and the fabrication of axehammers. Near the coasts, the settlement process intensified. The houses were made of wood, skins and branches. The adoption, in the fourth millennium, of pottery with either a pointed or conical bottom, decorated by punctiform (made by points) impressions, characterized the oldest Neolithic groups in the Nordic region. Breeding (oxen, swine, ovines) and agriculture could have appeared selectively, near the end of the Neolithic, in the areas southwest of the forest belt.

In Siberia, some communities of hunters and fishers appeared as early as the close of the Paleolithic, continuing to exist for a long time on their hunting economy. In the third millennium, near Lake Ossinovo, on the the Amur River, some sedentary communities lived by fishing and by the cultivation of millet. At the same time, the settlement process triumphed on the eastern coast. Ceramics and polishing were also known in the region of Lake Baikal (Ssakovo phase). Other recognized cultures include hunters and fishers (Yakuts, Western Siberia, tundra zone) or hunter-gatherers (in Mongolia). Metalwork developed toward the second millennium (Volga, Ural).

The Neolithic in China

China also was a center of the early emergence of the Neolithic. From the Mediterranean to Baluchistan, economic characteristics turned more and more to production, while, at the other end of the Asiatic continent, certain peoples engaged in a simultaneous, irreversible process that, in its turn, gave birth to agricultural communities. The specific aspects of putting into place a production economy in eastern Asia will be detailed later (see p. 145). There has been much debate about whether the Neolithic civilization in China emerged as a result of native dynamism in a more or

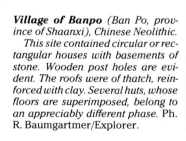

Village of Banpo (Ban Po, province of Shaanxi), Chinese Neolithic.
This site contained circular or rectangular houses with basements of stone. Wooden post holes are evident. The roofs were of thatch, reinforced with clay. Several huts, whose floors are superimposed, belong to an appreciably different phase. Ph. R. Baumgartner/Explorer.

less closed environment or if certain techniques (domestication, terra-cotta) were attributable to influences from western Asia. The strongly original characteristics of the most ancient Chinese farming cultures, their resource to indigenous plants and the long east Asiatic tradition of ceramics tend to support the first hypothesis.

Easy to farm, the loess lands of northern China were a cradle of agricultural communities as early as the sixth millennium. Subsequently, notably in the fourth millennium, along the Yellow and Wei Rivers, the Yangshao (or Painted Pottery) culture blossomed. Habitation was established on terraces and dominated the course of the river. The most well-known is that of the Banpo (Shaanxi), dating to the beginning of the fourth millennium. Enclosed by a ditch, the site yielded vestiges of round or quadrangular houses, with walls of wood, wattle and clay, while other central piles supported the framework and a thatch roof. Within the Yangshao cultures, pigs and dogs were bred, while oxen and sheep played a minor role. Ceramics were distinguished, in particular, by the presence of painted containers in black and red, with geometric or linear motifs, whose quality indicated a mastery of the arts of firing. Another group (the Majiabang) developed at the same time on the lower course of the Yangtze Kiang, where some earlier centers of rice cultivation were found (Hemudu). In the course of the third millennium, the Longshan (or Black Pottery) culture emerged, more strongly entrenched in the north, east and southeastern areas of China. From that time on, the habitations increase and reinforce their Neolithic character. The Chinese settlements were, within the scope of the Old World, another cradle for the cultivation of grains (rice and millet).

In southern China and in the continental area of Southeast Asia (Vietnam, Thailand, Burma), the local tradition at the end of the Paleolithic was characterized by a pebble industry, the Hoabinhian. These populations lived by hunting, fishing and gathering. The appearance of ceramics with cord-impressed ornamentation took place toward the sixth millennium in southern China and in the northern areas of Southeast Asia. Some sedentary villages of cultivators are noted in Vietnam in the fifth millennium and in northeastern Thailand in the fourth millennium.

Paleofarmers of Europe: Techniques and Dwellings

Let us return to Europe, a cultural area where the Neolithic is particularly well documented.

How did the farmers of prehistoric Europe work? Fire was their principal aid. The large forests of temperate Europe were cleared by stone axes, a technique that was augmented by the use of fire. The clearing of the land made possible the propagation of an agriculture on tracts of burned forest. On the light soils widely scattered along the terraces of rivers, a pioneer front developed, from Czechoslovakia toward the Ukraine, Poland, the lower Rhine and the Parisian Basin. Polynological (pollen) analyses seem to indicate already enclosed fields in regular forms. A system for allowing the land to lie fallow allowed the terraces to regenerate. Perhaps the

exhaustion of soil led to piecemeal opening of new fields and the necessary displacement of the inhabitants. In the Mediterranean area, in more fragile soil subject to greater erosion, the farming advances led to a more rapid, irreversible evolution.

The soil was prepared by a hoe—a blade of stone or bone on a shaft of wood. Certain curved sticks in hook shapes were able to serve in tracing the fields and in cleaning the planted rows. Swing-plowing shown on the alpine engravings in the Camonica Valley, is certain only at the start of the third millennium. This technique is confirmed by the funerary tunnels at the beginning of the Bronze Age. Harvests were made with the help of sickles, of which a wide variety has been discovered.

At first, cattle were used to clean newly cleared fields or to haul away felled trees used for the frames and walls of houses. With the invention of the swing plow, they became the precious aides to ploughing. Finally, the widespread use of the wheel and chariots, in the third millennium, greatly advanced the transportation of commodities, although here the cattle, soon to be overtaken by domesticated horses, played an essential role.

Concerning the habitations of these first farmers of Europe, in the southeast of Europe (Greece, Cyprus) the houses had subbasements constructed of stone with walls made of crude brick. The plans were circular (Khirokitia, Cyprus) or quadrangular (Sesklo, Greece). In the heart of the European

Chinese Neolithic, Yong-Tsing site (Yangshao culture).

Large pot-bellied jar with cylindrical neck and a flat bottom, with two small handles. The upper part was painted with bands and curvilinear or geometric motifs. The quality of the ceramics of the Yangshao civilization reveals the technical developments attained by this culture, which research has recently dated (end of the sixth millennium). Some Neolithic sites, even more ancient, are already known in northern China. Kept in the People's Republic of China. Ph. Lauros-Giraudon.

continent, wood and adobe that constituted the principal materials for houses of the Neolithic. In the Balkan villages, which were developed at the center of rich agricultural soils, cultivated over several millennia, the homes of the first farmers were simple: square or rectangular, with an interior hearth, an oven, and a reserve area, where grain was stored in jars or in silos. In all of middle Europe, from the Ukraine to France and the Netherlands, the first farmers built elongated rectangular houses, varying from 30 to 120 feet (10 to 40 meters), sometimes more. These large buildings' double sloping roofs were supported by a line of solid posts matched by rows of lateral posts and dry walls, with surfaces reinforced by interwoven wattle faced with adobe.

In northern Europe, on the Orkney Isles, buffeted by winds, Neolithic farmers built sunken stone houses with rounded edges, low ceilings, one against the other and joined by narrow corridors. The particularly well preserved interiors are entered from the street level; stone was used to construct hearths, sideboards and cupboards, recessed into the thick high walls, the domestic oven and even beds enclosed by slabs of stone.

In the Alpine zones near lakes or in the regions of peat bogs, the Neolithic farmers initiated a form of habitat known as Lake dwellings. It was formerly thought that the houses had been constructed on piles, built on the water and linked to the mainland by a system of foot bridges for reasons of security. This somewhat romantic view has been refined by recent research. New observations, without excluding the possibility of houses on the water, have shown that most homes were built on land. Their eventual elevation had only one goal, to escape the dampness caused by wind currents and the occasional shifting of the shoreline.

Study of the lakeside sites has been fundamental to our knowledge of Neolithic Europe. Inside the bogs and silts, the tools and most varied remains are conserved much better than in any other terrestrial deposits, where the disintegration of evidence is generally rapid and unavoidable. Lacustrine sites have proven to be an exceptional conservatory of wooden objects, nearly totally destroyed elsewhere. A vast range of objects of all varieties, in wood, basketry, and unknown media is well known to us today, thanks to research in the bog and underwater environments: Picks, hoes, shafts for cutting, sickles, arrows, fish nets, spoons, baskets, ropes, remains of clothing, combs, wheels and yokes provide much data that help us understand the methods and daily existence of the first farmers. We also know much about the crops consumed: cereals (wheat, barley), legumes (peas, lentils), wild fruit (raspberries, blackberries, strawberries, hazelnuts, sloes, wild grapes, apples and acorns). We should also note that many Neolithic villages entrenched themselves behind ditches, stockades and ramparts, certainly a defense reflex

Overhead view of a Neolithic house of Skava Brae (Orkney Islands). In the islands of northwestern Europe, buffeted by winds, the Neolithic people constructed low houses, with stone walls, snuggled one against the other, linked by narrow corridors. Excavation has provided access to the well-preserved interiors of these prehistoric habitats, where stone was also an essential element in the internal fixtures: hearths, benches, cupboards and even beds edged with slabs. Ph. Picture-Point LTD.

but also the desire to mark off the boundaries of the village, to confirm its identity in space.

Megalithism: *Dolmens* and Collective Burials

An important stage in the evolution of Neolithic societies of western Europe is marked by the progressive shift from the individual to the collective tomb. Most of the complexes of the most ancient Neolithic rely on individual burial in a pit or a box. In the course of the fourth and third millennia, burial in collective vaults became the rule; large, megalithic tombs, nypogeum or natural caves were used as sepulchers. This phenomenon, of course, was not uniform on the entire continent. The regions of central and eastern Europe remained for the most part faithful to the individual burial in a pit or in a chest. On the other hand, the construction of collective tombs of large volume, built with the help of imposing slabs or dry stone, and encompassed in a constructed, protective burial mound, constitutes an essential cultural trait of certain Mediterranean or European peoples of the Neolithic. To these monuments are often given the name *dolmen* (from the Breton for "tables of rock"), a valuable general term but one that barely conveys the diversity of the architecture. The frequent use of slabs (or pillars) not only in the foundation of such funerary structures, but also in other monuments, (such as the raised stones or *menhirs*, elevated stones situated in circles or *cromlechs*, or monuments with a cultic character, such as temples) bring the whole of these monuments under the term *megalith*. The rise of megaliths thus designates the art of building with big stones. However, the term is intended also for monuments, of various heights, whose plans and function are identified with those for which blocks or slabs of considerable size have been used.

Many *dolmens* and megalithic tombs are found throughout Western Europe, from Portugal to the Black Sea. Their distribution seems to be greater in maritime lands or regions (the Atlantic coasts of Portugal and France, Ireland, Great Britain, Denmark, Sweden, Germany and northern Poland), but monuments exist in the interior countries (the Spanish Meseta, Silesia and Switzerland). The Mediterranean world also widely used these huge stone funerary constructions. Some megalithic tombs are known in the Near East (Syria and Jordan), in Bulgaria, southern Italy, Malta, Corsica, Sardinia, the French Midi, the northeastern and southeastern Iberian Peninsula and, finally, in North Africa (mainly eastern Algeria and Tunisia).

These settlements were not the result of the phenomenon of diffusion from a single region. Quite the contrary, the

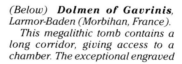

(Below) **Dolmen of Gavrinis**, *Larmor-Baden (Morbihan, France).*
This megalithic tomb contains a long corridor, giving access to a chamber. The exceptional engraved or sculpted ornamentation (arches, serpentiforms) that decorates certain pillars sometimes makes these tombs appear as a kind of temple. Ph. M. Levassort.

(Above) **Alignment of Palaggiu** (Corsica, Italy).
Alignments of raised stones (menhirs) appear in certain Neolithic European civilizations. Their purpose is not clear. It is thought that the alignments of Carnac could correspond to a vast system of astronom- *ical observation, but this is only one among many theories. Certain alignments in Corsica and Sardinia may have had a religious function. At Goni (Sardinia), some alignments are near tombs, where some authors have proposed an ancient cult. Ph. P. Tetrel/Explorer.*

European megalith is characterized by the diversity of architectural expression and nonconformity through time. Atlantic Europe has, in all likelihood, the most ancient monuments—built in the heart of the Neolithic communities still ignorant in the use of metal. In Portugal are found *dolmens* with polygonal chambers in front of a short corridor. In Vendée, in Normandy, colossal burial vaults with facades and steps were built, including several tombs accessible by long corridors. According to radiocarbon datings, this construction took place near the beginning of the fourth millennium, (near the middle of the fifth millennium in "calibrated" dates). In all of the Atlantic area, the preference for burials in huge stone crypts continued for nearly two millennia. The same is true of the Mediterranean world, which came to megalithism slightly more recently and marked by original construction.

Menhirs and Alignments

Another of the novelties of the western Neolithic is the establishment of numerous planted stones, or *menhirs*, in diverse forms and dimensions. The highest stone erected was certainly the Men-er-Hroech in Locmariaquer (Moribihan, France), a recumbent statue, now broken into five pieces.

This monolith originally measured more than 65 feet (20 meters) in height and weighed 350 tons. The highest *menhirs* still standing are about 33 feet (10 meters) above ground. Brittany is home to some of the most remarkable: Kerloas in Plouarzel (Finestère, weighing 150 tons), Kergadiou in Plourin-Ploudelmézeau (Finestère), Glomel (Cotes du Nord) and Champ-Dolent (Ille-et-Vilaine). These Armorican regions are also the best furnished in all of Europe.

Much has been written on the purpose of these erected stones: marker stone?; commemorative stelae? religious edifices? proof of a fertility cult? All this remains hypothetical. It is certain only that these monuments are all strictly contemporary. The most ancient Breton *menhirs* belong to an early Neolithic, true sculpted or engraved stelae. After having been erected and, over a period of time, venerated, these stones were then worn down and broken, and their pieces were reused in the construction or in the sealing of the megalithic tombs. All indications are that they were idols or the representations of some personage or dignitary. The breaking of the monuments signified the end of an epoch, the modification of certain religious or social structures or the loss of power of a long respected chieftain.

The alignments of Carnac are more difficult to date. These are some 4,000 stones arranged in three close groups, ending in nearby circles of stones (1,169 stones at Ménec,

Dolmen of Burren (County Clare, Ireland).

The whole of Atlantic Europe constituted, for two millennia, an intense megalithic center, with architectural types varying in function over time. The mound that protected the funerary chamber and the method of access to it have sometimes been totally dismantled by the alterations of the historic era. In one obscure chamber protected by a mound, there remained only a skeleton in a funerary cell, but it was preserved by the stone slabs that were utilized for this essential part of the monument. Ph. Roy/Explorer.

1,029 at Kermario, 594 at Kerlescan). It is thought the site once contained as many as 10,000 stones. The group near Kerzerho in Erdeven can also be cited, consisting of 1,129 *menhirs*, which can be dated by analogy to the fourth or third millennia. Their function is without doubt religious, but nothing more precise can be determined without veering into mere speculation.

The Neolithic Religion

Of the religion practiced by the first farmers, we can only make a few general suppositions. As early as the seventh millennium, the cult of the ancestors appears likely at Jericho, as is testified by the display of a number of heads with faces modeled in plaster. Elsewhere, in southeastern Europe, an abundant statuary favoring female idols (there also exist male or androgynous representations) with developed genitals and the breasts, is generally linked with a fertility cult. Certain authors believe that the Neolithic communities developed a pantheon dedicated especially to the forces of regeneration and agriculture—cults of fertility, cults of the natural elements, cults of the dead—and thus to the community's identity with the local environment.

Where were these religious beliefs expressed? Buildings with a religious purpose appeared early, as did the megalithic monuments. Their topographical location, the quality of their architecture, their immense size and their meticulous ornamentation, show that parallel to their role as tombs they symbolized the cult of the ancestors and the community's attachment to a productive region. Particularly noteworthy are the Cairn of Barnenez, measuring 230 feet by 82 feet (70 meters by 25 meters); the impressive *dolmen* of Gavrinis in Brittany with 23 decorated slabs; and the group of more than 30 monuments at Newgrange, county Meath, Ireland. This double function, as burial ground and sacred site, must have applied equally to certain hypogea (subterranean burial chambers) in the Mediterranean. Certainly, many of these tombs, dug by humans in the soft or hard rocks, were only simple vaults. However, some of the cavities rapidly attained grand proportions, benefited from very complex planning and were comprised of numerous chambers (the hypogeum of Calaforno, in Sicily contained 35 successive chambers!). Here too it is likely that the most spacious of these hypogea, those that have been decorated by paintings and elaborate sculptures, were at the same time both temples and tombs, such as the "tomb of the Chief," of the hypogeum of San Andrea Priu and hypogeum of Santu Pedru (both in Sardinia), and the giant hypogeum of Hal Safliéni in Malta, the most beautiful Neolithic tomb of the Mediterranean, of some 20 rooms containing 7,000 individuals. In certain regions, actual temples were built: thus the megalithic constructions of the Maltese Archipelago, characterized by a curved facade and trefoiled into three or five chambers (Ggantija, Tarxien).

Ggantija Temple, *Island of Gozo (Malta, Spain), third millennium, uncalibrated.*

Toward the end of the Neolithic era, the Maltese populations were erecting cultural edifices with very original trefoiled plans and with curved facades. The two temples of Ggantija, joined by a single enclosure with thick, piled blocks, rank among the most ancient monuments of the archipelago. Here is one of the chambers of the southern temple. At the base, altars were erected with ordered pillars. Ph. Travert.

The Rise of the Powerful

Enriched by agriculture and composed of prosperous communities, some towns of the European Neolithic rapidly progressed in technological innovation. Central and eastern Europe went the farthest, the fastest. The mastery of the uses of fire allowed, as early as the fourth millennium, the development of ceramic styles of exceptional quality patterned in graphite (the Gumelnitsa culture from northern Greece up to Romania), or painted (the Cucuteni and Tripolye cultures in Romania and the Ukraine). A similar brilliance born in the most ancient metallurgic hearth in Europe extended from the Black Sea to Hungary, from Macedonia to the upper Dniester. Supplied by the copper mines (Ai Bunar in Bulgaria, Rudna Glava in Yugoslavia), the workshops of this vast territory produced and exported large adzes, flat or perforated axes; daggers; numerous objects of adornment (twisted pins, pearls, rings, spiraled bracelets in copper, and gold pendants). This budding metallurgy involved the specialization of individuals as prospectors, mines, forgers and peddlers. Some individuals benefitted from these favored products and acquired elevated social status.

Thus Neolithic society, until then little noted for hierarchical organization, begins the process of stratification. In the necropolis of Varna (Bulgaria), in the fourth millennium, some notables were buried with ornaments or insignias of

(Above) **"The thinker of Cernavoda,"** glassy terra-cotta, the Harmangia (Romania) culture, fourth millennium, uncalibrated.

One wonders about the meaning of this idol, discovered in a burial site next to a female figure. Does its posture, with face in hands, depict the calm and the reflection that certain authors have suggested, or does it portray a mask hiding the superhuman nature of the figure? Bucharest, National Museum of Antiquities. Ph. Lauros-Giraudon.

(Left) **Hypogeum of Hal Safliéni** (Malta, Spain) third millennium, uncalibrated.

The Mediterranean Neolithic civilizations early developed the custom of digging funerary monuments (or hypogea) in rock to inter their dead. By their scope and the quality of the architecture, certain of these tombs were also temples, as was undoubtedly the case of the hypogea of Hal Safliéni. Here the access to certain rooms have been sculpted in a manner similar to megalithic posts and lintels. Even the arrangement of the roof, created by corbelling, is like those in contemporary Maltese temples. Ph. Ch. Lenars.

gold, a metal that was already becoming symbolic of wealth. One progresses from that period through the course of the third millennium, in Europe—as in Asia—to the ascension of powerful individuals whose status is shown by the accumulation of deposits of rare pieces (weapons, objects of prestige, jewelry) or by the exceptional personal property buried within the vault, such as the treasures known as "Priam's" in Troy, in Asia Minor, in the underground tomb of Maikop in the Caucasus. Next to these potentates, other signs indicate at the same time certain attempts at cultural unification and the appearance of social elites. The process is particularly clear in Europe, where two groups ably abetted this development: the Corded Ware culture, dispersed from the Pontic Steppes to the Netherlands, England and Scotland, and Globular Amphora culture, which spread abroad from Portugal to Poland, from Great Britain to Sicily. These groups maintained the era's new practices: the rite of individual burial underground and the adornment of the dead with social emblems or elaborate possessions like copper daggers, stone or metal axes, gold ornaments and jewels).

Now several millennia old, the Neolithic social organization is replaced, little by little, by the more stratified societies of the Bronze Age.

Varna necropolis (Bulgaria), fourth millennium.
The richness of gold objects (diadems, applique, jewelry) from this Chalcolithic necropolis and several tombs in particular, enable one to see the grouping in one well-defined section of the cemetery of a certain elite. "Symbolic" tombs, as is the case here, were built with a mask of terra-cotta and personal finery. Museum of Archaeology, Varna. Ph. Museum of Archaeology.

Suggested Reading

Chih, Chang Kwang. *The Archaeology of Ancient China,* 3rd ed. New Haven: Yale University Press, 1977.

Mellaart, J. *The Neolithic of the Near East.* New York and London: Thames and Hudson, 1975.

Mohen, Jean-Pierre. *The World of Megaliths.* New York and London: Facts On File, 1990.

Piggott, S. *Ancient Europe.* Edinburgh: Edinburgh University Press, 1965.

Renfrew, Colin. *The Emergence of Civilization: The Cyclades and the Aegean in the Third Millennium.* London: Methuen, 1973.

Renfrew, J. M. *Paleoethnobotany: The Prehistoric Food Plants of the Near East and Europe.* London: Methuen, 1973.

Tringham, R. *Hunters, Fishers and Farmers of Eastern Europe.* London: Hutchinson, 1971.

Ucko, P. *The Domestication and Exploitation of Plants and Animals.* London: Duckworth, 1969.

FROM THE FIRST TOWNS TO THE INVENTION OF WRITING

Table with proto-Elamite writing from Susa *(level 15A, circa 3200 B.C.). The document, which cannot be deciphered with certainty, surely describes quantities of commodities or rations and their destinations.* Ph. French Archaeological Commission in Iran.

At the end of the Neolithic, two major ways of life coexisted: the hunter-gatherers and the farmers. Farmers settled in sedentary villages on lands favorable to their agricultural practices, the hunter-gatherers continued habitation in vastly smaller numbers in the rest of the world. No towns or villages had populations of more than a few hundred. All were autonomous, although alliances of exchange or social contact existed, more or less weak. Each one existed on the land, probably possessed in a collective fashion, and all were illiterate. Life moved with the rhythm of the seasons, without history, that is to say, the importance of good or bad harvests were forgotten. Epidemics and natural calamities, quarrels with neighbors, went unrecorded. Now, 7,000 years later, more than half the inhabitants of the Earth (whose numbers had multiplied more than a hundredfold) now do, or soon will, dwell in cities. Already 75% of the population in the most developed areas live in cities, and some of these cities have 6 million inhabitants. Some states rule over hundreds of millions of people; illiteracy is considered a scourge in a world where 70 out of 100 adults know how to read and write. It is only in remote places that representatives of the way of life so close and yet so far away—Neolithic hunters-gatherers and farmers—are still found. The course of this incredible transformation continues to preoccupy archaeologists. How and why did it come about?

City, state, writing and warfare are the key themes. Writing, whose achievement traditionally marks the end of pre-history, appears in all of the societies of the world, and, through the study of its first expressions comes the question of the origin of the state. Philosophers, historians, ethnologists and archaeologists have for a long time reflected on the problem, and more particularly, on its causes. Soon, the necessity of war is invoked to take over, at a neighbor's expense, the lands required by expanding population, or the organization of irrigation networks, which will necessitate a central authority for the execution of great works and the distribution of water. Both would have favored the appearance of a hierarchy, either military or bureaucratic, at the

93

heart of the society. Partial explanations, however, for irrigation networks exist outside of the state's control, and wars are conducted by stateless societies (as in New Guinea). Ethnologists who offer these alternative explanations try to understand the appearance of the state in contemporary "archaic" societies, where the evolution process seems to unravel under their gaze, but the proof is quite elusive and difficult to interpret. Hierarchies appear to separate slowly into apparently egalitarian societies from the end of the Neolithic Period. These societies were unlikely to be "primitive democracies," as is sometimes imagined. Certain individuals had more power than others, without doubt, perhaps enjoying greater wealth. It was only a temporary status, however, as the individual was not able to transmit his rank to his heirs, and it was not deemed necessary, so it seems, to express it by a more important residence, or to pursue it

The rise of villages in the Near East and Asia

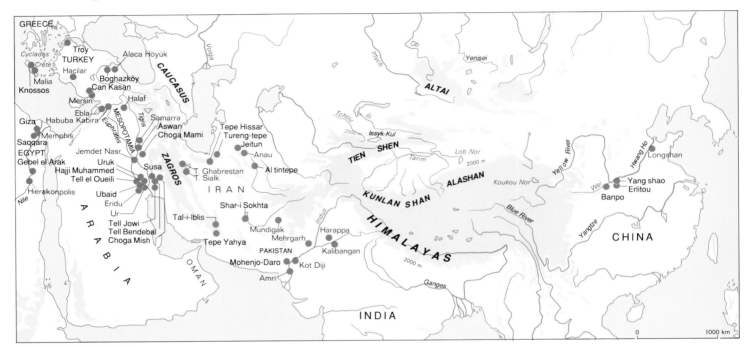

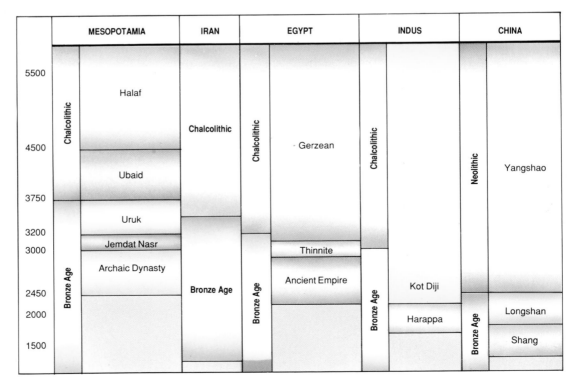

	MESOPOTAMIA		IRAN	EGYPT		INDUS		CHINA	
5500	Chalcolithic	Halaf	Chalcolithic	Chalcolithic	Gerzean	Chalcolithic		Neolithic	Yangshao
4500		Ubaid							
3750									
3200		Uruk	Bronze Age	Bronze Age		Bronze Age	Kot Diji	Bronze Age	
3000		Jemdat Nasr			Thinnite				
2450	Bronze Age	Archaic Dynasty			Ancient Empire				Longshan
2000							Harappa		
1500									Shang

beyond establishing a richer tomb. Ethnology reveals many examples of temporary war chiefs, without any power or particular status outside of the periods of conflict. There were powerful economic chiefs, like the "Big Men" of the South Pacific societies, whose might and wealth were constantly called into question and never bequeathed to their descendants.

When, at the start of the third millennium, the first texts that we can decipher give us some scraps concerning the social organization, everything has changed. Not only are power and wealth distributed in a very unequal fashion within the society, with several levels between those who become kings and those who will remain forever farmers, but these differences are hereditary. Put differently, a minority took over power and wealth, with the more or less forced consent of the majority, and the society now functioned to its profit. The riches are centralized inside places that we call cities. From there they are eventually redistributed by a central authority. Religious life, or at least the part of life that is concerned with the community, is organized into temples,

becoming the residences of the gods, to which is attached a clergy, itself hereditary. Writing facilitates the complex movement of property, while setting down a record of the transaction. It is perfected in order to take note of the religious myths and to immortalize the glorious acts of the mighty, among which is war, which allows the extension of the territorial base and humanity together. To this whole will be given the name of state, all the while noting that a definition as handy would certainly not satisfy all of the theoreticians. At least it will serve to better understand the events that mark the passage from prehistory to history, as well as archaeologists can reconstruct them.

The first states, so defined, appear in the third millennium, in the alluvial valleys of the great rivers: the Nile (Egypt), the Euphrates and the Tigris (Mesopotamia), the Indus (Pakistan and northwestern India), and a bit later perhaps, the Yellow River (China). These are the regions on which we have some light. Comparing them to find out if they all followed the same evolutionary pattern would be desirable, but the state of research is too uneven for such comparison to be fruitful. Writing from the Indus Valley has remained immune to attempts to decipher it; little is known about Egypt from the fifth to the fourth millennia and even less about China before the truly historic age. We will thus begin with the study of Mesopotamia, better documented, before briefly mentioning the other three. Then we will leave the great river valleys, cradles of the first empires, in order to concern ourselves with the appearance of writing in other regions and to settle a problem of great importance. Writing, which appears in Mesopotamia around 3300 B.C., is only known in the second millennium in Turkey and Greece, later in the Danubian region of Europe, or in Iran, where had existed for some time what some archaeologists do not hesitate to call a state, even if sometimes truth is only discovered in a city. Cities, states, writing and warfare are certainly terms that are associated with one another, but not everywhere in the same manner, thus leading to one of the most interesting questions.

The Prelude to Change: Village Communities of the Chalcolithic

Near 5500 B.C., all of the cultivable zones of the Near and Middle East are inhabited by sedentary agriculturalists grouped in villages. These farmers occupy the valleys and foothills of the mountains, fertile and well watered, eventually easy to irrigate. This is the case with Can Hasan and Hacilar in Turkey, Tepe Sialk, Tepe Hissar or Tall-i-Iblis in Iran, Djeitun and Anau in Soviet Turkmenia and Mehrgarh in Pakistan. Life differs scarcely from the end of the Neolithic, but here and there some changes appear that lead archaeologists to create a new term: Chalcolithic, literally, Copper Age. Thus the appearance of the first metal tools symbolizes the changes recognized as the premise of all subsequent evolution.

As far as we can determine, society still remains essentially egalitarian regarding the distribution of wealth; the plan of the crude brick houses varies from one region to the other, but remains remarkably constant within a village, where no buildings convey by their exceptional size or their opulence

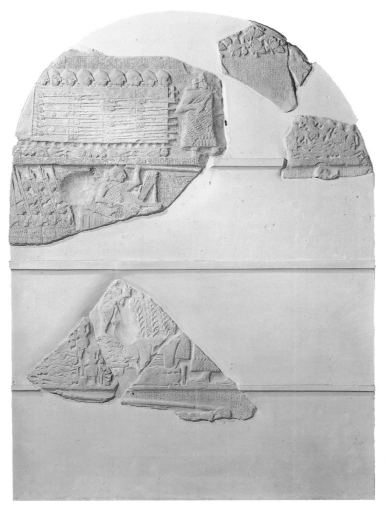

War scene "vultures" stella, discovered at Tello in Mesopotamia (around 2500 B.C.). Armed with lances, warriors of a city-state advance in closed ranks, protected by copper shields. Paris, the Louvre. Ph. Lauros-Giraudon.

the existence of individuals clearly richer than the majority of their fellows. The same impressions prevail for funerary rites. In two places, as far away as Tell al-Sawwan (Iraq) or Mehrgarh (Pakistan), no tomb is distinguished from another by a more ostentatious richness. The dead were accompanied by personal effects, but none took with them the symbols of pre-eminence within society. Painted pottery displayed the traditions of the previous ages: Decoration, always geometric, sometimes with schematic figurative motifs, was often very rich and of a real artistic worth. Each culture had its own style, painted in black on deep red, as in Sialk II (Iran), or in brown on cream in Turkey (Hacilar, Can Hasan). Some of these styles extended over vast regions, as did those of Samarra and Halaf in northern Mesopotamia and Eridu and Hajji Muhammad in the south. The great similarity of the forms and decorations, their uniformity from one village to another and the quality of their techniques, have caused some archaeologists to assume, as early as this age, the existence of specialized, perhaps itinerant artisans. This hypothesis cannot be completely confirmed, but ethnoarchaeological research on groups of contemporary patterns has revealed that very often pottery of high quality, specific to one precise typology, constitutes the partial occupation at the time of the women of a village, for example. One can reasonably assume that in this era each family or village had one or several potters, working in more than only agricultural activities. The diffusion of an identical pottery in a vast region would thus explain a certain identity of demand (or taste), for reasons which we must now examine.

The occupation of new lands

Religion also changed. We know nothing with certainty about such structures as temples, but the appearance of numerous figurines in the tombs, most often in terra-cotta, but sometimes in alabaster (as Tell al-Sawwan), allow us to suppose a progression in the attitude toward death and an evaluation of religious thought. A number of villages, such as Hacilar, Mersin, Tell al-Sawwan, are enclosed by walls, which could have had a defensive role. No object with a clearly warlike function has survived, and we are ignorant of all forms of conflicts, perhaps quarrels with neighbors, or combat with larger groups for the appropriation of cultivable lands. By identifying a pottery of the Halaf style and positing behind it a Halaf culture, the geographic distribution of elements of the stylized figurines of this culture can be traced. Archaeologists assume implicity a population, which from village to village, recognized certain links particularly those created by marriage bonds, fundamental yet invisible exchanges in human societies. That this culture extended itself in time toward the north (southern Turkey) and the west (northern Syria), in a manner never seen before the new style of pottery appeared, explains the advance of a population group at the expense of its neighbors, or that of a particular form of ornamentation and adornment taking root. Indeed, the two processes may be related. This is a question to which there are different responses, but it is clear that to each possibility there corresponds a different social organization

and this inability to determine is not the least measure of our ignorance of this era.

On the lower Mesopotamian plain, in the south, other groups fabricated a different pottery, with its own evolution, known under successive names as the Eridu and Hajji Muhammad. It was at the start of the age of Eridu, or a little before, that farmers began to settle on the plain. It was necessary for them to master the techniques of irrigation, because the rains alone were unable to assure abundant harvests. These farmers appear to have used the techniques on a relatively important scale. The most ancient irrigation canals were installed around 6000 B.C., at Choga Mami, in the foothills of the Zagros Mountains, and it is without doubt that in this environment new farming techniques appeared. The farmers mirror a new world in their culture, where they had to protect themselves against devastating floods from rivers, organize irrigation networks and drain marshes, as the excavations at Tell al-Oueili demonstrate. Agriculture in that area was largely augmented by the exploitation of marshes and by fishing. To these difficulties was added the remoteness of all sources of raw materials, except for clay. Flint tools, hard millstones and grinders all had to be imported from hundreds of miles/kilometers away, necessitating regular trade routes, more organized than in the Neolithic, for such items as obsidian. The agricultural communities of southern Mesopotamia were confronted with a situation much more hostile than those that manufactured the pottery of Halaf, or those that lived on the foothills of Turkey, Iran or Turkmania. Unfortunately, we know so little about them. Two surveys at Tell al-Oueili and Eridu and some slightly more important excavations to the east in Susiana, in a similar environment (at Tepe Jowi, Tepe Bendebal, Choga Mish) have been made. It is there that the evolution took place that, in three millennia, led from the village to the city.

The beginning of metallurgy

Before we see how this urban evolution was achieved, it is necessary to describe another fundamental aspect of the period: the increasing use of copper. It had been used occasionally in the native cultures in the preceramic Neolithic era,

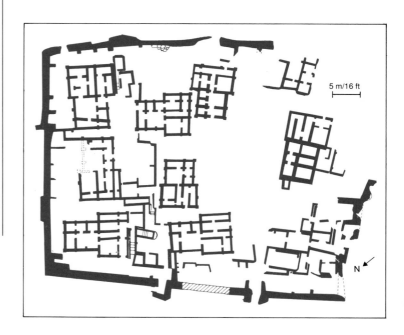

Plan of a Chalcolithic village in Tell es-Sawwan, in Mesopotamia. The village is surrounded by a ram- part and consists of large houses, similar in style, in a remarkably uniform arrangement.

but its use was an exception and did not constitute what could be called metallurgy. As early as the Neolithic, in Iran at Sialk I, some ornaments (pins) or small tools (awls, piercers) were produced by hammering abundant nuggets of native copper. These objects become more numerous with the passage of time and also more complex (headed pins and the needle). The first objects poured into a mold and flat hatchets and hoes appeared in the third period, around 4500 B.C., at Sialk, but also nearby at Tepe Ghabrestan, or more to the south at Tall-i Iblis. This is an important date in human history: The heat that humans already knew how to use to harden pottery and to change its color was for the first time exploited to alter the state of matter, to refashion it. It was necessary to possess ovens capable of attaining the temperature for copper fusion (about 1980°F/1083°C), which was possible with the ovens employed for pottery, and to invent the bellows that stoked the hearth to achieve the temperature and to maintain the heat for the required time. Some centuries later, a still more profound transformation of matter—the extraction of metal still within a block of ore—took place. No amount of debate has helped us determine when these processes, which allowed human beings to increase mightily their hold over nature, first took place. They were the result of repeated observations over generations, during the long hours spent in stoking the flames, manipulating the bellows around the furnace where the metal was formed. There were, without doubt, not one but many "firsts," not one, but many, inventors. Still it is only around 4500 B.C., in a number of Iranian villages, that flat hatchets, hoes and knives become more and more numerous, augmenting the tool kits of stone.

Rapid Transformations Leading to the Ubaid Period (4500–3730 B.C.)

4500 B.C. is the start of more and more profound transformations in Mesopotamia and Susiana. The Ubaid period is marked by the generalization of pottery over the whole of Mesopotamia, from the north (the ancient land of the Halaf) to the south. This pottery became standardized, produced in mass quantities, with a simplified geometric decoration, and became rare at the start of the fourth millennium. With a more decorated, naturalistic style, the Susiana followed a similar evolution.

The villages spread out along the traces of the rivers and the irrigation canals. As early as 4500 B.C., most of them possessed, next to homes and stores, vaster structures, often thought to be temples, less by reason of evidence discovered there than for their similarity to later ones. Some centuries later, the largest of these were erected at Uruk, Eridu and Susa, built on the summits of terraces, imposing masses of crude brick several feet/meters high. Monumental architecture was thus born. Also important was the appearance of a progressive differentiation in the size of the villages, of which certain ones, those in which the most spectacular buildings were located, clearly surpass others.

The world of the plains remained poor in raw materials and its economic effort pursued two main paths: the intensification of the productivity of available resources and the augmentation of trade with the outside. The copper, imported from the region of Sialk in Iran, according to archaeometric analyses, was commonly used in Susiana, as numerous flat hatchets discovered in the tombs of the "necropolis" there indicate. Metal

Monumental group of E-Anna at Uruk, in the fourth period (about 3400 B.C.). The function of this monumental group, made of crude brick in which certain buildings are more than 200 feet (60 meters) in length, is not clearly known. Generally interpreted as temples and adjacent annexes, the buildings could also be palaces, or a combination of the two.

Imprint from a seal, Tabet, Susa, proto-urban epoch (around 3300 B.C.). The scene represents the gathering of grain into a collective silo. It was stamped on a piece of clay sealing a jar or a package. Paris, the Louvre. Ph. Assembly of the National Museums.

Plan of E-Anna at Uruk:
1. Temple with the mosaics (level six)
2. Court (level four)
3. Square Palace (level four)
4. Temple D (level four)
5. Temple C (level four)
6. Grand Hall (level four)

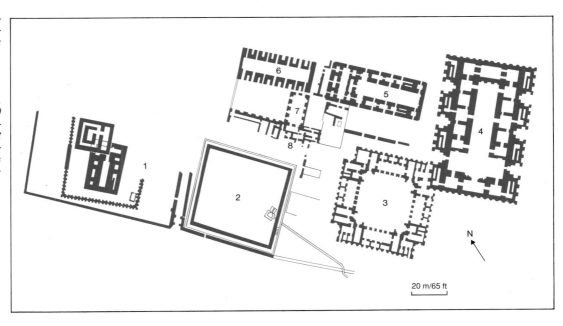

20 m/65 ft

remains, by contrast, very rare in Mesopotamia, where the humans began to fabricate in series the argil sickle, baked at very high temperatures (more than 2000°F/1100°C). The usage analysis indicates that these were used to cut vegetable stalks, thus replacing a local product of flint braces from earlier periods. Metal sickles perhaps already existed around this time. Some models of hatchets and hoes in terra-cotta have been found, but their usage is unknown. This short-lived technology, which would give way to metal when the commercial circuits became fully developed, illustrates the efforts made to utilize all of the available resources.

The digging of irrigation canals, monumental construction requiring a considerable labor force, was probably performed during the slow periods in the agricultural cycle, perhaps even at the expense of planting and harvesting. Who organized the digging? Was there already a form of government or were the old village organizational structures sufficient? The growing complexity of the techniques and the economy revealed by archaeology seem strongly linked to the increasing sophistication of society, which appears organized around the "temples." The style of stone, or baked argil, with geometric decorations, now very numerous on the sites, testifies to the early administrative activity. Was this the beginnings of a state-controlled production, sometimes called a "city-temple," or nothing more than the slow perpetuation of power in certain familial lines, who, by establishing traditional authority, transformed the life of society and perhaps diverted the functions to their own profit? Rather than the precursors of the large Mesopotamian temples, the "temple" of the Ubaid period can be viewed merely as a house larger than the others, the residence of one of the dominant lineages, which incrementally expanded its control of the direction of the economic, political and religious activities of the community. If such elites existed, as is very likely, they did not deem it necessary to stress their importance after death—all tombs of this period are alike.

The Period of Uruk and the First Cities (3750–3200 B.C.)

The differentiation of sites in their size and function is a practice begun at the start of the fourth millennium, no longer only in villages that dominate others, but for the first time in true cities. One does not hesitate to propose the figure of 10,000 inhabitants in Uruk, around 3750 B.C., though this maximum estimate should not be deceiving. A portion of the inhabitants of the city were farmers, cultivating the surrounding lands and fields. We have, however, sufficient evidence to confirm that in sites such as Uruk, Eridu, Susa or Choga Mish, some economic, religious and administrative activities were conducted on a regional scale, which allows us to describe such sites as cities.

Archaeology traditionally identifies this period by profound changes in pottery, whose manufacture can be qualified as industrial. The use of the pottery wheel, one of the first, if not the first, machines, came into general use at the same time that decoration disappeared completely. This industry was practiced on specialized sites and pottery, made by each family according to their needs during the Neolithic, and became an exchange product on a regional scale.

The countryside in the fourth millennium submitted to the authority of the cities and became the area of intensifica-

Large cultic vase in alabaster, Uruk, Mesopotamia (around 3400 B.C.). *The vessel depicts porters with offerings and agricultural scenes, attesting to the importance of agriculture in the economic life and ideology of the first cities.* Museum of Baghdad. Ph. Scala.

tion without precedent in the techniques of production and transformation—sometimes called a "revolution of by-products." The swing plough becomes widespread, as does the use of dairy products and the breeding of new stocks of sheep for sheared wool. This is suggested by the representations in the figurative scenes; perishable products of which archaeologists rarely recover traces, it is difficult to say much more. However, the use of milk products, for example, can be linked to the appearance of new forms of pottery (vases with pouring lips, churns, sieves). The productivity of the countryside, where the irrigation network had just been developed, increased the profits of the cities.

Monumental architecture is the most spectacular manifestation of these cities. It is especially well known in Uruk, where a group of large buildings made of crude brick with facades decorated by massive caves of multicolored stones were discovered. Certain of these buildings were probably temples, but others were no doubt residences or administrative centers. New techniques were born there, such as the cylinder seals that the functionaries rolled over fresh argil to seal jars, baskets and the doors of warehouses, to ensure their inviolability. Such invention marks the desire for central control, exercised by the "government" over the whole of economic activities. These cities were also the site of increasingly varied and growing artistic production, supported by the growing demand of the elite for objects of luxury and prestige: weapons, copper containers, rare jewels, furniture of exotic woods, sculpted or encrusted ceremonial vases, elaborate clothing, etc. Raw materials nearly always had to be imported from great distances: copper from the Iranian plateau, wood and stone from the mountains of Syria or Zagros, pearls from the Persian Gulf. The port of Habuba Kabira, created around 3500 B.C., on the right bank of the Euphrates River, in Syria, is a testimony to these diverse changes. Built on more than 50 acres (20 hectares), with an administrative center, houses aligned on streets, ramparts reinforced by square towers, the site illustrates the influence of the Uruk culture outside of its center in southern Mesopotamia.

The political system of the period can only be speculated about. On the cylinder imprints and on the first reliefs appears a bearded figure, conventionally called "priest-king," shown hunting wild animals, directing war, receiving gifts from subordinate figures and interceding with the divinities. His authority, and that of his entourage, extended to the territory controlled by the city, an area that he was able to extend by war with neighboring sites. Such a political system can also be described as a "city-state." The ownership of the land was still essentially collective, managed in the name of family groups of the old village structures. This much can be determined from the texts provided some centuries later, allowing us to piece together information about the system at the moment that it disappeared. Divinities are tied to the natural powers, and the figurative representations suggest the importance of agriculture within the cultic observances, thus confirming the agrarian character of the economic base of the first cities.

The Invention of Writing (about 3300 B.C.) and the Jemdet Nasr Age (3200–3000 B.C.)

Writing appears for the first time at the end of the Uruk era in the form of pictographic characters, schematized designs representing objects or activity. Evolving rapidly, they

(Left) **Seal imprint, Susa, proto-urban epoch** *(circa 3300 B.C.). Archers, at right, assail a temple situated on a high terrace, similar to the monuments found during excavations. The temple is decorated with horns, which also adorn the headdresses of the gods.* Paris, the Louvre. Ph. Assembly of the National Museums.

(Above) **Sumerian pictographic tablets** *(end of the fourth millennium B.C.). The signs are still very figurative, but could represent an inventory of property.* Paris, the Louvre. Ph. Assembly of the National Museums.

took on a syllabic value and served in the composition of words. Inscribed on tablets of wet clay that hardened while drying, the symbols quickly became prominent because of the clear constraints of the material. The *cuneiform* aspect (composed of drawings in the shape of nails), the modern name for this form of writing, continued for three millennia, until the time of Alexander the Great. In its first manifestations, writing was only an administrative tool, serving to record commodities, their quantity and their destinations. It was only some centuries later, after having been considerably perfected, that it was used to record literary texts, religions, myths and royal annals. They were written in Sumerian, the language of the lands of Sumer, a name that the inhabitants themselves gave to southern Mesopotamia.

History begins at Sumer, wrote the great specialists of this difficult language. But it is in the identical civilization of Susa that the state of research allows us to retrace the birth of writing best, as the result of a series of administrative procedures. It seems that the custom began, in the time of Uruk, to accompany commodities with a kind of "memorandum," a sphere of crude clay containing small tokens of different shapes, which symbolized the merchandise and the quantity. This "bubble" was closed, and the official who conducted the operation affixed his seal. It became common practice to reproduce on the surface of the bubble, by impression in the fresh clay, the image of the tokens that it contained. Numerous steps had already been taken in this regard. The following stage was merely making do with stamping signs on a simple small plate of clay (where a seal was always affixed), while more and more diversified symbols clarified the information necessary to the nature of the commodities. The two systems coexisted at one time. Writing was thus born as a means to track the circulation of commodities and goods inside the city-states. It is significant that at the moment of its beginnings, writing had the two different models, Uruk and Susa, set down two different languages, Sumerian and Elamite, and with two systems of different signs, with a similar foundation. The economic and social structure was the same and, in fact, favored its invention. At the start of the third millennium, perhaps for reasons of political domination, perhaps because it was less practical, the "Proto-Elamite" writing of the Susiana began to disappear.

Following discoveries in Uruk's monumental structures, it had been thought that writing was used only by the religious and political elite. However, at Susa, some documents were found in private homes (which had not been excavated in Uruk). Certain tablets pertain to quantities of commodities and relatively small numbers of livestock. Writing thus appears as a method of managing commodities, which affects the whole of society, even if its management is in the hands of a few specialists. It continued this function in Mesopotamia during the historic eras, where copies of contracts and transactions were maintained and duly registered by an official, even if he was incapable of reading or writing them.

The beginning of history

The period at Jemdet Nasr, from which arose the first improvements of writing, was also the height of early urbanization. A more elegant ceramic, now painted, was used alongside the usual undecorated wares. The art of statuary, cylindrical in shape, improved and diversified. Metal working evolved to such a degree that certain centers rivaled in techniques and quality products from the areas of the metal's origin. Copper, lead, silver and gold were worked, and natural alloys like copper and arsenic were supplemented in the first experiments to produce new alloys, with lead, antimony and tin. The successful manufacture of bronze led to its generalized use around 2500 B.C. The influence of southern Mesopotamia extended a long way, to the peninsula of Oman to the south, which became, at the start of 3000 B.C., the principal source for copper, up to Shahr-i Sokhte, at the Irano-Afghani border, the most easterly point of the diffusion of administrative practices invented in the fourth millennium: cylinder-seals and writing. Northern Syria also came under strong influence, and perhaps even far-off Egypt was affected.

At the start of the third millennium, the city-states of Mesopotamia already had a history, not yet written but one that is divined in the evolution of their archaeological layers. The social stratification, strongly rooted, was marked in tombs and their furnishings. The royal and religious func-

Seals and counters from the acropolis of Susa *(level 18, circa 3400 B.C.). Early administrative "documents." The imprints from small sticks and circles on the surface of* the seal probably represent the counters it contained. Ph. French Archaeological Commission in Iran.

tions differentiated more and more, even if the king kept a number of ritual attributes, as is suggested in the royal tomb in Ur, around 2500 B.C. In the 24th century B.C., Sargon founded the Akkadian Empire, the first state encircling all of the lands of the two rivers. The texts, long intelligible, provide the identity of the kings and their places of battle, the titles of their officials, the names of their cities, those of their gods and their attributes. We have entered history.

Cuneiform tablet from Lagash, Mesopotamia (circa 2400 B.C.). Writing had been in use there for several centuries, becoming the clas- sic "cuneiform" phase, which we can now read perfectly. The text concerns the contract of a slave sale. Paris, the Louvre. Ph. Ch. Lenars.

The Nile Valley

Egypt experienced a similar evolution, of which we are still somewhat ignorant. Its brilliant civilization seems to start around 3000 B.C. The society of the Naqada and Gerzean periods, in the fourth millennium, would be comparable to that of contemporary times in Mesopotamia. The scenes of war and the mythological scenes sculpted on the ivory handle of the Jebel el-Arak knife, for example, recall the representations on the vases and cylinder seals of Uruk. Some similarities suggest a Mesopotamian influence, or at the very least some contact between the two regions at the end of the fourth millennium, to which, however, it is not necessary to attribute a large role in Egypt's later development. The struggle for power between the city-states (or the Egyptian equivalent) lasted until the Thinite Period (approximately 3100–2800 B.C.) and the first attempts at unification. Egyptian historians have learned of Menes (or Narmer), a king of Upper Egypt from Hierakonpolis, where an important Gerzean group is found. At the junction of the Nile and the Delta, he founded Memphis—the first capital of Egypt. The pharaohs of the first two Egyptian dynasties were certainly already theocratic monarchs, as were their successors. Hieroglyphic writing appeared in this period, gradually acquiring its classic form. Work in stone, metal (copper, gold) and wood, etc., attained a high level of technical and artistic quality and sculpture its first expressions. With its particular character, Egypt, as early as the Old Kingdom (starting 2800 B.C.), was a unified state, capable of enormous mobilizations of manpower, like that which was required for the construction of the Step Pyramid at Saqqara for Pharaoh Djoser (around 2750 B.C.), followed by the grandiose group at Giza (2650–2550 B.C.).

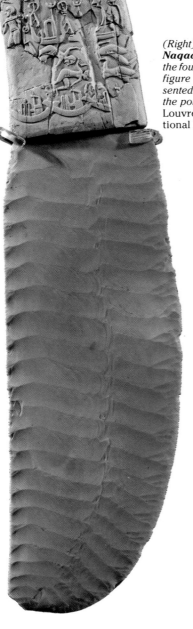

(Left) ***Jebel el-Arak knife, Egypt*** *(middle of the fourth millennium B.C.). The handle, made of ivory, of this very beautiful flint knife shows hunting and war scenes, themes that reflect the preoccupations of the upper classes of society.* Paris, the Louvre. Ph. Lauros-Giraudon.

(Right) ***Painted vase of the Naqada culture, Egypt*** *(middle of the fourth millennium B.C.). A human figure and an animal are represented on a boat, a common motif in the pottery of this epoch.* Paris, the Louvre. Ph. Assembly of the National Museums.

Stela of the "King-Serpent," Abydos, Egypt *(first dynasty, circa 3000 B.C.). The falcon, symbol of the god Horus, and the serpent form hieroglyphic writing of a royal name and are represented atop the serekh. Paris, the Louvre. Ph. Lauros-Giraudon.*

The extraordinary continuity of Egyptian texts allows us to return to the first dynasties, and the remarkable preservation of archaeological documentation in the Egyptian soil makes reasonable hope for a fruitful elaboration on our knowledge of the passage from prehistory to history, based on much needed excavation.

The Indus Valley

The civilization of the Indus Valley is still little known, although it left imposing ruins: Mohenjo-Daro on the middle course of the Indus, Harappa and Kalibangan in the Punjab. Even the date of these cities is still debated, 2100–1700 B.C. being a reasonable estimate. The excavations of Mehrgarh suggest an important contribution of the Chalcolithic cultures of Baluchistan to the development of the brilliant handicraft of this civilization, and it is at least certain that, as early as 3500 B.C., some agricultural villages already occupied the alluvial plains, periodically submerged by violent floods from the Indus and its tributaries, whose courses were not yet fixed. This natural phenomenon strongly influenced the occupation of the region, where one imagines very mobile villages due to the seasonal displacements of the river and its multiple branches. The large cities of strong baked brick, with several tens of thousands of inhabitants, sometimes built on artificial terraces, such as Mohenjo-Daro, are the ultimate result of a long history of which little other testimony survives. This is the case at Amri, where the continuity is evident between the pottery of the Kot Diji style and that of the large cities, characterized by a painted decoration executed in black on deep red.

The Indus Valley civilization remains an enigma. Writing is known there by the brief inscriptions, notably on square seals in steatite (soapstone), but their translations, like the language, continue to elude us, despite numerous attempts at decipherment. Unlike in Mesopotamia, Egypt or China, no evident historic continuity emerges to help reconstruct the society. Neither tomb nor palace has been excavated there,

although their existence is very probable. The tombs reveal no social differentiation, although the impression of the whole, from the plan of the cities to the remarkable uniformity of the material culture on a vast geographic level, belies the existence of a very structured society. One would like to be able to clarify its differences from those of Egypt and Mesopotamia, in order to better understand the variety in early human societies.

The Origins of Chinese Civilization

The roots of the Chinese civilization are still little-studied, and it is certain that the division into periods now defined does not fully reveal the phenomenon of urbanization or the appearance of state-controlled societies. The farmers of the "Neolithic" Yangshao culture (4000–2400 B.C.) perhaps practiced a cyclic agriculture. The major cultivated plant was millet and inhabitants were already established in villages, which recall the beginnings of the Chalcolithic in Mesopotamia. On nearly 25 acres (10 hectares), Banpo in the Wei Valley (Shaanxi) is surrounded by a ditch and has in its center a large construction (a "temple," communal house or a chief's residence?) while the diverse styles of painted pottery (found over vast geographic areas) resemble somewhat those of Halaf and Obeid in Mesopotamia. A little after 2400 B.C., the

(Left) ***Aerial view of Mohenjo Daro, Pakistan.*** *Two constructions in baked brick, the most well known in the large city: a series of platforms, at the right, often identified as a collective granary, and a basin, bordered by porticos, at the center, known as the "great basin." Although the interpretation is contested, it probably represents a cultic administrative section of the city.* Ph. G. Helmes, German Research Project, "Mohenjo Daro."

(Above) ***Tablet from Mohenjo Daro, Indus civilization*** *(circa 2400 B.C.). In soft stone (steatite) like most tablets, this one depicts a fantastic unicorn before an "altar." Above, four writing symbols, as yet undeciphered, from the Indus civilization.* New Delhi, National Museum. Ph. J.-L.Nou.

Longshan culture, with its black turned pottery and sites enclosed by a rampart of earth formed around a central building, occupies the eastern regions, in the great plain of the Yellow River, this culture was already familiar with writing.

One traditionally places around 1850 B.C., the appearance of the Bronze Age with the Shang Dynasty (1850–1112 B.C.). As early as the first phase (1850–1650 B.C.), named after the site of Erlitou, systems of state and urban control had evolved, of which a brilliant culture presents a continuity with the Longshan. Metal appears and its usage develops rapidly, as early as the following phase, the Erligang (1650–

1400 B.C.), with the appearance of an industry of a massive quantity of luxury items. This is also the time of the first manifestations of writing, with characters traced on animal bones, utilized for some divinatory practice suggesting circumstances completely different from the processes in Mesopotamia. It is likely that this sudden flourishing is only one episode, masking a very long evolution that began as early as the fourth millennium. The divisions of the past adapted by Chinese archaeologists highlight a fact that must not be forgotten: that the immense majority of the population under the Shang Dynasty lived in a way that differed little from the Neolithic. That important point probably applies as well to the farmers of the third millennium in Egypt, Mesopotamia and the Indus. The agricultural economic base that allows the development of social hierarchies and state-controlled societies dates to the end of the Neolithic. It remains predominant in numerous areas until our own time.

Outside the Great Plains

One could not end a discussion of the dawn of history by limiting oneself to these four regions. Some societies with marked social hierarchies appeared almost everywhere in the third and fourth millennia, at the start of the local Chalcolithic cultures. Iran and Central Asia, for example, experienced an urban phase whose height was achieved a little after 2500 B.C., at Shahr-i Sokhte, Tureng Tepe, Altyn Tepe and Mundigak. These four sites, among many others, occupied an area greater than 125 acres (50 hectares). They were fortified, dominated by a monumental group with a high terrace of a religious nature like the other buildings of great size. These true cities do not seem to have been familiar with writing, with the exception of a short-lived episode around 3000 B.C., at the start of their development, where some tablets in Proto-Elamite characters accompanied by cylinder seals of the Susian type have been found at Shahr-i Sokhte, Tepe Sialk and Tepe Yahya, thus explaining the strong influence exercised by Susa on the region. These cities were the centers of local state-controlled systems that doubtless

(Above) **Tripod "U" vase in copper, excavation of Tcheng-tcheon, Honan, China** *(Shang era, middle of the second millennium B.C.). This example attests to the perfection attained as early as this era by copper metallurgists of China.* Paris, Cernuschi Museum. Ph. Lauros-Giraudon.

(Right) **The high terrace of Altyn Tepe, Soviet Turkemenia** *(circa 2500 B.C.). A hypothetical reconstruction. The terrace dominated the city and was probably the religious center.*

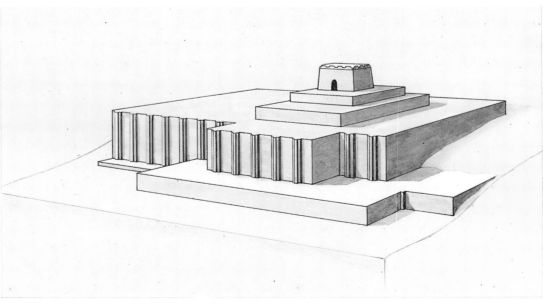

played a large role in the commerce of raw materials created by the great plains (such as lapis lazuli, found from Afghanistan to Egypt) but they followed their own evolutionary process. None of them gave birth later to centralized states, and writing did not reappear until around 500 B.C., during the Achaemenids (the Persian Hakhamanishiya) Empire.

Cities developed very late in the third millennium in Syria and in Palestine, subjected to strong influences of their powerful neighbors, Egypt and Mesopotamia. Those of northern Syria, such as Ebla, used cuneiform writing and became powerful in some eras toward the middle of the third millennium. But the pressures of their neighbors proved too strong for any state to surpass them on a regional scale. One hesitates to talk about cities in Turkey and the Greek world, as well as the Cyclades in the third millennium. The monarchs who ruled over Troy, leaving such rich treasures, or Alaca Hüyük, where tombs are known for providing us with an abundance of precious personal property, resided in fortified market towns, of which Troy II gives an excellent example, rather than in true urban centers. Writing does not seem to have been used. It is only around 2000 B.C. that relatively important states appear in this region: the Hittites in Turkey, the Cretan civilization and the Mycenean civilization, a little later in Greece. The first two developed under strong outside influence from Mesopotamia and Egypt and adopted writing. Cuneiform writing was used by the Hittites, writing called linear was used in Crete and Greece. Boghazköy, the capital of the Hittites, in central Turkey, Mallia or Knossos in Crete, are true cities, and the very elaborate art of Crete captured the imagination when it was discovered at the start of the 20th century.

In the course of these pages, we have presented only one hypothesis, one that now allows greater understanding of the information gathered from excavations. It insists on local evolution, minimizes external influences, does not take into account eventual migrations of people, often put forward by archaeologists tempted to explain the appearance of a new pottery and forms of architecture. Sumerian migration toward Mesopotamia has often been discussed. It was not our intention to repudiate these influences, nor to maintain that the migrations of populations never took place. But we have preferred to emphasize the importance of internal factors in the evolution of societies, factors that help us truly comprehend the great tendencies of human evolution that is prehistory.

Suggested Reading

McAdams, R., and H. J. Nissen. *The Uruk Countryside: The Natural Setting of Urban Societies.* Chicago: University of Chicago Press, 1972.

Mellaart, J. *The Neolithic of the Near East.* New York and London: Thames and Hudson, 1975.

Redman, P. L. *The Rise of Civilizations, from Early Farmers to Urban Society in the Ancient Near East.* San Francisco: W. H. Freeman, 1978.

Disc of Phaestos, Crete (circa 1650 B.C.). This document in baked clay bears an inscription in "linear A," which remained undecipherable until recently and which is linked to the palatial system of Crete in this era. Heraklion Museum. Ph. M. L. Maylin.

PREHISTORY OF AMERICA

The term "prehistory" assumes a particular significance for the American continent. In effect, if one preserves the classic sense of this word—the "history of humanity since the most distant times until the appearance of written accounts," according to M. Brézillon (1969), the prehistory of America goes back to the 25th century B.C., only ending with the "official" discovery of the New World by Christopher Columbus in 1492. The innumerable and brilliant civilizations—the Olmecs and Teotihuacan in Mesoamerica, the San Augustín complex, the Quimbaya and Tairona cultures in Colombia, Chorrera and La Tolita in Ecuador, and the Chavín, Nazca and Tiahuanaco in the middle Andian regions—to cite just a few of the most widely known, would be included under this definition. They succeeded each other, in Mexico and along the Andes, from the second millennium to the start of the 14th century A.D., several attaining an urban stage. Even "empires" stretching over vast regions, like the Aztec and the Inca, would thus be classified as prehistoric, without having, it is true, passed the technical stages equivalent to the Bronze Age, their social and cultural evolution surpassed in many fields that of the European groups of the second millennium B.C. Another contradiction: the Olmecs and Aztecs of Mexico would be considered prehistoric because they had no writing, but not the Mayas, successors of the first and predecessors of the second, who possessed a very elaborate glyphic writing style. As for the Incas of Peru, depending on whether or not one accepts the thesis of an ideographic writing as some textiles suggest, they would be either prehistoric or historic.

The Americanist prehistorians thus often favored another criterion to define their field of research: the appearance of the first ceramics. The term "preceramic" is sometimes used and, according to cases, will encompass forms of sociocultural organizations very different and unequal—from groups of predatory hunters, gatherers or fishers, having scarcely passed the technical levels of postglacial Europe, up to production societies (agriculturists and breeders), which advanced and became hierarchical and sendentary. Often, but not in a systematic manner, the first methods preceded the second. Finally, it is necessary to emphasize that the appearance of baked clay containers does not constitute an absolute chronological dateline for pottery appeared in diverse places of the continent at highly varied times: at the end of the fourth millennium on the northern Pacific coast (from where it spread toward the north and south); around 2000 B.C. in Mesoamerica and in Peru; in 1000 B.C. in North America; and only in 500 B.C. in Argentina. The tribes of the extreme south, like the fishing people of the southern coast of Chile or the Magellanic Archipelago, never used it; others like the Tehuelches of the Argentine Patagonia, only adopted it in the 12th century A.D.

The sequence defined here, and the one we will adapt is certainly convenient since it restores the upper chronological limit of American prehistory to date more or less comparable, with some exceptions, to those of the rest of the world. It is also questionable inasmuch as the appearance of pottery, although undoubtedly an important technical innovation, is nonetheless only a minor phenomenon, which did not deeply modify the social and cultural habits of the people who invented it or adopted it from others.

It remains now to clarify the lower limit of the preceramic period and, there again, the profound originality of America is evident. Its roots are, in effect, much shallower than in the rest of the world and, in our present state of knowledge, 50,000 years constitute the extreme age that can be attributed to an American human population. Still, the oldest sites are few in number and often, alas, rather ephemeral. It is often a question of a logically admissible age rather than a proven one.

American prehistory is a young science. The first truly scientific research is only half a century old, and the sum of our knowledge is minute in regard to that which remains to be yet discovered.

108

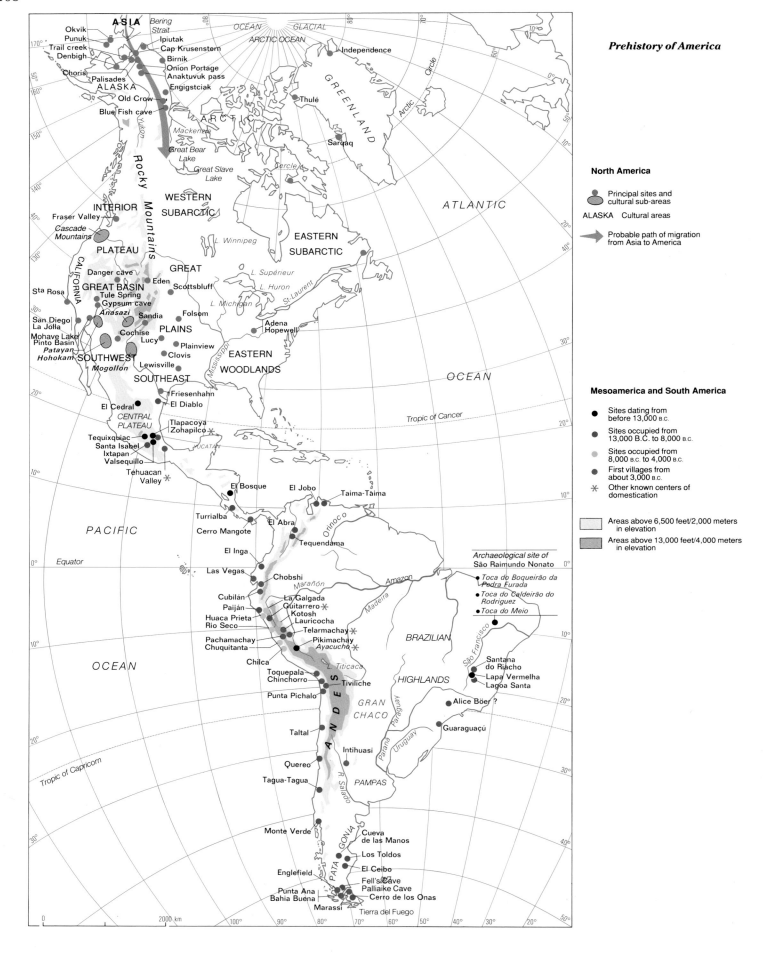

Prehistory of America

ASIA
Bering Strait
OCEAN GLACIAL
ARCTIC OCEAN
Okvik
Punuk
Ipiutak
Independence
Trail creek
Denbigh
Cap Krusenstern
Birnik
Choris
Onion Portage
Anaktuvuk pass
Palisades
Engigstciak
ALASKA
GREENLAND
Old Crow
Thulé
Blue Fish cave
Yukon
Mackenzie
ARCTIC
Sarqaq
Great Bear Lake
Great Slave Lake
Cercle
Rocky Mountains
WESTERN SUBARCTIC
ATLANTIC
INTERIOR
Fraser Valley
Cascade Mountains
L. Winnipeg
EASTERN SUBARCTIC
PLATEAU
CALIFORNIA
GREAT PLATEAU
Danger cave
Eden
GREAT BASIN
Tule Spring
Gypsum cave
Scottsbluff
L. Supérieur
L. Huron
St-Laurent
Sta Rosa
Anasazi
Sandia
Folsom
L. Michigan
San Diego
La Jolla
Cochise
Lucy
PLAINS
Adena
Hopewell
Mohave Lake
Pinto Basin
Patayan
Hohokam
SOUTHWEST
Mogollon
Plainview
Clovis
Lewisville
EASTERN WOODLANDS
OCEAN
SOUTHEAST
El Cedral
Friesenhahn
El Diablo
Tropic of Cancer
CENTRAL PLATEAU
Tlapacoya
Zohapilco
Tequixquiac
Santa Isabel
Ixtapan
Valsequillo
YUCATAN
Tehuacan Valley
El Bosque
El Jobo
Taima-Taima
Turrialba
Cerro Mangote
El Abra
Orinoco
PACIFIC
Tequendama
El Inga
Equator
Las Vegas
Chobshi
Marañón
Amazon
Madeira
Archaeological site of São Raimundo Nonato
Toca do Boqueirão da Pedra Furada
Cubilán
La Galgada
Guitarrero
Kotosh
Paiján
Huaca Prieta
Rio Seco
Lauricocha
Telarmachay
BRAZILIAN
Toca do Caldeirão do Rodriguez
Toca do Meio
Pachamachay
Chuquitanta
Pikimachay
Ayacucho
São Francisco
Santana do Riacho
Lapa Vermelha
Lagoa Santa
Chilca
Toquepala
Chinchorro
Tiviliche
HIGHLANDS
OCEAN
Punta Pichalo
L. Titicaca
GRAN CHACO
Alice Böer ?
ANDES
Paraná
Paraguay
Uruguay
Guaraguaçú
Taltal
Intihuasi
Quereo
R. Salado
PAMPAS
Tagua-Tagua
Tropic of Capricorn
Monte Verde
Cueva de las Manos
Los Toldos
El Ceibo
Englefield
Fell's Cave
Palliaike Cave
Cerro de los Onas
Punta Ana
Bahia Buena
Marassi
Tierra del Fuego
PATAGONIA

0   2000 km

North America

Principal sites and cultural sub-areas

ALASKA   Cultural areas

Probable path of migration from Asia to America

Mesoamerica and South America

Sites dating from before 13,000 B.C.

Sites occupied from 13,000 B.C. to 8,000 B.C.

Sites occupied from 8,000 B.C. to 4,000 B.C.

First villages from about 3,000 B.C.

Other known centers of domestication

Areas above 6,500 feet/2,000 meters in elevation

Areas above 13,000 feet/4,000 meters in elevation

CHAPTER EIGHT

Jean-François Le Mouël

PREHISTORY OF NORTH AMERICA

Ivory comb with sculpted face; Dorset culture, Maxwell Bay, south of Devon Island, Northwest Territories, Canada. National Museum of Man, Ottawa. Ph. R.-J. McGhee, National Museum of Man.

Regardless of the school to which they belong, all archaeologists accept that the Bering Strait was the conduit for all that is from the Old World—both people and objects—in North America. This does not exclude some transoceanic contacts, trans-Pacific in particular, which could have taken place in certain periods. Let us eliminate, however, the theories of those who, like Greenman, suggest that in the glacial period some prehistoric Europeans were able to take advantage of the ice pack to cross the northern Atlantic. Such a hypothesis raises the problem of a journey of 3,700 miles (6,000 kilometers) in a hostile environment, whose destination is the shores of Iceland and Greenland. Finally, we have no proof that this was the case.

"Early-Man": the First American

Whatever their origin, the first Americans penetrated into an empty continent inhabited only by animals, which clearly drew the humans to these sites. What landscapes offered themselves to these first humans? What paths did they follow? In such an immense, empty space, they probably followed the easy trails. These routes are a function of topography.

A cross-section of the American continent, from west to east, reveals a narrow coastal band, running along the Pacific, the abrupt heights of the Cordillera (which is divided into the Pacific Chain and the Rocky Mountains in the north and the Sierra Madre in the south), hemming in the high plateaus, the low central lands (plains and prairies, Canadian Bouclier and the Mississippi basin, and the lower elevations of the ancient chain, the Appalachians), and finally an Atlantic coastal band. The spread of humanity into America must have been along a north-south axis along a relatively simple geographic pattern. The river basins probably played an important role in the communication routes.

In the length of time that we will consider (tens of thousands of years), the vertical relief of the continent remains stable; at most modified by some erosion of the mountains, the build up of lacustrial or fluvial terraces, the superficial

Great North American Cultural Tradition

chronology of lithic points

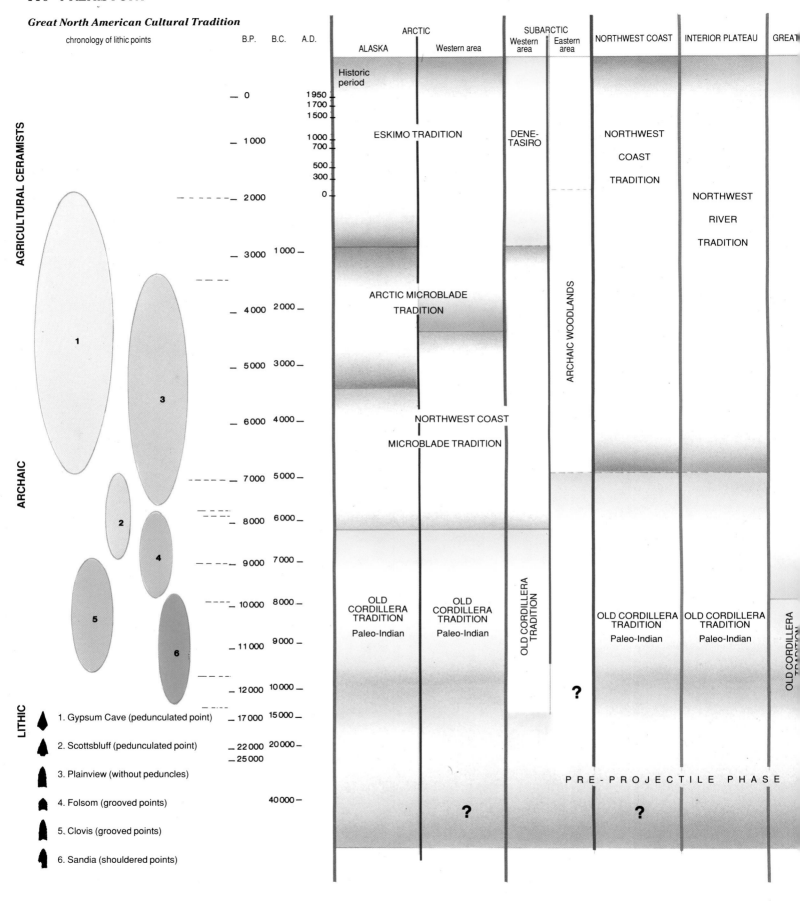

1. Gypsum Cave (pedunculated point)
2. Scottsbluff (pedunculated point)
3. Plainview (without peduncles)
4. Folsom (grooved points)
5. Clovis (grooved points)
6. Sandia (shouldered points)

Chart (after Willey)

	GREAT PLAINS AND PRAIRIES	CALIFORNIA	SOUTHWEST	EASTERN WOODLANDS
	PLAINS VILLAGE TRADITION		SOUTHWEST TRADITION	MISSISSIPPIAN
	WOODLANDS TRADITION	COAST TRADITION AND VALLEY TRADITION		EASTERN WOODLANDS
DESERT TRADITION			DESERT TRADITION	ARCHAIC TRADITION
	BIG GAME HUNTING TRADITION Paleo-Indian	BIG GAME HUNTING AND DESERT TRADITION		
Paleo-Indian	?	?	BIG GAME HUNTING TRADITION Paleo-Indian	BIG GAME HUNTING TRADITION Paleo-Indian
	?		?	?

deposits, etc. On the other hand, the oscillations of the climate were numerous and important and, therefore, the coastal plains have advanced or receded to the rhythm of the warming and cooling periods.

The Climatic Fluctuations

In the course of the fourth glaciation, the Wisconsin, (the Würm in Europe) about 18,000 years ago, Canada and Alaska were again covered by the large Cordilleran and Laurentian glaciers. At its apex the Laurentian had an estimated thickness of 3,200 to 4,000 feet (1,000 to 1,200 meters) and the Cordillera attained at least 8,200 feet (2,500 meters) at its center of expansion, situated on present-day British Columbia.

During formation, a glacier accumulates enormous amounts of water from the atmosphere, which causes a drop in the worldwide (eustatic) sea level. This drop in the general level of the oceans is relative to the immediate proximity of the glaciers, whose weight bends down the Earth's crust (isostasy). It is estimated that in the coldest periods of the Altonian or the Tazewell, the coastline corresponded approximately to the zone of the continental shelf, submerged today under 330 feet (100 meters) of water; during milder periods, the ocean levels rose again. Thus it is known that in the hottest period of the postglacial era (the Altithermal), the ocean's level was about ten feet (three meters) higher than it is today. Thus, the movements of the ocean waters have, in certain periods, allowed passage over the coasts, while forbidding them later. The sites that would testify to all of this are still liable to be submerged today.

The problem is more complicated, however. In fact, the level of the oceans is the same at one time for the whole world, but the magnitude of isostasic phenomena works against this uniformity, with the result that relative sea levels depend on local factors as well such as the elasticity of the rocky substrate and the weight of a nearby glacier. Today, one cannot be certain that two beach fossils in two regions of the world, at the same level, are the same age!

Finally, it is necessary to remember that isostasic movement is slow, slower than eustatic, which means that as a glacier melts the water level rises more rapidly than the Earth's crust flattens out. However, the final height of the Earth's crust is higher than the marine transgression.

The result of all of these movements is a progressive exundation of beaches, whose series, in certain well studied regions, will constitute true "flat stratigraphy," the most ancient being the highest and the farthest from the present coastal level. Thus the land and passages used by humans are not the same during the glacial peaks as in the warm or temperate periods. Also as a consequence of this phenomena, in some periods, islands were linked to the continent and where today exists a strait, an isthmus was formed, such as the Beringian Isthmus, which joined for a time America to the Eurasian continental mass.

Beringia

Today, the Bering Strait is nowhere deeper than approximately 160 feet (50 meters). In the coldest periods of the Wisconsin, the strait was exposed on several occasions when the level of the sea dropped. Investigators have tried to isolate these moments when the strait became an isthmus linking America to Asia by a true land bridge called Beringia. This bridge was over 900 miles (1,500 kilometers) wide in certain periods, so that the people who used it passed from one continent to another without even taking notice of its shape.

Tundra covered this new land, which was occupied by mammoths, reindeers, musk ox and wild horses. In the pursuit of these game animals, the Siberians ventured far deeper into Alaska, leaving base camps for their movement into the New World. What paths were open to them to move even more deeply into these new lands?

After the theories of David Hopkins, certain scientists believe that during the coldest periods the two glaciers, Laurentian and Cordillera, joined together to form a single icecap, a glacier that covered the entire North American continent, from east to west. Thus, at least in certain eras, the MacKenzie Valley—the preferred corridor of north-south communication—was blocked by an enormous wall of ice. According to Hopkins, this blockage was complete on two occasions: from 70,000 to 28,000 B.C. and from 25,000 to 13,000 B.C., at least during the coldest peaks. A these times Beringia was opened to Alaska, whereas migrations toward the south were impossible. Hopkins himself recognizes that a corridor could have been formed in certain periods of a milder climate, in between these phases, and he thinks it existed between 28,000 to 25,000 B.P., and in a way continued to the start of 13,000 B.P.. Many of the details of Hopkins's theory are debatable, but most geologists agree that for two long periods, from 75,000 to 45,000 B.P. and from about 25,000 to 14,000 B.P. the Bering Land bridge was exposed. This 2,500-mile (4000-kilometer) passageway was hardly an easy corridor, with wind and avalanches. Thus it appears that when Beringia was existed, one could not pass south because of the union of the glaciers, and, when Beringia disappeared under the water, making dry foot passage no longer possible between Asia and America, the route toward the south was open. Finally, for some decades the problem of the passage from Asia to America "with dry feet" has been raised, overlooking that in some periods when human beings were able to pass during the Wisconsin era these adventurers would have had to possess a good mastery of ice. With or without the formation of Beringia, the passage from Asia to America (18 miles/30 kilometers) was clearly possible.

For an equal length of time, applying the conception of European prehistory, the question of navigation by boat inside the strait was not suggested. Now the example of the peopling of Australia around 30,000 years ago furnishes some arguments to those who advance the hypothesis of possible passage of the strait several millennia ago, regardless of the formation of Beringia.

In studying the penetration south from Alaska, certain scholars have proposed an advance along the Pacific Coast. They claim that on the rim of the coast the glaciers were never very thick and, indeed, that outside of the glacial maximum of the Wisconsin, the Pacific coast would have been free of ice. Some islands and promontories, also free of ice, could have served as stepping stones from Beringia to America. These scientists conjecture that the inland refuges, benefiting from the warming influences of the Pacific, had to have been areas rich in marine fauna and land mammals like the caribou. This hypothesis remains unproven, since the places capable of having been occupied during the last glaciation are today under water. However, the hypothesis is logically supportable.

The Oldest Sites

The question of an earlier Paleolithic in America

The presence of humans prior to the Wisconsin period has been supported by certain authors, who rely alterna-

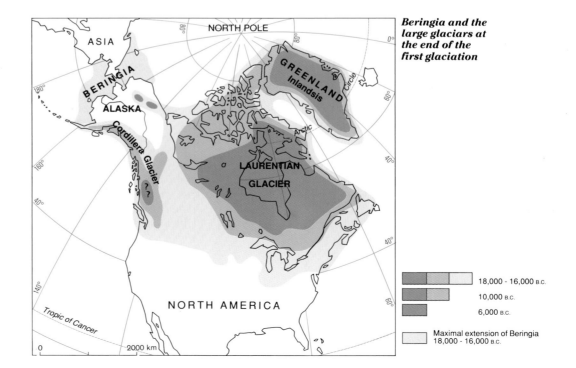

Beringia and the large glaciars at the end of the first glaciation

18,000 - 16,000 B.C.

10,000 B.C.

6,000 B.C.

Maximal extension of Beringia
18,000 - 16,000 B.C.

tively or simultaneously on geological facts and typological analyses of materials found, to which is attributed great antiquity.

To the north of the Sierra Nevada, on the fossil terraces and, in particular, on the banks of Lake Lahanton, samples of very water worn lithic materials have been found, which by their shape appear very old (choppers, chopping tools, bifaces and planes) and share similar characteristics with remains of the ancient cultures of southeastern Asia. Thus, some authors suggest an Asian origin for America's peoples before the Wisconsin period. However, neither the coarse appearance of these tools nor the patina can be used as criteria for age. It becomes obvious, in fact, that some techniques disappeared and that more recent artifacts have a less-finished appearance than those of the more ancient periods. Finally, there is no agreement on the presence of humans in America before the Wisconsin.

The preprojectile phase

On the other hand, myriad sites have furnished dates estimated at between 70,000 and 15,000 B.P., before the traditions of the projectile points originated, on which archaeology bases a large part of its prehistoric chronologies. This research has not reached a definitive conclusion to date, although the weight of supposition grows each year. The groups of this phase are defined in a negative fashion at first: They contain no bifacially retouched tools, no knives, no projectile points. They characterize a horizon prior to the projectile point. Still, the geological context of the layers is Pleistocene, as are faunal remains, with which, in the best instances, they are associated. These sites are found for the most part in Texas and California (Lewisville, Friesenhahn grotto, Santa Rosa, La Jolla, San Diego), Nevada (Tula Spring), Wyoming and Mexico (Tequixquiac, Tlapacoya, Valsequillo).

At Old Crow, near the Alaskan border, on the banks of the Porcupine, a subtributary of the Yukon, Canadian scientists discovered numerous fossil animal bones from the glacial era in some collections that seem to have suffered strong "blows." Among the 18 species of mammals represented (wooly mammoth, American lion, wild Yukon donkeys, goats,

great horned bison), the mammoth bones particularly had been chosen to support the idea of this "industry." The most spectacular was incontestably a tool made from a caribou tibia, with a denticulated front. It was deemed a "flesher" because of its striking resemblance to tools still used by numerous Amerindian groups for the cleaning of skins. It was originally dated to 27,000 B.C.

In the years that followed, Old Crow became one of the most elating and costly archaeological adventures in all North America. The scientific world passionately debated the reality of the industry and the authenticity of the proposed dating (29,000 B.C.). The skeptics advanced at first geological difficulties. The bones had been transported from their original sites by flood waters and thus could not be attributed to any geological strata. Of the bones themselves two major problems were raised: How could scrapes and impressions worked by people be distinguished from those left by predators or natural causes? And, if one admitted human markings, what could be determined about the age of the tools? Finally, once the bones were dated, the puzzle remained as to whether the bones were worked when they were fresh, or "green," or if they were already fossilized. To answer these questions, an experiment was conducted. Hundreds of bones, some fresh mammal bones and some fossilized bones, were broken. The fractures were filmed by ultrafast cameras and examined. Some bones were frozen to examine the effects of cold, others submitted to the prolonged, repeated action

"The oldest tool in America," *a piece found at Old Crow on the collapsed banks of the Porcupine River. Made of a caribou tibia, this tool shows a denticulate front unusual for the very ancient date (27,000 years B.P.) attributed to the scraper. Similar tools existed until recently in numerous Amerindian cultures, who used them for the preparation of skins. (Length: 8.7 in/22.5 cm.) Ottawa, National Museum of Man. Ph. from the Museum.*

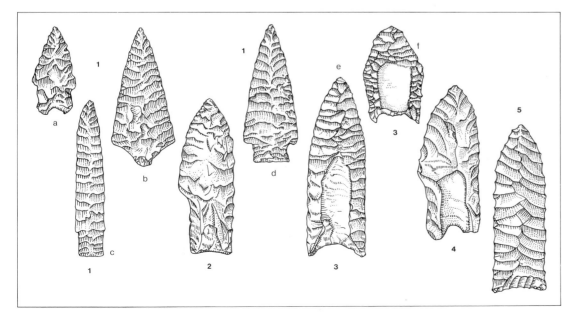

Arrowheads of North America

1. Lanceolate points with penduncles and rhomboidal points:
  a. *Pinto Basin*
  b. *Gypsum Cave*
  c. *Eden*
  d. *Scotsbluff*

2. Shouldered points:
  Sandia

3. Lanceolate fluted points:
  e. *Clovis*
  f. *Folsom*

4. Shouldered, fluted points:
  Lucy

5. Lanceolate points without penduncles:
  Plainview.

of acidic water. Bones gnawed by large carnivores were examined. At each stage, agreement was reached on certain points, skepticism on others. As is frequent when experts confront one another, the cause is only rarely understood. As for the flesher, even its dating is contested—one recent, highly sophisticated radiocarbon test gave a reading of only about 1,300 years ago.

However, about 40 miles (64.4 kilometers) from Old Crow, the excavated site at Bluefish Cave has yielded some cut stones in the sediment beds, containing the butchered bones of mammoth, horse, bison, elk and caribou. The dating by ^{14}C places them at 13,000 to 11,000 B.C.. Stone tools, including biface flakes, microblades and a wedge-shaped core were found mixed with the animal bones. The discoverers have been struck by the similarity with the remains from the Upper Paleolithic of northern and eastern Asia, including the Dyukhtai tradition of Siberia. Archaeologists believe that the inhabitants of Bluefish could be representatives of a migration of Asian hunters across Beringia and Alaska, up to northwestern Canada. If these hunters or their descendants expanded toward the south, to the interior of North America, is unknown.

The Time of the Great Hunters

Around the 16th millennium North American prehistory becomes more tangible, when humans are present at least in the southwestern United States. At the start of this era their diffusion throughout the whole continent is extremely rapid. It seems that the demographic density thus increased the network of sites, which become tightened throughout the entire continent. The term "Great Hunters" actually gathers together two cultural traditions: the Big Game Hunting Tradition and the Old Cordillera Tradition.

The Big Game Hunting Tradition
These predators, still far from becoming agriculturalists continue to adapt to their environments: for the Big Game Hunters, in the prairies of the southwest of the United States at the end of the Pleistocene, drawn by their game of mammoth, bison, horses and, for those of the Old Cordillera Tradition, in the mountainous region of the United States.

Stone projectile points and the forms that develop from them, shoulder points from Sandia (New Mexico) and various types under the term of Plano, are guide fossils or "cultural markers" of the Big Game Hunter. From 7,000 to 8,000 B.C., later in certain isolated and mountainous regions or at higher latitudes, this tradition will fade away when the climatic conditions change radically preceding the warmer and drier climate that marks the end of the Wisconsin and the entry into the postglacial period. However, the old traditions of hunting will remain vigorous, notably in the prairies, where the presence of the bison, after the disappearance of the megafauna of the Pleistocene, will cause minor adaptations of hunting traditions rather than radical upheaval. Clearly, in certain lowland areas, the great hunters will remain much like their predecessors until around 4000 B.C. However, these

artifacts supply little information on the hunting methods themselves.

Certainly the massive, heavy points of the Big Game Hunters were used to tip weapons of the javelin or spear type thrown with a throwing stick, the *atlatl*, and not arrowheads (the bow seems to be unknown in this era). Finally, it is impossible to believe that the hunters could kill mastodons or mammoths with one blow of a spear or javelin. It has been noted that where the bones of these mammals are abundant, they are located in the swampy zones or in former shallow lakes, where these enormous stranded animals became the prey of the hunters.

The Old Cordillera Tradition
The second tradition of the Great Hunters is based on the chronology developed from the typology of lithic points, but less detailed. (See table p. 113) Several kinds of projectile points are associated with it: Cascade points, points from Gypsum Cave, Pinto Basin, Lake Mohave, etc. In addition to these points, the Old Cordillera Tradition contains crude tools, pebbles, chipping chisels and planes. The OCT appears all along the Pacific coast, on the interior plateau, as well as in the Great Basin, the states of Washington, Oregon, California and also in Mesoamerica, up to the Arctic zone.

Its first manifestations on the northwest coast are identified around 10,000 B.C. in certain regions, notably the interior plateau, where it lasted until around 500 B.C. The ethnographic data offered by the excavations of sites of these OCT hunters are poor, but do show that they gathered vegetables and fished and hunted marine mammals (seals) on the coast.

From Predators to Producers:
The Rise of Regionalism

While the traditions of these two large groups of hunters were established at the height of the Wisconsin glaciation, they continued until the postglacial period. They thus underlay cultures that manifested adaptations to more differentiated environments, at a time when an important number of large animals were disappearing. This rapid and radical transformation of the environment is difficult to explain. The postglacial change into the more varied climate gives, from that point on, greater weight to regional factors. The progressive passing from nomadic hunters to agricultural societies contributed to reinforcing the regional characteristics.

The Northwest Coast: from California to
British Columbia
The epiglacial marine transgression (the incursion of the sea over the land) covered traces of the first occupants with water. It is known that the Old Cordillera Tradition population lasted until circa 5000 B.C. To the exploitation of terrestrial resources is added progressively the profit gained from marine resources. During this period, to the north of the region, archaeologists identify an Early Northwest Coast Microblade Tradition that is characterized by small blades of flint and obsidian. The linking of this lithic tool group and its

techniques of production to that of the Paleolithic peoples of the Old World is quite obvious. On the other hand, the relations that existed between these two traditions (the Old Cordillera and Microblade Traditions) are not easily established. All the same it is believed that they contributed, first the one and then the other, to the developments of the more recent occupants.

Scarcely any further data exist for the 2,000-year period that follows. However, around 3000 B.C., the change in coastal occupation is evident. Whereas before the relatively small sites were briefly occupied by small groups, sometimes perhaps just nuclear families, from that point on important masses of shells (middens), indicating a lengthy period of settlement, is characteristic: To account for the radical change, it has been proposed that the stabilization of marine levels allowed an increase of salmon stocks and thus reserves of food for groups that were able to become rather sedentary, grouping in time into villages occupied for generations. In their mass of detritus, one finds bone tools, and sometimes, in their lacustrian deposits, pieces of wood and vegetal fibers. An adaptation to coastal life appears more and more successful: harpoons with barbelates for the hunting of marine mammals, fish hooks and weighted nets, projectile points and polished stone cutters. As to the lacustrian sites, they produced some needles and spacers for the fabrication of nets, objects in basketry and woven boxes and chests, very similar to those that are found 5,000 years later among the Amerindians.

The era's the funerary monuments suggest differences in the treatment of the individual, implying a social hierarchy. Certain burials, of men only, appear to be for ritual warriors and contain some broken skeletons and some skulls with cranial damage. Artistic objects abound (numerous pearls, labrets, earrings). Along the Frasier River, six great cultural periods have been identified: Locarno (3500–2500 B.P.), Marpole (2500–1500 B.P.), Whalen II (1500–1350 B.P.), Pre-Stselax (1300–800 B.P.), and Stselax circa A.D. 1200, until the final historic period.

The interior plateau

The prehistory of the interior plateau is extremely obscure and badly documented. Sites are few, but the collection of projectile points indicates that its more ancient occupants arrived from the plains and had to adapt their hunting techniques to the new game of their adopted territory (bison, wapiti, caribou). Between 8000 and 3000 B.P., the region was inhabited by groups skilled in producing microblades and that seem to have been related to the groups of the interior of the Yukon and the western sub-Arctic.

Around 3000 B.P., a major change occurs, and certain populations begin to construct semisubterranean houses, with facings of peat, which suggest passage to a more sedentary life. At the same time, exchange routes are established, and these Paleolithic groups are opened up to the outside world. They begin to sculpt in stone and their funerary monuments denote a hierarchical society: The social order seems founded on the possession of material goods and the capacity

to demonstrate such riches. Perhaps the "potlatch," an elaborate gift-giving ceremony, lasting several days, originated during this period.

Until the historic period, the exchanges are strengthened with all of the neighboring populations, those of the coast, the plains and the plateau. This contact satisfactorily explains the great cultural diversity of the Plateau Indians.

The Great Basin

For this region archaeology cannot supply a detailed chronology either. It is simply possible to establish two great cultural phases. One, prior to 10,000 B.P., is similar to the Old Cordillera Tradition; the other, which succeeds it and lasts until the 19th century, belongs totally to the Desert Tradition characterized by a successful adaptation to the arid, zones of the western United States.

The survival of the populations rests on plant (wild grasses) and animal (small mammals) life. The human groups are of modest height and practice a sort of cyclic nomadism over the area gathering vegetables. Other than some stone points, with shoulders and notches, excavations have unearthed some coarse grindstones and pestles for the preparation of seeds; baskets, sandals and nets attest to the mastery of basketry and weaving. In this long tradition several cultural periods are recognized: the Great Basin, Danger Cave II, III, IV, and Lovelock I and II.

The Great Plains and Prairies

Only in this immense and continuously uniform period (nearly 10,000 years) are the Paleo-Indian techniques conserved (the Big Game Hunting Tradition). When the large herbivores of the glacial age became extinct, the bison sur-

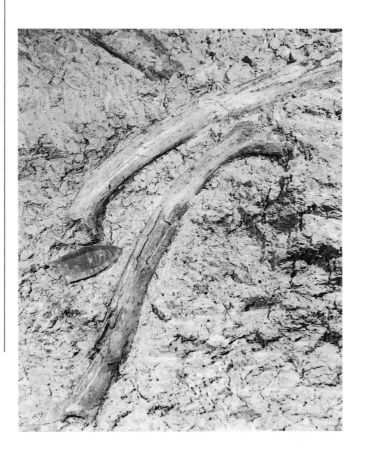

Near the Folsom site in New Mexico, American archaeologists discovered, in the 1930s, this fluted point stuck between the ribs of a bison. It is rare—if not extraordinary—for an archaeological dig to bring to light an association so evident of the game and the weapon that brought it down. Denver, Museum of National History, Ph. Robert R. Wright.

vived. Its continued hunting did not require any major change of technique. Wild plants complete the alimentary regime, until then primarily carnivorous.

The typology of the lithic points provides a general chronology. Around 7000 B.C., points of the Clovis type were replaced by those of the Plano tradition (Scottsbluff and Eden), which existed in the north until approximately 5000 B.C. Hunters of the Barren Lands, between the large Bear Lakes and the Hudson Bay, used them against caribou.

From 3000 B.C. onward, different groups developed new techniques of hunting bison, communal techniques that involved the stampeding of herds between corridors of stones that led to cliffs, from which the herds were driven over the edge. Then, diverse influences altered this unified tradition, emanating from the forest lands to the east. At the start of the 10th and 11th centuries A.D. populations of the Valleys of the Mississippi and Missouri (the Plains Village Tradition), practiced horticulture and agriculture on the river banks.

In the Canadian provinces, at the start of the first millennium A.D., the bow appears: Small projectile points in flaked stone replaced the voluminous and heavy lithic material. Some funerary practices came from the south, as seen in the construction of mounds (south of Manitoba in particular), which seems to indicate contacts with the agriculturalists of the Missouri Valley.

The upheaval in the prehistoric life of the Plains from the seventeenth century onward, stems from the conjunction of two factors: on one hand the progressive northward spread of the horse after the Spanish settlements—they reached the northern frontier of the United States around 1730—which carried along a revolution in the indigenous techniques of hunting, traveling and war; on the other hand, the "winning of the West" by the European settlers pushed before it the tribes of the wooded lands of the East in the 18th century.

California

If one sets aside the finds that attest to the existence of a very ancient peopling, it is in California and Texas that the oldest datings have been advanced for human presence in America. The most undisputed traces of humanity of those regions are linked to the Old Cordillera and Desert Traditions. Affiliated with these two traditions, the cultural evidence from 5000 B.C. to the European conquest (18th century) form the Coast Traditions and the California Valley Tradition. Two elements characterize them: an adaptation to the marine environment more and more successfully, and the economy of abundance that it creates and manages—marine resources for the coastal populations and plant stores for the groups of the hinterland valleys. To the very evolved techniques of cutting stones is added that of polishing for the manufacture not only of tools but even ceremonial ornamental objects. To this richness is also owed the increase in population: A significant number of true coastal villages arise. The bow and arrow replace the javelin and lance. The use of ceramics spreads from the Southwest before the historic period eventually replacing the locally produced steatite wares.

However, one fact stands out: The Californians remained impervious to agriculture and did not adopt it from close neighbors in the Southwest. The causes of this renunciation are unclear: The Californians, spoiled by the abundance of their regions, were perhaps victims of their own success. Unless the principal cause is to be found in the Mediterranean type climate, with burning and dry summers and rainy winters little favorable to the cultivation of grains?

The famous site of Mesa Verde (Colorado) houses the remains of the most spectacular villages of the Anasazi culture. In the covered shelter of a sandstone cliff, a great number of houses, towers and "kivas" were discovered. Long covered, these served as silos. The function of the tower, either religious or defensive, is still unknown. Ph. Conklin -Cocorific.

The Southwest

The dry climate is one of the most constraining factors of this region, which extends as far as Mexico (States of Sonora and a major part of Chihuahua). The first manifestations of humans in the region belong to the Big Game Hunting Tradition and integrate later some elements of the Desert Tradition.

At the start of the eighth millennium, a series of transformations takes place: arrival of cultivated plants from Mesoamerica, population growth, increasing sedentism, and introduction of ceramics. All of these transformations lead to the development of the Cochise culture. A more detailed chronology allows the division of it into features: Sulphur Springs Phase (7300–6000 B.C.), Chiricahua Phase (until c. 1500 B.C.), and San Pedro (1500–500 B.C.). In this region is best seen the passage from the stage of predation to that of production. Little by little, hunting of large game adapts to smaller species, supplemented by plant gathering. While plants are becoming increasingly important in the diet, a seminomadic pattern of returning to certain sites on a regular basis is established. Finally, agriculture is born at the time when storage pits and earthen houses appear, evidence of a sedentary way of life. With ceramics, the true Southwest cultures emerge.

At the start of the first century and until the historic period, archaeologists have traced the parallel development of four main cultures: the Patayan (in the lower Colorado Valley), the Hohokam (in central and southern Arizona near the Gila and Salt Rivers), the Mogollon (in east central Arizona and west central New Mexico near the Mogollon Mountain Range) and the Anasazi (in the "Four Corners" area of the Colorado Plateau). It is in the region of the Anasazi, one of the best known prehistoric cultures from such sites as Mesa Verde and Chaco Canyon that the Mesoamerican influence on agriculture is most perceptible. The Anasazi (whom archaeologists have divided into several "Basket Maker" and "Pueblo" phases) lived in villages of oval log huts with flat roofs. Baskets, woven sandals and other artifacts have been perfectly preserved by the dryness of the climate. The Anasazi cultivated corn, squash and oats and adopted the use of ceramics. At the beginning of the seventh century, during the Pueblo stages, crops like cotton and beans were added. An irrigation system and permanent dwellings were constructed, which the first Europeans discovered, abandoned, in the 16th century.

The Eastern Woodlands

This immense, forested region stretches from the Gulf of Mexico to the provinces of Ontario and Quebec. In the south, the pines are scattered over the coastal plains, cypress and tupelos at the bottom of the valleys, to the north, oaks. At even higher latitudes conifers become more numerous, together with beech and birch. Considerable climatic differences exist between the south, quasi-tropical, and the north, which borders on the sub-Arctic area. Food resources (deer, small game, fish, mollusks, walnuts, wild grains, roots) seem unlimited; agriculture is aided by satisfactory rainfall.

Four primary cultural periods succeed one another:
—the Paleo-Indian period, which dies c. 8000 B.C. and which includes the Large Game Hunting Tradition;
—the Archaic period, including the Early Archaic, 10,000 B.P. to 7000 B.P.; Middle Archaic, 7000 B.P. to 4000 B.P.; and Final Archaic, 4000 B.P. to 3000 B.P.;
—the Burial Mound period extends from 1000 B.C. to A.D. 700, subdivided into the Burial Mound I (1000 B.C. to A.D. 700) and Burial Mound II, including the Woodlands Tradition from A.D. 300 to A.D.700;
—the Temple Mound period, from A.D. 700 to A.D.1700, divided into Temple Mound I (A.D. 700 to A.D. 1300) and Temple Mound II (A.D. 1300 to A.D. 1700).

THE ARCHAIC TRADITION is characterized by the hunting of small game, fishing in rivers and lakes, collecting shellfish and mollusks, the gathering of walnuts, berries, acorns, the harvesting of maple sap in Canada and, later, wild rice in the south. It appears today as a long period in the course of which the population grows and social life becomes more complex. On the technical level, it is accompanied by the development of new points, bone harpoons and a range of woodworking tools. In the Canadian facies (the Archaic Shield, Laurentian Archaic), copper is worked for tools and ornamental pieces.

EASTERN WOODLANDS CULTURE appeared about 3,000 years ago. To the Archaic, which it succeeded, it added new elements, a typical ceramic style (domestic implements, objects for ceremonial use, funerary pieces) and an agricultural tradition based on corn. In the Mississippi and Ohio Valleys, the Adena and Hopewell cultures (about 700 B.C to A.D. 400) spectacularly emerge, extending their influence as far as the Great Lakes, Ontario and Quebec. The Adena built great earthworks in the shape of circles, squares and pentagons and constructed burial mounds (the most famous in Miamisburg, Ohio), where grave goods, such as copper ornaments and pipes have been found. The later Hopewell culture built upon the Adena tradition and grave goods became even more elaborate: copper jewelry, axes and cutouts; ceramics; stone animal effigy pipes; and many other artifacts. The extraordinary Serpent Mound in Ohio may be Adena or Hopewell.

THE MISSISSIPPIAN tradition (about A.D. 800 to 1500) was greatly influenced by Mesoamerican cultures to the south. Based initially in the Middle Mississippi Valley, local variants extended across much of North America. This culture constructed true towns, fortified by walls, of greater size and density than any known before. Ceremonial mounds suggest a complex social organization and the existence of a politico-religious hierarchy.

Alaska

Although it was the passageway from Asia to America, notably when Beringia linked one continent to the other, Alaska has nonetheless yielded no site that attests clearly to its occupation during the glacial period.

Some finds (Trail Creek, Engigstciak, Anaktuvuk Pass) dated from 16,000 years B.P. fueled speculation about the presence of large game hunters. The certainties are supported by the well-developed stratigraphy (30 feet/9 meters deep) of the deposits of Onion Portage, in the center of Alaska on the Kobuk River, excavated in 1965–66. At the base was uncovered the Akmak Complex, characterized by a lithic industry of large obsidian cores and scraper blades. The very characteristic microblades are similar to those of the industries found in Siberia, Mongolia and Japan. By ^{14}C, the Akmak Complex has been dated to 10,000 B.P. However, practically nothing is known of these hunters.

The name Northern Archaic Tradition is given to the caribou hunters who left remains from 6600 to 4200 B.P. at Tuktu and Palisades. At Onion Portage were discovered numerous open hearths (placed at the center of the tents?) and some foundations: floors of wooden logs laid over a slight hollow in the soil, a framework in flexible willow, hearths in the form of an oven. Until then, the inhabitants of Alaska seem to have been interested primarily in the resources of the hinterlands, principally the terrestrial fauna. At the start of 4200 B.P., the fish-filled rivers and the sea attracted them. In this epoch are seen for the first time the manifestations of the Arctic Microlithic Tradition, which will spread throughout the Arctic.

Entirely oriented toward the sea, without tangible links to the cultures that preceded them nor those that will succeed them, the Old Whaling culture flourished around 3800 to 3700 B.P. on the shores of the Bering Sea, particularly in the region of Cape Krusenstern. In addition to long retouched blades of flint, which armed the harpoons and lances of these hunters, their arsenal contained arrow heads some of which recall those discovered in the eastern United States. The Old Whaling culture, with its origins and destiny unknown, appears as an anachronism in the Alaskan fresco, especially because its emergence did not interrupt the development of the Cape Denbigh (Microlithic) culture that followed it c. 3500 B.P., which in turn evolved toward the Choris culture. In certain aspects, the Choris still belongs to the AMT but slowly abandoned the production of microblades (burins in the shape of mittens, polished burins, pseudo-burins) and adopted decorated pottery and large points, similar to the Plano type. The economy of Choris is based on the hunting of seals as well as land and marine birds, while eighty percent of the bone remains from their sites belong to reindeer, which by their size appear similar to domestic Siberian reindeer. In the process of settling, the Choris were Siberian breeders who crossed with their animals over the strait in skin boats. Their habitats recall as well those of Tchouktches breeders. Finally, they practiced scapulomancy, a divinatory technique using shoulder bones.

Around 2500 B.P., the Norton hunters invaded their territory. They lived principally by hunting seals, without abandoning, at least seasonally, the hunting of caribou. Technicians, with notable artistic ability, the Norton culture, foreshadowed the Eskimos, equally great craftsmen. At the start of the first millennium A.D. the Norton culture waned, just as that of the Ipiutak flourished with a remarkable artistic exuberance at Point Hope, on the southern coast of Alaska. The Ipiutak artists are famed for their carvings on bone, ivory, and antler, exquisite human and animal representations, in a Scytho-Siberian style. Some purely ornamental, these foreign objects preserve the secrets of their symbolism.

At the end of the Ipiutak, around the fifth century, on the borders and islands of the Bering Strait, appear cultural elements that will much later be found among the Eskimos. This new culture, the Birnik, produced harpoon heads for seal hunting, barbed harpoons, lures and fish hooks, as well as spears and bolas for catching birds, bows and arrows for the hunting of caribou and cut or polished stone tools (such as adzes for the working of bone and wood). Through the heritage of earlier cultures (Punuk, Old Bering Sea, Okvik), the Birnirk inherited some Siberian elements.

The Subarctic

The Subarctic corresponds rather narrowly to the rocky mountainous taiga that Indian ethnic groups of Canada inhabited when the Europeans arrived, and the Arctic to the treeless lands (tundra) in the territory of the near contemporary Eskimos. It is best to divide this long band of land into an eastern and western Subarctic, at the imprecise borders somewhere between Saskatchewan and Manitoba.

During the first five centuries A.D., *hunters of Ipiutak, on the northern coast of Alaska (Point Hope), produced an extraordinary quantity of objects, many associated with burials. The eyes and openings of the nose were plugged with ornaments made of walrus ivory. It is* thought that the cult of the dead was developed among the Ipiutak and it seems that this mask—somewhat "Asiatic"—was part of their funerary liturgy. New York, American Museum of National History. Ph. from the Museum.

THE EASTERN SUBARCTIC On the Atlantic coast and in the maritime provinces of Canada, some tenuous remains attest to the presence of Big Game Hunters or Paleo-Indians, here around 10,000 years B.P. The study of the lithic industry suggests a late transition between all of the first manifestations of human habitation and those of the Archaic tradition, which succeeds it around 6000 B.C. and attests to its passage over the shores of the Belle Isle Strait to the south of Labrador. On these coasts the marine character of the tradition, as early as its emergence, earned it the designation of Maritime Archaic. At Anse-Amour, a tumulus about 7,500 years old, yielded, in addition to a tooth and an object made of walrus ivory, a detachable harpoon head similar to those that will appear much later and already evolved from the Arctic cultures. During the following 2,000 years, this population, the only coastal one, developed a specifically marine way of life of which some barbed harpoons and fishing equipment (lines and fish hooks, weighted nets) attest. Their elaborate funerary sites are true cemeteries, with tombs containing mortuary objects, covered with red ochre. These elements are found as far as the maritime provinces and New England. Without doubt the Mic Mac and Beothuc Indian tribes met by the first Europeans owe much to these coastal people of prehistory.

Between 4000 and 2500 B.P., the populations of the Maritime Archaic left the coasts of Labrador pushed south by the Paleo-eskimos of the Arctic (the Dorset culture) and by other groups of the Archaic, who were moving toward the east from the area of Bouclier as far as the Saint-Laurent Valley. The Dorsets descended as far as Newfoundland and toward 1500 B.P. abandoned in their turn their former territories, except the extreme northern point of Labrador.

At the southern limits of the Subarctic band, some influences from the south are seen at the start of the fifth century B.C., when ceramics arrived. This was not the only influence from the south; in the funerary mound of Angustine, at the limit of the forest lands, objects imported from the Ohio Valley (Adena culture) have been discovered.

THE WESTERN SUBARCTIC to the west of the Mackenzie, it is believed that today we can recognize two distinct human occupations at the start of the Postglacial period, dated respectively 10,000 and 7000 B.C. The first is known only by lanceolate projectile points characteristic of the Big Game Hunters. The second was that of groups whose techniques are similar to those of the Northwest Microblade Tradition of the Northwest, subdivided into three phases: Little Arm (7500 to 6000 B.P.), Gladstone (6000 to 4000 B.P.) and Taye Lake (4000 to 1800 B.P.). It is believed that from this Northwest Microblade Tradition the Athabascan Indians borrowed numerous elements of their culture through another cultural tradition, that of the Denetasiro, a tradition of hunters-trappers-fishers.

The Arctic

Around 6000 B.P., the Arctic Microlithic Tradition appears. It spreads from the Bering Strait to Greenland, where it will survive until around 800 B.P. It owes its name to small tools, finely worked by pressure, burins, retouched blades, graters, thin-bladed drills and small retouched blades. Flint with a fine texture, obsidian and jasper form the raw materials of this industry. The meticulousness of the industry is

Anthropomorphic statuette of the Okvik culture (300 B.C. to A.D. 100). In contrast to the hunters of the Old Bering cultures, those of Okvik (Saint Laurent Island), who shared the same shores and islands of the Bering Strait at about the start of the Christian era, preferred to sculpt in walrus ivory human forms rather than animals. Their statuettes, with cylindrical bodies, lacking arms and legs and with faces scarred with tatoos, have an enigmatic expression, characteristics, perhaps, of their distant Asiatic origin. Bern Museum of History. Ph. Georges Bandi.

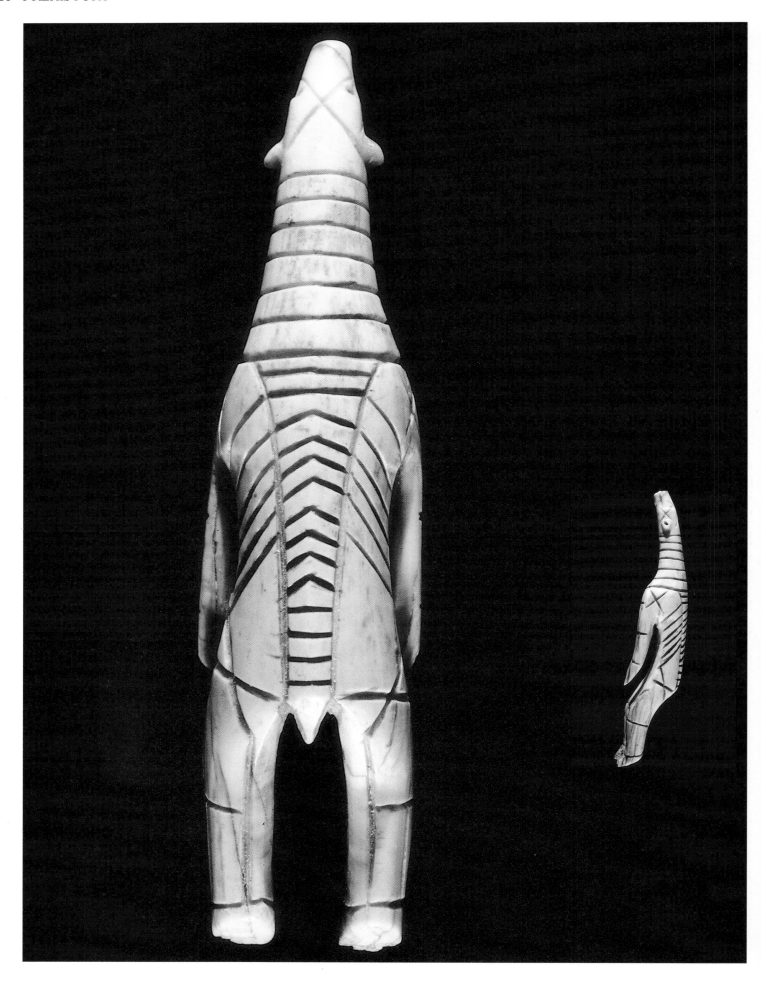

such that even the handles of burin spalls a few tenths of an inch (millimeters) long and wide are worked to produce tools destined for the carving of wood, bone and ivory. On the shores of the Bering Sea, where the Denbigh Culture was discovered at Iyatayet, no traces of habitation remain and the ethnography of the Denbigh is little known. It is known only that they hunted marine mammals.

On the origin of the Arctic Microlithic Tradition, of which the Denbigh is in fact only a single manifestation, conjecture abounds and certain archaeologists suggest that it has its roots in the Siberian Paleolithic or Epipaleolithic, while others posit a long evolution on the site. Its destiny is associated with that of the hunters who, by successive waves, invaded the Arctic as far as its most extreme regions. From 4000 to 3500 B.P., the hunters of Independence I set up their tents, of which remain only simple hearths and gravel used to hold down the skin covers. The bone remains show that these groups hunted, probably small game such as foxes, hares, ducks and geese. Certain others, like those from Peary and Ellesmere Island, had become specialized in hunting musk ox, while, more to the south, on some islands of the Arctic archipelago a marked preference for the hunting of bears and marine mammals is observed.

The following wave, the Pre-Dorset, from 3700–2800 B.P., descended upon other regions: Those more abundant in game in the Fox Basin, to the north of the Hudson Bay, where they left the most numerous remains. They profited there from the faunal richness of the Arctic: caribou, fish, birds, populations of local seals (mottled and bearded seals) and migrant seals (Greenland seal), walrus, belugas and narwhales. Their lithic tools belong to the same tradition as that of the Independence hunters; however, they are often even smaller, in particular, small polished blades and burins. Their more numerous and important encampments outnumber those of Independence I. The living structures are oval or circular. They possessed oil lamps rather than fixed hearths. They constructed the igloo, of which no trace remains. A certain conservatism characterizes this culture, whose material elements evolved little in 1,000 years.

The Dorset

Around the start of the first millennium B.C., changes until then little perceptible accelerated. Habitations become massive and the microblades more numerous and knives and lithic ore were made with notches to allow the attachment of handles. Lamps and cooking utensils appear. Knives for cutting ice and making igloos and sleigh runner treads indicate an adaptation to winter hunting on the ice fields. We have been able to establish that the seasonal cycle of the Dorset was somewhat similar to that of the Eskimo. Spring and summer were spent on the coasts, and the hunters devoted themselves to hunting marine mammals in the ice fields, then

in open water. In the middle of the summer certain groups gathered together near lakes and rivers in places favorable to spearing Arctic chor. In autumn, families holed themselves up in semisubterranean houses, generally rectangular.

The Dorset may not have used the kayak, though two pieces of wood found on Bylot Island to the north of Baffin Island resemble frames. Hunting in open water, if it ever existed, was done at the icefield rim, because Dorset harpoons are not equipped with a floater, used by the Eskimo to exhaust and locate harpooned marine mammals. They used the sleigh, but differently from the Eskimo: Their sleighs are small and, as dogs were still not trained and harnessed, it is believed that the people themselves pulled them. It is by their art perhaps that the Dorsets best survive. Its symbolism evokes magic and shamanistic activities: wooden masks, sculpted collections of animal teeth, shaman drums. Numerous sculptures of bears and humans have a hole in the thoracic cavity or in the throat, often containing a small piece of wood and a small bowl of red ochre, perhaps expressions of magical or religious rites.

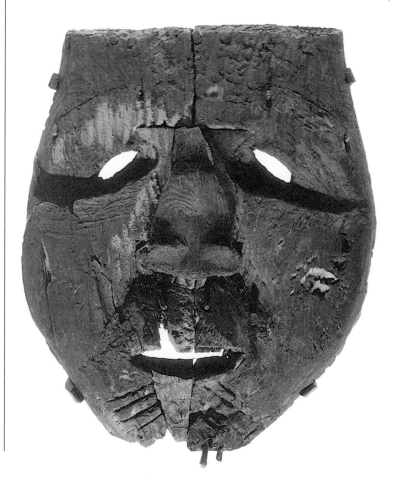

Dorset culture (800 B.C.–A.D. 1000), the site of Alarnek, Igloolik region, Canadian Arctic. The animal sculpture is far more numerous among the Dorset. The "decoration" in the form of a skeleton is not a true skeleton but a skeletal "X-ray," projected on the outside of the animal. Bear sculptures will evolve, diminishing in size until used as a harpoon head, perhaps a magical design or symbolic form of an "animalized" weapon, using the image of the greatest predator of the Arctic, the polar bear. National Museum of Man, Ottawa. Ph. R. J. Megnee.

This Dorset mask in driftwood, found by Guy Mary-Rousselière at Button Point on the Island of Bylot in the eastern Canadian Arctic, is one of the rarest and most important anthropomorphic representations. For what use was it made? The magical properties associated with red ochre, which covered it entirely, suggest a magico-religious purpose. National Museum of Man, Ottawa. Ph. R. J. Megnee.

The Thules

Quite different from the Dorset culture are the new arrivals. Aggressive invaders, the Thules inherited and improved upon a long hunting tradition on the shores and islands of the Bering Strait. They began their eastward migration when their major game, the right whales, began to expand their own migratory routes because of a climatic warming that disrupted the Arctic ecology in the tenth century A.D. Aboard their *umiaks*, skin boats so large that they allowed entire villages to relocate and on their efficient dog sleds, they traveled in some decades over thousands of miles/kilometers separating Alaska from eastern Greenland. The captains of these boats, the *umialiks*, gained considerable social standing.

With their technological inventions, the Thule culture was so extraordinarily well adapted to the Arctic climate that it advanced rapidly, and they left their remains from one end of the Arctic to the other. Their houses, dug into the beaches and facing the sea, were massive and comfortable. The sea-side opening, sloping downward from a central room, functioned as a cold "trap door," preserving the warmth of the inner areas. A platform, sometimes of wood, sometimes simple flat stones covered by a cushion of twigs and skins, provided areas for sleeping and certain domestic tasks, such as sewing clothes with bone and antler needles. Lamps and cooking utensils, first in pottery and then in steatite, were stored in a corner of the room. The roof was made of drift wood or large whale ribs to produce a framework covered by skins, peat and gravel.

Around A.D. 1200, a climatic cooling put to a test the marvelous forms of adaptation of the widely scattered group. Without doubt, the whales became rarer, which may account for the disappearance of some groups. From the archaeological evidence, one notes the cultural uniformity of the group was replaced by a mosaic with a regional character. In the Canadian west, on Victoria Island and in the central Arctic, certain groups concentrated during the summer on fishing the Arctic char and hunting caribou in the interior lands. They sometimes established stone storage facilities far from the coasts, which reflect their search for a balance between their marine and terrestrial resources. During winter they moved onto the ice fields, hunting seals at breathing holes in the pack ice. On the western coast of Greenland, the Thule began to hunt small mottled seals when the large whales disappeared.

In this region, eastern bands of the Thule culture evolved toward the Inugssuk culture, who experienced the first meetings with the Europeans who had arrived by about A.D. 1000 *Skraellings* ("barbarians") was the name given to them by the Norsemen.

The Thule culture persisted into historical times so imperceptibly that the moment when the Thule became Eskimo cannot always be defined. Perhaps certain descriptions from the first European voyagers to the Arctic are of Thule groups who, among the last in North America, thus passed from prehistory to protohistory.

The interior of a circular house often flanked by one or two alveola (pits) in a clover-leaf plan in the soil, sheltered a nuclear family. The excavation of this dwelling surrounded by a wall made of stones and bog, has led to the discovery of areas for domestic activities (cooking, sewing, the preparation of skins, platforms for rest and sleeping). The structure in this photo displays a particular feature of the Thule Culture— the use of driftwood for the house frame. Ph. J.F. Le Mouël.

Suggested Reading

Acatos, Sylvio, and Maximilien Bruggmann. *Pueblos: Indian Cultures of the Southwest.* New York and Oxford: Facts On File, 1990.

Fagan, Brian. *Incredible Journey: The Peopling of Ancient America.* New York and London: Thames and Hudson, 1989.

Fiedel, Stuart J. *Prehistory of the Americas.* Cambridge: Cambridge University Press, 1987.

Jennings, Jesse D., ed. *Prehistoric Man in the New World.* Chicago: University of Chicago Press, 1971.

Mac Neish, R. S. *Early Man in America: Readings from Scientific American.* San Francisco: W. H. Freeman and Co., 1973.

PREHISTORIC CULTURES OF MESOAMERICA AND SOUTH AMERICA

Zoolith of the Sambaqui culture *(Brazil).*
The animal sculptures that sometimes accompany the burial in the sambaquis *(mounds of shells), represent a varied and often maritime fauna. The forms are often geometric and very stereotyped, but sometimes naturalistic pieces are found, such as this large, very flat fish, characteristic of the Laguna region, which contains a cavity on the left side and incisions on the fin.* Ph. P. Jungueira.

If the most ancient evidence of a human presence in North America goes back about 20,000 years, perhaps 30,000, one would expect early man finds to be of later origin as one moves toward the south, because an essential fact of the peopling of the New World—a thesis admitted today and each day better substantiated—is that people moved from north to south.

The Conquest of the Southern Continent

Nevertheless the first known human manifestations in Mexico and even in Brazil are as ancient, if not more so, than in the extreme north. Whether the remains are better preserved in the sometimes very dry tropical environment, or if the occupation of the entire continent was very rapid, perhaps favored by a vegetal cover less dense than today at the end of the Pleistocene, the antiquity of the remains discovered stretches from between 30,000 and 15,000 B.C. As early as 11,000 B.C., the whole continent was occupied, and humanity was established in its southern extremity in Patagonia and Tierra del Fuego.

The period between 30,000 and 15,000 B.C. corresponds to the last part of the final glaciation of the Quaternary, the Wisconsin (more or less contemporary with the European Würm). The fauna was then numerous species extinct today—the mammoth (as far as Mexico), the mastodon, American horse, diverse kinds of large edentates (giant sloth, mylodon)—which were the first game hunted by human beings.

Of the early humans we know very few details, other than that they existed. However, the signs of their presence, still very scarce, seem to have one common trait: In all of the habitations or hunting sites discovered, the stone tool kit lacks any finely worked pieces, particularly flaked and retouched arrow heads, as will be found in abundance later. The equipment is of a very crude appearance, most transformed from lithic objects of a large size, among which the

123

choppers, very thick bifaces or large flakes, little or unretouched (to bring out a sharp edge or a pointed extremity) are sometimes found with tools of bone or wood.

The existence of the first stage, called "Lower Lithic" or simply "Lithic" by some, "Stage I" by others, was for a long time in doubt, although it has been defined as early as 1954 by the American, Alex Krieger, under the name of "Pre-projectile Phase." At the time, the data cited for this stage were far from satisfying. A crude lithic material was found on the surface and was undatable (the deposits of Garzon in Colombia, Ghatchi in Chile), or of doubtful dating, obtained by correlation with the supposed sites from which the objects were taken (Rio Pedregal in Venezuela, Chivateros in Peru). In most cases it was proven subsequently that the objects were from quarries or workshops for the flaking techniques (from whence the "unrefined" appearance of the objects derived); prehistoric certainly but of a more recent age. Or some data concerned objects of stone with a flaked appearance, but that proved to be the result of recent grinding (Exacto and Manantial in Ecuador, now the site of a quarry workshop, or Chuqui in Chile, along a former caravan trail). All of this "evidence" is thus discredited, although still mentioned in many works.

Some better-supported discoveries have very recently been made, however, confirming the reality of this first peopling and refining the definition of the term. In Mesoamerica, the oldest remains seem those found at El Bosque (Nicaragua) and, in Mexico, at Tequixquiac, Valsequillo and other sites around Puebla, at El Cedral. In all of these cases, which would correspond to encampments in the open air, lithic tools were discovered, rather crude and worked on one side only, sometimes accompanied by bone instruments and Pleistocene animal remains (mammoth, mastodon and horse). The dates obtained range from 35,000 to 22,000 B.C., although some are disputable. One of the most reliable deposits of remains are at Tlapacoya, in Mexico, on the shores of a Pleistocene lake: two hearths, unifacial tools and faunal fossil remains, which attest to a human presence about 22,000 years ago.

In South America, it is the northeastern part of Brazil that has yielded the most ancient remains for the moment: in Piaui several grottoes or shelters with a very ancient occupation were discovered; at Toca do Boqueirão da Pedra Fura da, the age of the deep levels ranges from earlier than 30,000 to 23,000 B.C. The remains of laid out hearths and about 15 or so tools (pebbles or fragments of quartz or quartzite) testify to the passage of hunters, but no bone remains were preserved. More to the south, in the region of Lagoa Santa, famous for its fauna fossils and human remains (then supposed contemporaneous), work conducted there as late as the 19th century

by a Dane, Peter Lund opened the shelter of Lapa Vermelha, which contained more than 45 feet (14 meters) of material. The remains there are, however, scarce even in bones and human caprolites; three mylodon claws and a pebble of flaked quartz attest to the utilization of the shelter as early as 22,000 B.C. Finally, in Piaui, several other grottoes (Toca do Caldeirão do Rodriques, Toca do Meio) were occupied a little later, between 18,000 and 12,000 B.C.

In Peru, the grotto of Pikimachay has produced artifacts more difficult to interpret. According to its finders, the occupation would have started 25,000 years ago, when small bands of hunters came to track large game (large cervidae, horses and giant sloths). The tools were of the most rudimentary fashioning: clippers, very crudely worked pebbles, hammers and some worked bones. However, all but four of these "tools" are made of tuff, rock forming the grotto itself (strong and difficult to cut). For a number of specialists these chipped and more or less shapeless fragments were only bits detached from the wall (the four "exogenous" tools constitute

an intrusion). As to the giant sloth's remains, they prove only its presence, possibly seeking refuge there in order to die, perhaps before the arrival of humans in the region. Thus, the reality of this first "Pacaicasa" stage (23,000 to 13,000 B.C.) cannot be accepted uncritically. It is, however, somewhat certain that around 13,000 B.C. humans occupied the grotto.

This is all that is known about a prehistory before 13,000 B.C., evidently very little, yet its existence, if contested not long ago, no longer in doubt. Only the concept of "preprojectile" is debatable, to a large extent where there have been found artifacts in bone, wood, even stone at sites with a clearly separate function. As to human remains, they are still rarer. Chimalhuacan Man, recently discovered in Mexico, is 28,000 years old. In South America, only the shelter of Lapa Vermelha has rendered some long bones, a mandible and a portion of a cranium, dispersed in a deep but badly dated strata. There is little available to reconstruct the physical appearance of these first hunters.

The Last Great Hunters of the Pleistocene

Between 12,000 and 8,000 B.C., the landscape and the conditions of life slowly transformed. Until then, the glaciers covered all of the Central Andes above 13,000 feet (4,000

(Left) ***Toca Shelter do Boqueirão da Pedra Furada*** *(Paiaui, Brazil).*
It is at the foot of these enormous red sandstone cliffs, in northeastern Brazil, that the shelter where the remains of a human occupation dating to about 30,000 years B.P., were discovered. Though this date is not accepted by all specialists, if confirmed, it would be the most ancient occupied site known to date in South America. Ph. N. Guidon.

(Left) ***Toca Shelter do Boqueirão da Pedra Furada*** *(Paiaui, Brazil).*
The excavation yard of the Franco-Brazilian mission on the exterior bank of the shelter. Here, archaeologists clear a level of occupation dated to around 20,000 B.C. Ph. N. Guidon.

Santa Isabel *(Iztapan, Mexico).*
A clearing of the skeletal remains of a mammoth. Ph. D.R.

meters) and, at the southern extremity of the continent, extended to the ocean. After one last advance of a short duration (contemporary with the North American Valders), the warming began, the glaciers retreated and the environment slowly modified, while the level of the ocean rose as a consequence of the melting of large ice caps. From the dry, sometimes semi-arid regions to the tropical zone, the climate became more humid, and the vegetation changed. In the very open landscapes, formed by savannahs to that point, the forest took slow possession of the land. As a result of these climatic phenomena and perhaps also, as certain authors argue, of an overly efficient hunting technique, the

Pleistocene megafauna gave way to the present species: cervids in all of the regions, camelids (vicunas and guanacos) in the Andes and the pampas in the south, numerous carnivores and rodents of various sizes, all species that will henceforth be found in growing proportions amongst the hunted game.

Humans continued to occupy the same grottoes and natural refuges, or established themselves in open-air encampments, but the deposits found, much more numerous than those of the preceding period, now allow one to better imagine, and to reconstruct, although only in a partial manner, daily human activities. The most spectacular discovery made in 1976, is that of an open-air habitation at Monte Verde, in southern Chile. Dated at approximately 12,000 B.C., it provided the well-preserved remains of a dozen habitations with thin wooden frames. Some partial skins, apparently mastodon, were found (near some perch,) suggesting the use of tents, somewhat similar to that of the Alacaluf Indians of the Magellanic Archipelago. A number of hearths, with a pit hollowed out and covered with clay, were laid out between these tents, and one of them preserved even the imprint of the foot of eight-to-ten-year-old boy. In the surroundings the bones of at least five mastodons were dispersed, some with signs of having been butchered, mixed with rudimentary tools of wood—chisels, rods, and even hand tools—and of stone. Some balls were found, perhaps used as projectiles (the most ancient *bolas* of America), some cut instruments (choppers or crude chipping tools) and two scrapers with handles intact, as well as often naturally broken pebbles that were used as tools. Finally, three wooden mortars, supported by posts and several grinding stones attest to the use of plant resources, while, on the floor of the tents, and in the hearths

(*Above*) **Prehistoric camp of Monte Verde** (*southern Chile*).

The remains of a horseshoe-shaped structure can be distinguished at the rear, formed by a mound of sand and compressed gravel, which supported a round frame of branches, covered with skin. In the foreground, in front of the probable entry, tools of stone and the remains of branches and various organic matter were scattered, exceptionally preserved by the peat bog, which formed above it. The whole site, dated to about 12,000 B.C., constitutes one of the oldest remains of human habitation discovered to date in South America. Ph. T. Dillehay.

(*Right*) **Fell's Cave (Chilean Patagonia)**.

This cave, one of the oldest occupied spaces in the extreme south, is dug into the flank of a thick volcanic outflow and dominates the small valley, well watered by the Rio Chico. Measuring 40 feet (12 meters) wide and 30 feet (9 meters) deep, it was, as early as circa 9000 B.C., inhabited by hunters of guanaco and (in the earliest phases of occupation) the horse. Ph. J. Emperaire.

there still rested the remains of wild apples and various berries and grains. The encampment of Monte Verde, which accommodated about 50 people for several seasons in a row, is for the moment unique, but its discovery was enough to modify the somewhat simplistic image that had been put forth about the "primitive" hunters of South America.

Arrow heads in flaked stone are absent in the various layers dispersed from Mexico to Tierra del Fuego until around 9000 B.C., even when the game is no longer solely now-extinct species. While in two encampments in central Chile a tool kit exclusively of bone (at Quereo, 9150 B.C.) or stone pebbles (at Tagua-Tagua, 9430 B.C.) accompanies some remains of mastodons and horses, the game found in the grottoes of Los Toldos and El Ceibo (Argentine Patagonia, c. 10,500 B.C.) is almost entirely composed of guanaco, a present-day species. However, the tool kit still only contained pebbles, more or less retouched. The same thing was noted in the shelters of Colombia at Tequendama and El Abra (c. 9000 and 10,500 B.C.), when cervids and rodents replaced guanacos.

Some New Weapons and Tools

The most ancient bifacial points are perhaps the large lanceolate "El Jobo" points, characteristic of northern Venezuela. At Taima-Taima, the headless skeleton of a young mastodon, dated to around 12,000 B.C., carried half of one of these points in its pubis. Most of the deposits with points are, however, later and scarcely date to the ninth millennium.

In Mesoamerica, where they are in the majority, foliated (leaf-shaped "Lerma" type) points still accompany some fauna fossils, as at El Diablo and Santa Isabel Iztapan, in Mexico, where they were associated with some articulated mammoth remains, or at Turrialba in Costa Rica. In South America, next to deposits with foliated points, "Ayampitin" type, the most numerous, or perdunculate ("Paijan") type, are also found in some places—such as El Inga in Ecuador and Fell's Cave and Palli-Aike Cave in Chilean Patagonia—"fluted" points, carry on each face scars of their vertical removal from the rock, doubtless designed to facilitate its insertion into a shaft. Such points are familiar in North America, where they characterize the Clovis, then Folsom, cultures around the 10th millennium. In South America the points of a slightly different shape are called "an abrupt end," appearing later but giving evidence of rapid diffusion. Despite the poor reputation attached to diffusionist theories, it is difficult to assume that a technical trait, or a characteristic, was invented centuries apart in two locations as far apart as the Great Plains of the United States and Patagonia. Other specimens have been found on the surface throughout Mesoamerica (Mexico, Costa Rica, Panama) and in South America (Brazil, Peru, Uruguay and Argentina).

There is evidence of many diverse types of points, finely flaked on the sides, with handles at the end of wooden or reed shafts, forming very efficient weapons used as projectiles—javelins or arrows launched with propulsion because the bow was still unknown—or held in the hand like long lances. Their appearance surely reflects changes in hunting techniques, putting into perspective the progressive disappearance of the large fauna, which became rare after 9000 B.C. They also attest to a progress in the manufacture of stone instruments, which henceforth included carving with a "soft" hammer (of wood or cervid antlers) and retouching. Other new tools are

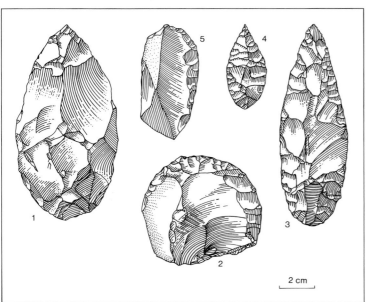

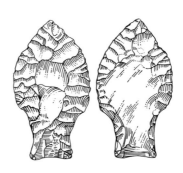

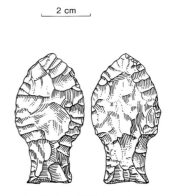

Various lithic tools of the Peruvian Andes:
1. *Biface (cutting tool used to cut, carve or scrape)*
2. *Scraper (used to scrape skins)*
3. *Large biface point (used as a spearhead)*
4. *Bifacial arrowhead*
5. *Scraper (small multipurpose cutting tool).*

Doc. French Archaeological mission of Junin (Peru).

Arrowheads from Fell's Cave from Journal de la Société des américanistes.

2 cm

2 cm

2 cm

also fabricated, more and more finely elaborated and apparently specialized: scrapers and scraper-knives of various types that allowed for the better cutting of game, scraping and trimming skins; some stone fragments with notches, piercers, in some instances burins, all well adapted to working in wood, bone or on supple materials. There were also multiple bone instruments, flesh cutters, smoothing tools and needles. Finally, and becoming more abundant, are grinding instruments, millstones and mortars, sometimes intentionally polished, which attest to a greater systematic use of resources other than those gained by hunting. The collection of berries, grains and wild turkeys was undertaken, small mammals and birds were trapped and mollusks were gathered—easily completing a dietary regimen where all the resources are put to good use.

The Conquest of the Andean Highlands

About 8000 B.C. begins an era in which the climate warms noticeably, causing the retreat of the glaciers that had covered the high regions and freeing vast expanses that soon became habitable and even very favorable, despite the cold and the altitudes (10,000 to 15,000 feet/3,500 to 4,500 meters), for some hunters. The rapid extension of pastures favored the increase of large herds of ungulates—cervids and camelids—and the natural refuges of the high plateaus were utilized as seasonal hunting rest places. At Lauricocha Pachamachay, Telarmachay (Peru), humans settled in shelters immediately after the retreat of the glaciers. There, where no natural refuges existed, they established, as in Cubilán (Ecuador), encampments in the open air. Everywhere these occupations of lands situated above 9,800 feet (3,000 meters) are dated between 8000 and 7000 B.C. In the habitats that they chose, always well positioned and close to a water source, people spread out their domestic space in a manner that sometimes was very elaborate. The site was limited and protected from bad weather by low walls of stone,

as in Telarmachay, by rows of poles supporting a wind break of skins and vegetation. Hearths of different types were built for a variety of tasks (various cooking methods, or more technical uses). The humans also gave themselves spaces for various activities in the "house," which was normally the same from one abode to another. The core of such activities was the exploitation of animals, involving the fabrication of weapons, tools for hunting and other tools for the preparation of the products of hunting (meat, skins, bones, tendons, etc.). The tool kit continued to be augmented and diversified with some new varieties and also objects made of skin and basketry, of which some fragments are still preserved. The variety of arrow heads is evidence of different adaptations to available resources and game.

Dietary requirements were satisfied by hunting cervids and camelids, because edible vegetation was rare in these altitudes. If the cervids dominate among the bony remains in the northern Andes (for example, at El Abra and Tequendama, in Colombia), camelids—vicunas and guanacos—become more prominent in the central Andes at an early stage (Peru,) and in the southern Andes (Chile) will grow in importance. The behavior of these animals may even have favored the progressive specialization of the hunters. Vicuna, for instance, live in small family groups (one male with four to seven females with their young) in the interior of

Prehistoric dwelling at Telarmachay *(near Junin, Peru).*
Detail of a floor, dated to around 2500 B.C. At the foot of a rocky wall (at bottom) a circular hearth was dug and then covered with small limestone slabs. Next to it was a pit sealed by a slab that contained the articulated remains of several young camelids. The presence of numerous newborn animals in the habitat indicates the existence of domestic camelids at that time, kept in an enclosure. Ph. D. Lavellée.

Las Vegas *(Santa Elena Peninsula, Ecuador).*
A trench in the soil from the implantation of a circular hut, about seven feet (two meters) in diameter. The vertical stakes mark the probable placement of a superstructure of organic material. At the center of the construction a burial was found, while, in front of the door, there were two stone pestles (foreground, at left) and various alimentary wastes (shells, bone remains). This structure was dated to circa 7000 B.C. Ph. K. Stothert.

a defined territory that is constant from one year to another, which they defend against intrusion by other groups. Guanacos have a very comparable behavior, although less stable. Humans finding these animals in such conditions would have understood the need to reduce trapping to protect the females and the young as stable and regular sources of nourishment. Cervids, on the contrary, were more often solitary animals, difficult to track, no longer a significant supplement to the diet, as were rodents, small carnivores, birds and even frogs, in a system of hunting becoming more specialized.

Alpaca and Llama

This growing familiarity between humans and their game is probably, in large part, at the origin of the "control" that began to be exercised over the herds of wild camelids, leading in barely one millennium to the appearance of domesticated animals. These centers of domestication were many, although certainly limited in the Andean high plains (altiplanos), but the process has still been revealed and studied in only one deposit, that of Telarmachay, situated at more than 14,000 feet (4,400 meters) on the central Peruvian high plateau. In this shelter, until that time visited by hunters of vicunas and guanacos, one observes among the innumerable long fragments accumulated in the occupied layers, a growing proportion of newborn animal remains at the start of 4000 B.C. How does one explain hunters, concerned with preserving their principal source of food, striking down the younger members of a herd? In fact, this apparently absurd percentage reflects nothing more, according to archaeologists, than the appearance of stocks in the process of domestication, replacing in the diet the wild, hunted animals. Grouped together in the enclosure, where they are more easily surveyed and protected from predatory animals, the very young, clearly born during the rainiest months, suffered from filth and overcrowding. Bacillary illnesses decimated them (a frequent phenomenon even in herds today). The animals themselves are in the process of evolution as their morphology and their dentition alter as can be detected in a deposit. They are no longer vicunas and guanacos, but alpacas and llamas, which, starting between 3000 and 2500 B.C., are clearly domesticated, while their wild counterparts suffer increased depletion. The hunt, as the principal activity of subsistence, progressively gives way to a pastoral economy that will supplement agriculture, developing more or less in the same era. The llama and its cousin, the alpaca, with its long and silky wool, becomes the main work animal of the Andean farmers. In this continent where no Old World animals exist,

it provides meat, wool, leather, bone, tendons and excrement (used as fuel). It is not only its milk which will be used. Very hardy, the llama can also carry loads over long distances and even before the preceramic period ends (circa 2000 B.C. in Peru), there are probably caravans of llamas that move various products between the highlands and the littoral, items such as salt, corn and fish, as well as more precious goods such as spondyle shells, used in numerous rituals.

The domestication of camelids remained, however, a phenomenon local to the central Andes. The guanaco of the Pampas of the south is never domesticated, and in the northern Andes, only the guinea pig, which in its wild state, became a substantial part of the hunters' diets at the El Abra and Tequendama sites as early as 5000 B.C. in Colombia. It is possible that it was rather quickly domesticated, as bone remains testify to a progressive increase in its size and certain modifications in its skeleton. Around 3000 B.C., the guinea pig has also acclimatized itself to Peru, where it quickly becomes the regular associate of the Andean farmer. As for the dog, its origin is problematic. Although some believe that it was domesticated in North America, others suggest that it arrived already domesticated with the first waves of Siberian hunters from Asia. However that may be, no wild dog remains have been discovered in tropical America, but the domestic dog is rarely found before the appearance of an agricultural or pastoral economy, and the remains of it are extremely rare in the Preceramic. The Andes are the only region of America where, with the llama and alpaca, domestic animals truly play an economic role. In Mesoamerica only the turkey was domesticated, in Mexico, and at a much later date.

The Art of the Hunters

Sometimes, on the walls of grottoes and shelters that they frequented, man painted scenes of game and the hunt, and indeed, in Patagonia and Brazil, more elaborate compositions with abstract elements. These depictions are at times several tens of meters long, in an often rich chromatic range. By their schematicism and the dynamism of the scenes, they evoke at times the art of the Spanish Levant or that of North Africa.

(Above) **Shelter Toca da Entrada do Pajau** (Piaui, Brazil).
 A painted scene, from the Northeast Tradition, of human silhouettes, several of which appear to be dancing around a tree. At the bottom left, one can make out a portion of a head and a cervid body. Ph. N. Guidon.

(Right) **Shelter Toca do Salitre** (Piaui, Brazil).
 Behind a large representation of a cervid stands a very schematized human silhouette. The scene painted on the shelter belongs to the Northeast Tradition, characteristic of northeastern Brazil, where it appeared around 10,000 years ago and lasted until about the fifth millennium.

With few exceptions this art is difficult to date. Most of the works were executed on the walls in the open air, isolated from other cultural remains. This is the case, for example, of the innumerable painted figures, generally in red ochre, that are found in the limestone reliefs in the Andes of Chile and Peru. They most represent camelids in diverse perspectives, associated with or without human figures, who always remain schematic and offer scarcely any elements for chronological diagnostics. Elsewhere, on the high plateaus of Colombia, there are geometric pictographs or very stylized human silhouettes.

Nevertheless, some examples can relate to a prehistoric occupation. In Brazil, again at the shelter at Toca do Boqueirão da Pedra Furada, the most ancient evidence has been brought to light on South American cave art. According to the archaeologist who discovered them, on a piece of wall, detached and bearing traces of red paint, remains of mineral colors and fragments of yellow and red ochre were contained in an archaeological bed dated from between 26,000 and 22,000 years B.P. They are very slim proofs, indeed; the walls of the shelter contain some magnificent scenes painted in red, white, grey, yellow and black, with figures of humans, cervids, jaguars, armadillos and lizards, often superimposed one on top of another, next to geometric motifs and "signs"—triangular motifs, "suns," concentric circles—that remain undecipherable. Large compositions depicting hunting scenes, warfare, dancing, sexual scenes (mating and childbirth) or the curious "tree scenes" (men surrounding a tree in a kind of circle), characterize the northeast tradition, whose origins possibly go back to the tenth millennium and that last until the fourth millennium. Proper to the northeast part of Brazil, where it has been identified in numerous sites, it is perhaps at the heart of the other figurative traditions of Brazil.

In Peru the grotto of Toquepala contains archaeological levels dated at between 7500 and 3000 B.C. and some wall paintings, which could depict the oldest occupation: more than 50 figures painted in red, yellow, green, black and white compose scenes of hunting camelids and cervids. Near some very realistic animals are found silhouettes of armed men, one with a sort of a club, the other with a raised baton, perhaps a projectile. The chronological correlation rests only on a tenuous sign: the presence in the deepest layer of two rods topped by balled bits of wool, saturated with red orchre, interpreted by their discoverer as brushes.

In Argentine Patagonia, the extraordinary pictorial composition formed by the "negative" (silhouetted) hands from the Cueva de las Manos (where dozens of handprints are outlined in black, red, yellow, violet and black) is the work of guanaco hunters of Los Toldos (9000 to 7000 B.C.), because some fragments of painted rock have been found in the dated levels of the grotto. The other rock art works of South America seem more recent. Thus the numerous paintings of the region of Lagoa Santa (Brazil) are linked with the Planalto tradition, characterized by animal figures, often monochromatic which do not seem to date past 4000 B.C. Nor do the innumerable geometric figures and other more or less schematic tracings that are found from one end of the country to the other, most often in red, sometimes bichromatic or trichromatic (red, yellow and black). This geometric tradition overlaps with evidence a number of regional features, of very different ages and for some, Postceramic designation.

Hunting scenes, Toquepala Grotto (near de Tacna, Peru).
Along with animals—camelids and cervids—are seen silhouettes of armed humans, one with a club, another with a baton—a projectile—held vertically. More than 50 figures, some of which must date to circa 7500 B.C., have been found in this grotto in southern Peru. Ph. P. Rojas Ponce.

Cave paintings and engravings also abound in Mexico, in Baja California and in the Sonora. Nearly all appear to be from the ceramic period, except perhaps the very beautiful polychrome scenes from the Sierra de San Francisco or San Borjita (Baja California), where enigmatic figures of men with their bodies pierced by arrows are found. There are also some kinds of "supplicants" surrounding large cervids, all in a very naturalistic style.

American cave art has a long existence. Appearing as early as the end of the Pleistocene, it continues until the European conquest and its study poses the same problems, often insoluble, as that of the prehistoric arts throughout the world. Although certain themes denote a stage or date of execution, as the llamas restrained by a halter in the Andes or the corn plantations in Brazil, others are of all eras and regions. Abundant and varied, this art, still undeciphered, forms an exciting field of study that may illuminate the origins of certain ethnic groups or the routes that they followed during their migrations.

Fishers and Seal Hunters

Until now, we have often mentioned some established societies inland, living on terrestrial resources. Nevertheless, very early some groups began to settle down near the marine shores, specializing in the exploitation of sea products. Of the settlements established along the beaches, only those from approximately 3000 B.C., after the end of the great post-glacial rise of the ocean have been preserved, while others, more ancient, situated at some distance from the shoreline, were able to be studied. The first would be those of the north coast of Peru, where as early as 9500 B.C. small groups of mastodon hunters also gathered mollusks, which were abundant in the coast mangroves (Amotape phase). After the disappearance of the megafauna, they lived almost completely on marine resources (Siches phase), as did the groups established at the same time or a little later on the coasts of Panama at Cerro Mangote, and in Ecuador and northern Chile. At Las Vegas, in the semidesert peninsula of Santa Elena (Ecuador), as early as 8800 B.C., a sedentary group hunts cervids, pecaries and foxes, gathering mollusks from the mangroves and wild plants. Their equipment seems very poor: no fishing gear, no finely fashioned tools, only barely retouched stone fragments, pebbles and some objects of bone and shell. The impression of a circular hut has been found, made from rushes and rattan, near which were buried 200 skeletons, the most ancient cemetery of South America.

In Chile, the numerous habitats established at more or less great distances from the shores, between the seventh and fourth millennia—Tiviliche, Taltal, Punta, Pichalo, Chinchorro—surround a richer panoply, with increasingly

advanced fishing gear: fish hooks of cactus spines, then shells, stone or bone, harpoons of bone and barbed harpoons, nets with gourd floaters and stone weights.

From the fourth millennium, all of the inhabitable littoral zones were occupied, with the various modalities, from Cen-

Cueva de las Manos Pintadas *(Rio Pinturas, province of Santa Cruz, Argentina).*

On the wall of the cave, one of the most famous sites of rupestrian art in America, are hundreds of "negative" hands, made by applying black, red, yellow, violet and white color around a hand pressed to the wall. They were probably the work of guanaco and horse hunters of the Los Toldas culture, between 9000 and 7000 B.C. Ph. F. Gohier/Explorer.

tral America, Venezuela, and its islands down to Tierra del Fuego. However, the most numerous and most important encampments were those on the coast of Patagonia and Brazil, where innumerable masses of shells (*conchales* in Spanish and *sambaquis* in Portuguese) show signs of an intense exploitation of the ocean. In southern Chile, hundreds of *conchales* are slowly built by fishing people and seal hunters, who move ceaselessly in vessels in the labyrinthine Magellanic canals. Originally, as early as the sixth millennium, small oval tents and rudimentary tools were used at their

brief stopping places: simple bone harpoons and mussel shells, approximately 20 centimeters long, that serve as knives. Later, habitations became more solid and larger, slightly submerged in a pit. The occupantions grew longer, by greater numbers of people, and the mass of wastes became more significant. The nomadic hunter-fishers utilized large harpoons in whale bone, and a beautiful industry of flaked stones with bifacial points began. The deposits of Englefield Island, Punta Ana and Bania Buena, dated to the third millennium, show this evolution. It is a scene rather identical to the one seen by the first European navigators in these waters. Along the Atlantic, hundreds of *sambaquis* line the coast of Brazil, from the mouth of the Amazon to Uruguay. Some of heights greater than 20 meters (sambaqui de Guaraguacu), these piles are formed by various shells, with which bird bones, fruit, and grains are mixed, found together with bone tools (awls and needles), stone shell grinders, thick graters and arrow heads and often polished axes. Also found are burials and beautiful animal sculptures in stone, "zooliths," probably ritual containers. Certain *sambaquis*, with bases now submerged, could date to the sixth millennium though most are from 3000 to 2000 B.C. Some were occupied during the ceramic epoch and perhaps even until the arrival of the Europeans.

Beans, Squash and Maize: The Beginning of Agriculture

The domestication of plants was not, as long believed, a "revolution" that took place in one unique center (the Near East), but was a long evolution that began at many different times in various parts of the world. Two of these "nuclear areas" are Mesoamerica and the Andes (including the Amazonian foothills), which introduced several plants to the world, both edible and nonedible, the most important being maize, potatoes, beans, tomatoes, peppers, cotton and tobacco. The history of this domestication is complex and difficult to summarize. The small amount of data that survive, for the most from the highlands of Mexico and the coast of Peru, regions that are very dry, where organic remains have been preserved. The reality was doubtless infinitely complex, the centers more numerous and the advances more varied.

In Mesoamerica, and more particularly, in Mexico, the signs of primitive agriculture appear as early as the sixth millennium, following diverse paths according to whether it arose in semiarid zones or the more temperate environments of the interior or the littoral. Thus at Tlapacoya -Zohapilco, in the Mexican Basin, the diversity and the proximity of different biotopes, joined to the abundance of natural resources that were exploitable throughout the year, seem to be at the heart of an early settlement process, accompanied early on by agricultural practices. Among the first plants utilized were amaranth, green tomatoes, and frequently (circa 5000 B.C.) a cereal resembling maize and its probable ancestor, teosinte. In the dry Tehuacan Valley, on the contrary, the seasonal nomadism practiced for millennia by small bands of hunters and gatherers of wild plants will take place only later, towards 3000 B.C., at the settlements of permanent housing. Hunting, gathering and trapping, combined in a wise method of alternating the exploitation of various resources, remain for a long time the surest means of subsistence. The evidence of horticulture appeared ap-

(Above) **The sambaqui of the Florianopolis littoral** (state of Santa Catarina, Brazil).

Formed by the accumulation of alimentary wastes, principally the remains of mollusks and fish, Brazilian sambaqui can reach 100 feet (30 meters) in height. Dated for the most part to a period between 3000 B.C. and the beginning of the Christian era, they conceal previously inhabited areas and abandoned tool kits. They are particularly numerous in mangroves, and at the bottom of deep bays, where the maritime resources could augment those of the river and the littoral forests. Ph. P. Junqueira.

(Right) **Evolution of corn in Mesoameria**

At left, from top to bottom, a series of ears of corn (of which only the cobs remain after the seeds have been eaten), from scarcely more than an inch (2.5 centimeters) to progressively larger ears. These examples were discovered in the successive archaeological levels of the Tehuacan Valley in Mexico. The oldest, apparently already cultivated, are dated to circa 5000 B.C. These cobs of corn reveal the modifications of the plant attributable to selective cultivation and successive hybridizations. Ph. Salvat Editores S.A.

proximately 5000 B.C.—avocado, amaranth, squashes, finally maize during the Coxcatlan phase—and may owe much to some exterior contributions, notably for maize, rather than to local innovations.

In Peru, cultivated plants appear earlier still, in the zones of middle altitude. The hunters who occupied the grotto of Guitarrero cultivated beans as early as the seventh millennium, then, around 5000 B.C., squash and gourds. It is even possible that they cultivated another species of maize before 5000 B.C. On the coast horticulture arrives later. Beans are found as early as 3000 B.C., but they become common only around 2500 B.C. Cucurbits (edible gourds and gourds used as containers) are cultivated in most coastal sites circa 3000 B.C. as well, at the same time as peppers, avocados, ground nuts, sweet potatoes then cotton, which henceforth allows the fabrication of materials (at first intertwined and then woven) nets and cloths of all sorts. In those regions where the economy was still often based on fishing, maize appears only around 2500 B.C.: at Los Gavilanes, the inhabitants cultivated sufficient crops to be able to store some of the ears in pits.

Where was this Andean agriculture born? According to some, in the dry basins of the Andes, between 6,500 and 10,000 feet (2000 and 3000 meters). Others, who advance the fact that nearly all of the plants are, according to botanists, originally from the tropical lowlands, propose a different chain of events: The first attempts at agriculture would have taken place to the east of the Andes, somewhere between Venezuela and Ecuador, and as early as the start of the Postglacial period, when the vegetation cover was less dense than it is today. Subsequently, the warming of the climate and the expansion of the forests forced people to look for other lands. They then went to the courses of the large rivers, crossing the Andes to reach the coast and bringing with them agriculture. The theory is certainly attractive, but far from being unanimously accepted, although its merits include the explanation of the relatively late arrival of coastal agriculture in comparison with the highlands.

However that may be, in Mexico, as in Peru, the introduction of new species and agricultural techniques started around 2500 B.C., giving agriculture a primary role based on

the trinity of squash, beans and maize, with complementary nutritional values.

Elsewhere in South America, agriculture seems to have come later, despite some recent discoveries with dubious datings: maize in Argentina as early as the seventh millennium, in Chile, around 5000 B.C. In Brazil maize is cultivated only in the northeast, circa 2000 B.C.; manioc later still, and then the pottery appears. More to the south, the vast plains of Uruguay and Argentina will remain, until the settling of the Europeans, the quasi-exclusive domain of the guanaco hunters.

First Villages, First Temples

In Mesoamerica, as in South America, when agriculture becomes sufficiently productive (c. 3000 to 2500 B.C.), then people built large permanent villages, quite superior in size and number to the small semisedentary or even sedentary hamlets of the preceding periods. In Mexico, some small villages with houses made of daub were erected in the Tehuacan Valley, starting around 3000 B.C. However, nowhere will the cultural flowering be as brilliant as on the coast of Peru. Along this desert (a band 1,400 miles [2,250 kilometers]

Preceramic textile from Huara Prieta. From Nawpa Paccha.

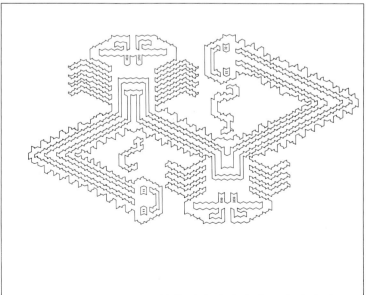

Las Vegas *(Santa Elena Peninsula, Ecuador).*

Double burial from the preceramic era, called "the lovers of Sumpa." The tucked up leg of the man (at left), rests on the hip of the extended woman (at right), and her hand is on his waist. The two individuals, aged around 20 years, were buried together, and covered with six stone slabs, doubtlessly to protect their remains. Ph. K. Stothert.

long, washed by one of the richest seas of the world in fauna thanks to the cold currents of Humboldt), and with oases generated by as many as 30 small rivers descending from the Andes, some permanent hamlets like that of Paloma, with habitations in semisubterranean pits, existed as early as 4000 B.C., sheltering a reduced population of fishers-gatherers-horticulturalists. Very quickly, however, establishments multiply and grow in size: Chilca, circa 3500 B.C., is a true village of conical huts of branches and reeds, while at Rio Grande huts of straw alternate with rectangular stone constructions.

The technical equipment was also varied and diverse,with fishing gear, wooden clubs and projectiles, tools of stone and bone, gourd containers and baskets. Neither maize nor cotton were cultivated yet; their appearance in the economy caused, it seems, a major demographic and economic expansion. Huaca Prieta, around 2500 B.C., sheltered several hundred individuals in small semisubterranean homes of pebbles, with roofs of wood and whalebones. At Rio Seco, more complex housing was built, able to accommodate about ten people, and some kinds of constructed pyramids with unknown purposes. Finally, at Chuquitanta, a stone

edifice containing 35 pieces is perhaps the most ancient temple in Peru (unless it functioned as a complex storage structure). The whole building, which had to have several phases of construction, was covered by a coating of smooth argil and was painted in ochre, white and red. A parallel evolution is taking place, in the highlands between 2000 and 1000 B.C.: centers like La Galgada or Kotosh, where the famous "Temple of the Crossed Hands" was raised (so named because it contains a low relief representing two human forearms crossed), are based on an agricultural economy supplemented by breeding.

In Mexico and Peru, and in Ecuador and Chile, this extraordinary cultural flowering of the final Preceramic period will be at the heart of the great Formative period: the Olmecs in Mexico, the Valdivia in Ecuador (where pottery was "invented" as early as 3000 B.C.), Chavin of Peru. These peoples will erect large politico-religious centers and develop new forms of societies, based on intensive cultivation of maize. Everywhere else in South America, where agriculture was practiced (the basins of the Orinoco, Amazon and Parana), permanent villages will only appear at the same time as pottery, roughly between 1500 and 500 B.C.

Suggested Reading

Coe, Michael; Snow, Dean, and Benson, Elizabeth. *Atlas of Ancient America.* New York: Facts On File, 1986.

Jennings, Jesse. D., ed. *The Ancient South Americans.* San Francisco: W. H. Freeman, 1983.

Patterson, T. C. *America's Past: A New World Archaeology.* Glenview, Ill. and London: Scott Foresman and Co., 1971.

Salmoral, Manuel Lucena. *America 1492: Portrait of a Continent 500 Years Ago.* New York and Oxford: Facts On File, 1990.

Bas-relief of the "Crossed Hands" *at Kotosh (near Huánco, Peru).*
In what appears to have been a small temple, built circa 1800 B.C. in the northern Andes in Peru by a pre- *ceramic people, this bas-relief in molded clay represents two crossed forearms, decorating the base of two small niches, fitted into the wall—perhaps to receive offerings. Ph. Kodawsha Ltd., Tokyo.*

CHAPTER TEN

José Garanger

OCEANIA AND INSULAR ASIA

An adze of the Baruya of New Guinea (*M. Godelier mission*).
The blade, fashioned out of polished volcanic rock, is fixed to a wooden handle, cut from the fork of a branch. The blade types vary throughout the Pacific, but the stone adze was the basic tool of all Oceanians, who may have used it for forestry, woodworking, the fabrication of tools and for canoes or sculpture. Ph. J. Garanger.

What the Europeans named Oceania, or the "fifth part of the world," is not geographically homogenous. It comprises, to the west, the old Australian shield, bordered by insular, tectonically active chains, part of the "circle of fire of the Pacific." Beyond lies the Great Ocean and its islands as numerous as stars in the sky, as the Polynesians say. Of volcanic origin, of varying age, they formed high islands, generally encircled by a lagoon limited by a coral reef or low islands, atolls that emerge only a few feet/meters above the surface of the sea. It is a tropical world, but eased by altitude (glaciers exist in New Zealand) and by latitude; many tropical alimentary plants, for example, could not be acclimated by the Polynesians in New Zealand or on Easter Island.

The prehistory of Oceania is itself heterogeneous. Australia and New Guinea were colonized by humans 40,000 years ago; the Australian Aborigines remained hunter-gatherers until the European period. The peopling of the Oceanic archipelagos occurred much later, only a few millennia ago to the west. These sailors were cultivators and also bred the dog, pig and chicken. They made pottery but did not use the wheel, weave or practice metallurgy. This island world was divided, in the 19th century, into three groupings: Melanesia, to the southwest, Micronesia to the northwest and Polynesia to the east. This subdivision is convenient but hides a more complex reality. If the dark-skinned people with fuzzy hair are the most numerous in Melanesia, while other populations with lighter skin and wavy hair predominate Micronesia and Polynesia, no geographic border really separates these groups who have a long history of contact with one another. The unity of their way of life, their beliefs and their language indicates that they forged a common "ancestral culture" before leaving eastern Asia to venture over the Great Ocean.

Australia During the Glacial Period

In the coldest periods of the Quaternary, the formation of glaciers led to a significant drop in the ocean level and Australia formed a single continent with New Guinea and Tasmania. The Asian continent extended then as far as Bali and Borneo. Between the two continental groups, respectively named Sahul and Sunda, a small archipelago still existed: the Wallacea, which Homo sapiens colonized during the Würm period. One after another, they crossed the arms of the sea, with a width of less than 38 feet (60 kilometers). Rafts, used to fish along the coasts, were perhaps sometimes diverted into the high sea. However they achieved landfall, humans reached the north of Sahul early on, discovering an environment scarcely different from that of Wallacea; with tropical vegetation and nearly identical fauna. Slowly, new lands were discovered by following the western coast of Sahul and exploring the valleys further inland. Around 38,000 B.C., some groups reached as far as the southwest of the continent and settled on the banks of the Swan River. Some 7,000 years later, the extreme south of Australia was peopled. Its riverine network was extensive, notably the Murray and the Darling, and numerous lakes,dried since the end of the Pleistocene, were well drained.

The whole region was favorable to these inhabitants, who lived by hunting, fishing and gathering. Their presence in such distant times was revealed in 1968 by the discovery, near Lake Mungo, of evidence of their activity: hearths, sea shells, lithic tool kits. Some graves were brought to light as well. Anatomically, these people were scarcely different from the present-day Aborigines, except for a larger jaw. Starting in 1969, numerous human fossils were discovered in the site of Kow Swamp, 200 miles (350 kilometers) south of Mungo. Although dating only from 13,000 to 9,000 years B.P., their cranial, facial and mandibular morphology indicated traits more archaic than those of the Mungo fossils, which poses a still unresolved paleontological problem. Whatever the explanation, the tool kits of these populations do not vary throughout the Sahul and for all of the Pleistocene. A kit consisted essentially of scattered pebbles, fragments and large scrapers. Starting in 25,000 B.P., new tools were added: large serrated blades and polished blades with sharp cutting edges, of which the most ancient were discovered in the Arnhem Land.

The appearance in Australia of polished stone in such an ancient period amazed the prehistorians. They thought that it had arrived more recently and was proof of South Asian

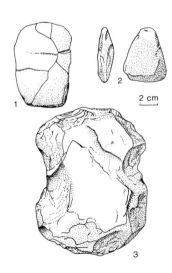

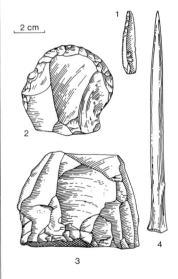

Lithic tool kit of New Guinea and Australia, Pleistocene.
1-2. Polished cutting blades from the Oenpelli region, northwest of Arnhem Land, northern Australia, around 20,000 B.C.
3. Blades with lateral indentations, Kangaroo Island, southern Australia.

Aboriginal tool kit of Australia
1. "Bordi" point (recent)
2. Rounded blade (recent)
3. Nucleiform scraper (Pleistocene)
4. Awl of bone (Pleistocene).

Kuk site *in the Highlands of Papua New Guinea, one of the first areas of excavations studied by the prehistorian Jack Golson. The darker sediments correspond to ancient trenches surrounding islands of cultivation (clear zones). The entire site, dated to circa 6000 B.P., is crossed by more recent rectilinear pits. In the same site, several series of similar plans were discovered, older and less complex, the first dating to 9000 B.P. Ph. J. Golson.*

Neolithic influences. In fact, the Aborigines of *Sahul* could well have been the first of the world to discover this technique. Their material security was not their only concern. They clearly were preoccupied with aesthetic and religious practices. The Aboriginal funerary rites were sometimes very complex, as exemplified by the young woman found on the site of Mungo: after being incinerated on a pyre, her bones were carefully broken and placed within a pit with hearth stones from the fire. At Mungo as well, the body of an adult human was buried in an elongated position, covered by ochre. These pigments have been observed in numerous sites, not all from burials. Were they utilized to decorate some objects or used for body paintings? Bone pearls have been discovered in the "Devil's Lair," a cave south of Perth, dating from 12,000 years B.P. Some 8,000 years earlier, networks of grooves had been engraved on the walls of a cave of Koonalda, in southern Australia, and at Laura (York Penin-

sula) picked images made 13,000 years ago, represented human and kangaroo footprints.

Sahul

In the 10th millennium B.C., the slow warming of the globe modified, as elsewhere in the world, the environment of the *Sahul*: an evolution of the regional ecosystem and significant marine transgressions, which isolate New Guinea and Tasmania from Australia. Some 6,000 years ago, the shore lines were nearly the same as those of today. In this epoch, we also begin to see a divergence of cultures over the Australian continent and on the two islands that were once joined to it.

In Australia, contacts and exchange intesify from one territory to another, sometimes over great distances. This

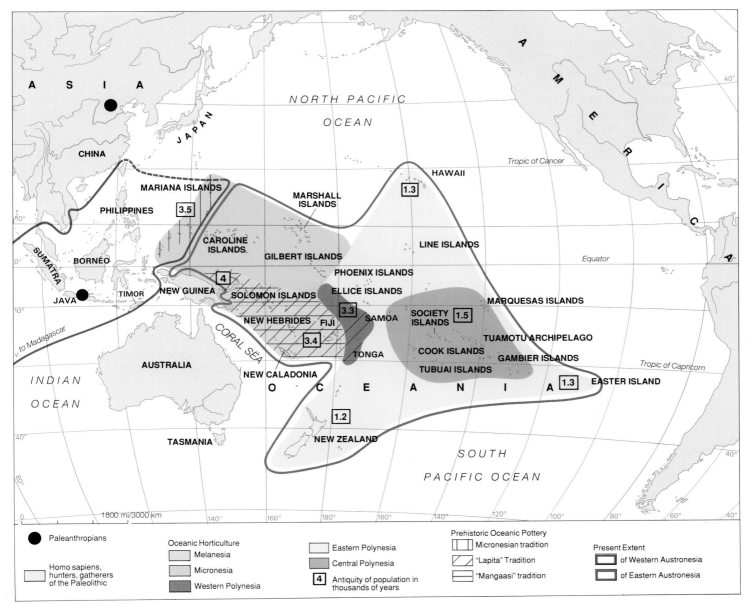

General map of Oceania

mobility may have been caused by an increase of the population and the necessity to reach new resources, alimentary or other. The lithic tool kit is refined and diversified: Its technical and aesthetic qualities are comparable to those of the Upper Paleolithic of western Europe or northeastern Asia. Excellent materials are needed to cut tools according to preconceived forms, to obtain blades, bladelettes, points and microliths and to finely retouch their edges and surfaces. Resins were used to assure the proper fitting of a handle, and pigments were needed to decorate them. The origin of this new tool kit, which expands very fast into the entire Australian area, presents a still unresoved problem. Were these improvements a local innovation or an external contribution? Their equivalent is found nowhere in New Guinea or in Southeast Asia.

The dingo, the hunting companion of the Aborigines, first appears in Australia, though from where and how it was introduced remain unknown. From this epoch the projectile and the boomerang also date, as well as the first wall paintings. Isolated from Australia by the Bass Strait, the Tasmanians do not achieve a similar evolution. Their lithic tool kit remains somewhat the same as that of the Pleistocene and probably their lifestyles as well.

Little is known about the ancient prehistory of Papua New Guinea, and that of Irian Barat (most of this immense island remains unexplored). The first occupants likely settled some 50,000 or more years ago, in the lowlands, submerged today by the Arafoura Sea, or they perhaps passed it by to inhabit the vast southern plain. Here, a coastal site on the Huon Peninsula has been dated at 45,000 years B.P., but the bulk of the known Pleistocene sites are in the highlands, colonized by humans 30,000 years ago. Their tool kit is similar to that of the *Sahul* of the same era, with some variations caused by the resources of the local natural environment.

The end of the glacial period and the warming of the climate, as elsewhere, have important consequences for the inhabitants: expansion of the littoral plains and lower valleys and the increase of vegetation in the various altitudes. The peopling of the mountainous interior intensifies and the first early attempts at cultivating the useful plants of the area are begun. This was accomplished for the first time at Kuk, at an altitude of 5,200 feet (1,600 meters). Where some 9,000 years ago a vast marshy zone was drained for the cultivation of plants. About 3,000 years later a true horticulture develops, with systems of drainage and irrigation allowing agriculture in dry and humid lands. At the same time the semidomestication of swine appears. It is a warmer period, from 8000 to 4000 B.P., than today, and humans were able to colonize regions formerly uninhabited. Some exchanges were also maintained with the populations established in the lower mountains and on the coast, as is proven by the presence of sea shells in several sites in the high altitudes. During the second or third millennia B.C., the first sailors, who would colonize the oceanic archipelagos on the northern coast of New Guinea, arrive.

Origin of Insular Oceania

The European navigators who discovered the islands of Polynesia were amazed to find people so far from all continental land and wondered where they had come from. Three hypotheses were then advanced: a local origin, an Amerindian origin and an Asian origin. The supporters of the first theory believed that a distinct human race had lived on a ancient continent, today swallowed up by the ocean and of which there remained only the highest summits of its mountains, the islands of Polynesia. What is now known about the depths of the Pacific Ocean goes against such a hypothesis, and the theory of multiple origins is discredited. The theory of an Amerindian origin is also dated, but nonetheless has received considerable support since 1950 when Thor Heyerdahl, on his expedition on the raft *Kon-Tiki*, sailed from the coast of Peru to the islands of Tuamoto. His publications greatly influenced the general public, but he has not convinced scientists who, while admitting the possibility of episodic contacts between the eastern Polynesians and the Amerinds, remain unanimous in citing Asia as the homeland of the Polynesian populations for a number of reasons. All of the Oceanians speak languages similar to Austronesian, which is linguistically related to the languages spoken in Taiwan, Philippines, continental and insular Southeast Asia, and as far as Madagascar, but not in the Americas. The plants cultivated and introduced into the Pacific are all originally from Southeast Asia, except for the sweet potato (from America), and sugar cane (from New Guinea). This is particularly true of the principal plants (breadfruit, a berry plant, taro, yams, banana and coconut) as well as dogs, pigs and chickens. Archaeological excavations since 1960 have only served to confirm Asiatic influence on the Polynesians.

The question of the origin of the Melanesians, considered racially distinct from the Polynesians, has also been debated. Their archipelagos were not very far from New Guinea or Australia, a distance that could have been crossed overland one theory goes, during the regression of the ocean during the Würmian period. This is, however, improbable. No trace of a Pleistocene peopling has yet been discovered in insular Melanesia, no land bridge, or even narrow sound, which could have allowed such pedestrian migrations, no evidence of rudimentary navigation, as was probably used by the first colonizers of *Sahul*. All of this suggests that the Melanesians are also from Southeast Asia, but the question remains as to whether or not they preceded ancestors of the Polynesians in the Pacific islands. This last point is generally admitted, and the only question now concerns whether or not the Polynesians frequented the Melanesian islands during their first migrations "toward the rising sun," or if these adventurous sailors passed farther north, through still uninhabited Micronesia. The feats of the Polynesians were suggested by Peter Buck in his 1938 work, *Vikings of the Sunrise*, and the idea of the superiority of the Polynesians is an old prejudice. One cannot deny the existence in Polynesia of people with

Melanesian features, and others, in Melanesia, with Polynesian features, but this is explained as the result of more recent contacts between the two groups as western Polynesians explored the Melanesian archipelagos and took on Melanesians, perhaps by force, during their departure toward eastern Polynesia. This thesis of a first peopling by a Micronesian route was still defended by the anthropologist William Howells in 1973, based, in particular, on the archaeological data: the sites with Lapita ceramics (considered Proto-Polynesian) were more ancient to the east of western Polynesia than in northern or central Melanesia.

New archaeological finds contradict this theory. Those who peopled the islands of the Pacific passed by Melanesia, not Micronesia, which would have been impossible for them. Central and eastern Micronesia, except for small mountainous islands, is formed only from atolls that were nearly submerged until the last oceanic regression of ten feet (three meters), which started only around 3,000 years ago. Western Micronesia, however, only comprises chiefly high islands.

Prehistoric pottery indicates that they were peopled as late as the 16th century B.C. by sailors coming directly from the Philippines. Their ancient prehistory is different from that of the rest of Oceania, as some linguistic studies have shown as well.

Lapita Pottery and the Polynesians

Lapita pottery is distinguished from other prehistoric patterns in the Melanesian area by its shape and decoration. It was first discovered at Watom (New Britain), by an amateur archaeologist, R. P. Otto Meyer, in 1909. He thought that it was technically too elaborate to be of local origin and could well have been Peruvian. In 1947, pottery was discovered on the Island of Pines, to the south of New Caledonia, resembling the Watom pieces. In the same year, the American archaeologist, E. W. Gifford, uncovered more samples in the Fiji Is-

Petroglyphs from the Sundown Creek site, on the northwestern coast of Tasmania. These geometric figures, whose significance remains unclear (perhaps astronomical sym- *bols?), have been chiseled in the rock. Similar ones exist all over the Australian continent, dated by radiocarbon to the Upper Pleistocene. Petroglyphs or polychrome wall* *paintings in a different figurative style, succeed them in Australia but not in Tasmania. Ph. J. Garanger.*

lands that date to several hundred years B.C. In 1952 he explored the prehistory of New Caledonia, excavating among others, a site where pottery had been discovered at the turn of the century near Lapita. Since 1960 the excavations have been multiplied in the Pacific, and Lapita culture sites have been discovered in the whole of Melanesia and in western Polynesia, dating from the eighth century B.C. The idea slowly gained credence that the makers of the pottery, the "People of Lapita," were the ancestors of the Polynesians.

According to the classic theory, the "People of Lapita" left southeastern Asia around the end of the third millennium and infiltrated the archipelagos of the southwest Pacific, already occupied by the Melanesians. Sea people, they settled on the coasts and traded with the Melanesians, who were

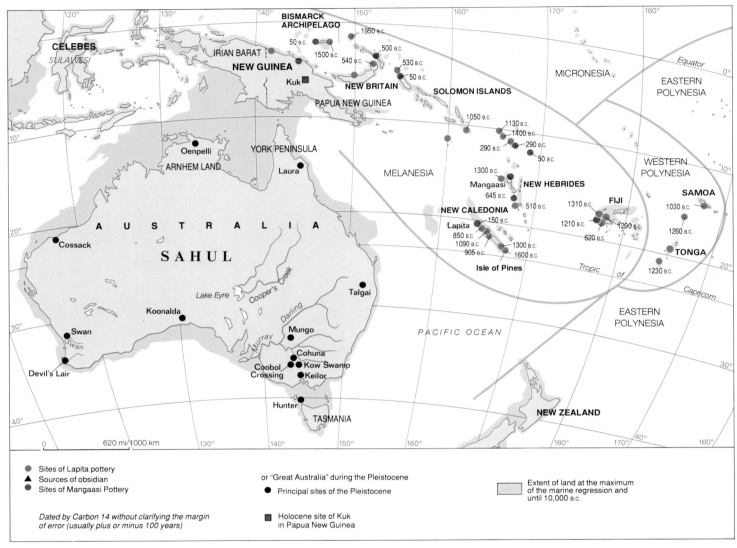

- ● Sites of Lapita pottery
- ▲ Sources of obsidian
- ● Sites of Mangaasi Pottery

Dated by Carbon 14 without clarifying the margin of error (usually plus or minus 100 years)

or "Great Australia" during the Pleistocene
- ● Principal sites of the Pleistocene

■ Holocene site of Kuk in Papua New Guinea

Extent of land at the maximum of the marine regression and until 10,000 B.C.

Southwestern Pacific

New Caledonia: irrigated taro field.
Taro (Colocasia) is a tuber plant originating in Southeast Asia, introduced into the Pacific islands by the Oceanians. It is now one of their main alimentary plants. Numerous botanical and horticultural varieties exist, cultivated with or without irrigation, or in naturally humid or shady places. Ph. J.-C. Galipaud.

land people, breeders and agriculturalists. They established networks of interisland relations and because of their large canoes, early discovered lands previously uninhabited: Fiji, Tonga and Samoa. Having acquired or perfected the techniques of agriculture from contact with the Melanesians, they were able to support themselves and to continue exploiting the resources of the sea, while also cultivating the interiors of the islands. Toward the start of our own era, the high population density forced some of them to leave to seek to the east, uninhabited lands, those of eastern Polynesia. This exodus had become all the more necessary because the Melanesians in their turn, were colonizing Fiji as they had acquired through contact with the "People of Lapita" the techniques of oceanic navigation, as well as ceramic techniques.

This theory of population, very briefly summarized, is based on a certain number of archaeological finds, though some lack support while others are contradictory. It remains to be explained how the Melanesians were able to people the islands before mastering the techniques of long-distance navigation. And the idea that the "People of Lapita" only settled along the sea may be illusory as the interiors of the islands have been little studied. Likewise, "Melanesian" ceramics have been found in coastal areas. The opposition of sea farers and land dwellers is also difficult to maintain in light of recent discoveries that show that Lapita populations also practiced agriculture and breeding from their arrival in the western Pacific.

It is principally on a stylistic analysis of Lapita pottery, and its geographic and cartographic distribution, that theories of its role in the circuits of interisland relations of the "People of Lapita" are based. It had been thought later that the "Melanesian" pottery (the best known being that of Mangaasi, a site on Vanuatu, dating to the seventh century B.C.) was only used where it was made. Today, Mangaasi pottery is found throughout Melanesia and sometimes very far from its point of origin. It also entered into the interisland exchange networks. The disappearance of the first ceramic tradition during the first centuries A.D., then the second, at a later date, can be explained by the fact that as the production

of such ceramics proved unnecessary, the networks in which they were involved modified, weakened and then disappeared. Other ceramics, or other products, then took its place in different networks.

Ethnologists have studied these intertribal circuits, following the maintenance of political alliances through the exchange of products of uniquely symbolic value. The exchange of ceramic wares from island to island was too small for them to have had a large role in daily life. As in the era of the first European contact, the foodstuffs (meat, fish, often tubers and breadfruit) were roasted or cooked on heated stones, either on a flat wooden dish as starches became a liquid paste, or were steamed in subterranean ovens called *canaques*, the remains of which have been found in prehistoric sites. Other receptacles were used as well: coconuts, gourds and bamboo stems. Pottery was not used widely and its disappearance, and indeed its absence in eastern Polynesia did not a hinder the islanders. Ethnologists have shown that in Oceania artistic techniques, including pottery were the property of a small group of craftsmen. During the first

(Above) *Lapita traditional pottery.*
Some shards brought to light for the first time in the Pacific, at Watom (1909) and preserved at the Museum of Man (collection no. 34 188). Ph. J. Garanger.

(Left) *Mangaasi tradition pottery.* Shards, decorated by incisions and ornamental reliefs, from the lower levels of the Mongaasi site (seventh century B.C.). This ceramic tradition is today known in the whole of the southwestern Pacific. Ph. J. Garanger.

peopling of Fiji and western Polynesia, the dispersion of even a small number of Lapita pieces provides the illusion of a widespread Lapita peopling.

If we sum up the whole of this data, we must take note that the ancestors of the Melanesians and Polynesians had their comparable lifestyles as they arrived in the Pacific. They cultivated the same plants, bred the same animals, used identical tools and spoke languages all similar to the Austronesians. Sea farers as well as land dwellers, they developed networks of relationships from island to island, which they maintained until the Europeans arrived throughout the Pacific. Certainly, a diversity in the activities was then observable, engendered by the centuries of evolution in different environments and dispersal over an immense ocean. This evolution and its innovations had not prevented the persistence of a deep cultural unity, in artistic techniques, systems of alliance and the role of ancestors in social and religious life. It is thus difficult to maintain the hypothesis that two populations, of different origins and cultures, colonized the islands of Oceania separately. All had to have shared the same ancestral culture, slowly developed in eastern Asia before their arrival in the Pacific.

The Asiatic Cradle

The differences observed in the physical appearance of the Oceanians were often exaggerated and simplified in order to maintain that there were two separate "races." Today, no anthropologist would attempt to define a Melanesian or a Polynesian race. The physical appearances of the two can be varied—as they are in shades of color—but it is known that the apparent physical characteristics of a people are not nearly as permanent as was formerly believed. From what is known about more recent periods, one can, however, determine that in the Upper Paleolithic, populations with dissimilar physical appearances existed in eastern Asia: dark-skinned groups in the south, in the present Malay Peninsula, and brown-skinned and white-skinned in the north and

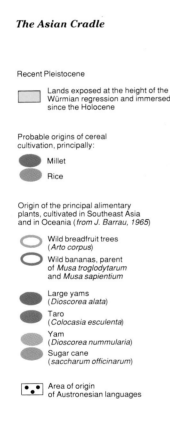

The Asian Cradle

Recent Pleistocene

Lands exposed at the height of the Würmian regression and immersed since the Holocene

Probable origins of cereal cultivation, principally:

Millet

Rice

Origin of the principal alimentary plants, cultivated in Southeast Asia and in Oceania (*from J. Barrau, 1965*)

Wild breadfruit trees (*Arto corpus*)

Wild bananas, parent of *Musa troglodytarum* and *Musa sapientium*

Large yams (*Dioscorea alata*)

Taro (*Colocasia esculenta*)

Yam (*Dioscorea nummularia*)

Sugar cane (*saccharum officinarum*)

Area of origin of Austronesian languages

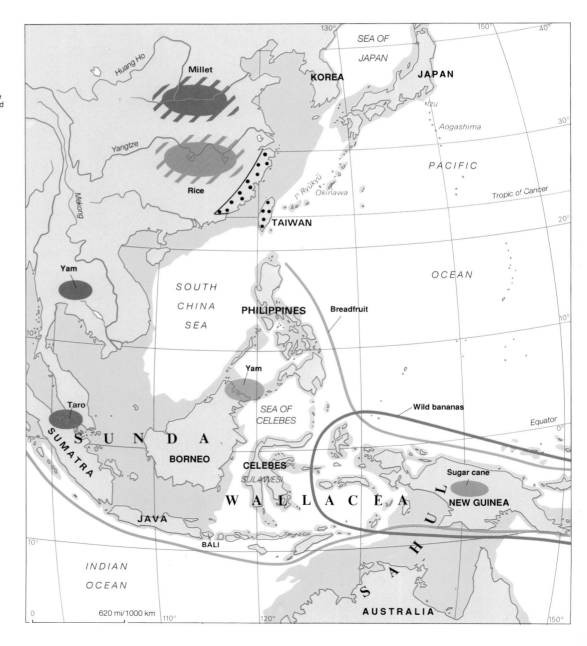

in the west. Their ways of life, still imperfectly known, had to be equally different, with the Würmian cooling subsiding considerably towards the south, as their technical artifacts illustrate. Lithic and bone tools were perfected in the northern regions (Japan, northern China and southern Siberia) and are comparable in technical qualities to the Upper Paleolithic tools of Europe. In contrast, the tool kits of the tropical zones remain very rudimentary. A rich vegetal environment always offered more abundant resources than elsewhere, and also materials such as bamboo, which made unnecessary the learned fashioning of points, knives and other weapons and tools in stone or bone.

The end of the glacial periods nonetheless had very important consequences for all of these eastern Asia populations. The sea slowly invaded the continental plateaus, submerging much of the littoral plains. The same transgression isolated the ancient lands of Sunda, of which only the Malay Peninsula and a multitude of small islands in the South China Sea remain today. More to the north, Taiwan separated from Asia, and Japan became an archipelago. The length of the entire coast line tripled. To the south, immense deltas formed at the mouths of the great continental rivers, which favor, with the settling of the monsoon climate, the growth of wild rice, as does the humid climate of central China. More to the north, the loess plains and a more temperate climate spurred a proliferation of other grasses, especially millet. In the remaining tropical zones the vegetation regained at higher altitudes the surface area lost in the submerged plains.

Toward New Ways of Life

Man adapted slowly to this transformation of the natural environment and concentrated his efforts on a small number of nutritional resources by beginning to domesticate animals and to control the reproduction of the most useful plants. The Neolithic evolutions are not identical nor synchronized from north to south in eastern Asia, and three principal areas should be considered: the cultivation grains (especially rice and millet), the importance of tuberous plants and the exploitation of marine resources. These activities correspond respectively to central China, Southeast Asia and the whole of the coastal regions.

Not too long ago, it was supposed that rice agriculture was born, either in Thailand (circa 10,000 B.P.) or in the deltas of southern China and northern Vietnam. These two hypotheses are rejected today. The first is archaeologically unfounded and the second untenable because it is impossible to control the production "floating" of rice in the naturally inundated deltas. Rice agriculture more likely began in southern China, in a central and humid region where irrigation was controllable, as early as 5000 B.C. More to the north, in the loess plains, millet was cultivated in about the sixth millennium (Yangshao, Neolithic). In both regions, pigs and dogs were already domesticated, to which were added the goat, sheep and ox, and to the south, the water buffalo.

In contrast to grain growers, agriculturalists of southeastern Asia did not use the germinative power of grains but only the possibility of vegetative reproduction of plants, particularly facilitated here by a warm and humid climate. These gatherers had to have undertaken for a long period the cultivation of steady growth in their agricultural plants: fruit trees (banana, breadfruit) and tuber plants (yams, taro and other roots). The preagriculturalists quickly improved their methods, not only through selective clearings but by transporting cuttings and tubers, which were then planted and given drainage or irrigation. This augmentation of the natural environment and the successive transportations slowly modified the plants. If certain of them lost their power of sexual reproduction in time, all of them augmented their nutritional qualities. In these regions, as later in Oceania, the dog, pig and chicken were also raised.

The population of the maritime plains of China and that of Japan's archipelago adapted differently to the transformations of their environments. With the softening of the climate in the Holocene period, the increased and diversified resources from hunting and gathering, required neither the domestication of animals (except for the dog, as early as 7000 B.P.), nor domestic crops until the last few centuries. It is only then that the grain production, particularly rice, begins to be manifest in southern Japan, probably under the influence of the Chinese Neolithic, and possibly through Korea. As early as 12,500 B.P., however, in these two regions, the same ceramics appear, probably the most ancient in the world. Their decoration, executed on the still soft clay with the help of a rolled cord (kaiten jomon in Japanese) will serve to designate this long Pre-Neolithic era and will persist during the first Neolithic times. Forms and decorations evolved in the course of time, but the various kinds of containers are generally

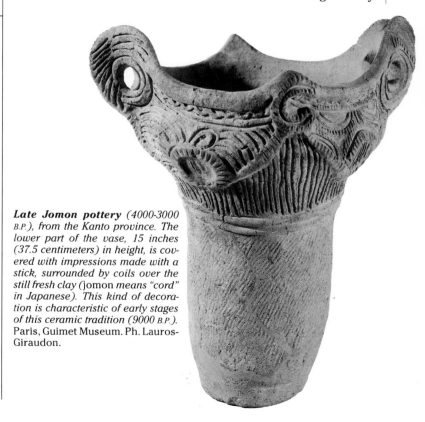

Late Jomon pottery (4000-3000 B.P.), from the Kanto province. The lower part of the vase, 15 inches (37.5 centimeters) in height, is covered with impressions made with a stick, surrounded by coils over the still fresh clay (jomon means "cord" in Japanese). This kind of decoration is characteristic of early stages of this ceramic tradition (9000 B.P.). Paris, Guimet Museum. Ph. Lauros-Giraudon.

small. Only a few would have been used for storage or for cooking vegetables, fish or game. (Such activities were heightened during the Jomon, as fishing weights and alimentary remains discovered in coastal sites attest, as do seagoing canoes dated to 6000 years ago.)

The effects of the Post-Würmian transgressions were here, and on the Chinese coast, responsible for the evolution of lifestyles with the loss of land, newly created islands, and the slow formation of an immense maritime zone with rich, and varied fishing resources. Exploration, always far from the coasts, is attested to by the presence of Late Jomon pottery (4000–3000 B.P.) in Okinawa and, earlier still, on the Islands of Aogashima, far south of the Izu Islands. Corded pottery from Taiwan appears to be of similar origin. It is probable that these were not the only ocean-going populations, in the south and Indonesia.

The prehistory of these regions remains obscure, but certain archaeological finds indicate that they pursued an indirect maritime relationship with the north through the intermediary efforts of interethnic and interisland links. Linguistic studies confirm this theory. Austronesian, had its birth in Taiwan and on the nearby Chinese coast at least 7,000 years ago. Some finds have been made in the Japanese substrata, but the culture extended primarily to Southeast Asia, then insular Oceania. One must conclude that a long commingling of these populations of diverse origins and ways of life, gave birth to the ancestral Oceanic culture.

It remains to examine the reason for the exodus of some of these people beyond the eastern horizon. The pressure of the populations of continental Southeast Asia on the dark-skinned peoples of the islands—dark-skinned peoples themselves started to infiltrate New Guinea early on, among the remote descendants of the colonizers of *Sahul*. The principal migration was around 6000 to 5000 B.P., and these same immigrants would have been already in contact with the Austronesian speakers. Some ancient elements of this linguistic family are found in the "Papua" languages today. Another impetus, farther north, would have been the pressure exerted by the populations of central China on those of the coastal regions. While probable, this is not a comprehensive expla-

Tomb of Roy Mata at Retoka (center of Vanuatu, formerly New Hebrides). The collective burial of this legendary hero (in the background, center) is dated to the 13th century A.D. His arrival, and that of his companions, into the center of the archipelago, caused an upheaval in the material culture: the abandonment of pottery and the introduction of shell tools of the Micronesian variety, replacing the lithic tool kit. We have here proof of the extensions into Melanesia of an ancient network of interisland "aceramic" relations coming from eastern Micronesia. Ph. J. Garanger.

nation. The influence of the Chinese Neolithic is here relatively late, later still in Insulinde, and the ancestors of the Oceanians left these regions before the cereal agriculture was introduced. The effects of this new marine transgression in Micronesia cannot be discounted. Although it was of some consequence for the island populations and is significant because it corresponds chronologically to the maritime expansion of the first Oceanians.

The Peopling of the Eastern Pacific

It is generally thought that the ancestors of the eastern Polynesians left the island of Tonga and Samoa near the start of the Christian era. The material culture of these two archipelagos had only slightly evolved in the course of the millennium that preceded this exodus, except for Lapita pottery, whose forms and decorations were slowly simplified before disappearing around 200 A.D., without being replaced, as in Fiji, by the two other Oceanic ceramic traditions: a stamped pottery, and the Mangaasi style. Notable in Samoa is an evolution of adze blades; formerly elliptic or biconvex, like those found throughout the western Pacific regions, they became triangular or quadrangular. However, this evolution was probably determined by the texture of the materials available—basalts, not andesite—rather than by an exterior influence. Some true architectural innovations will appear later in Samoa and Tonga with the vast ceremonial mounds and, in the eastern Pacific, lithic monuments in the form of stepped pyramids, destined to become the tombs of the most important chiefs, whose upper platforms support plazas for ancestor worship, religious ceremonies and the gatherings of the chiefs. Later still, in the eighth century, an amazing trilithon (stone arch) was built at Tongatabu, known as *Ha'amonga a Maui*, with a foundation (of coral sandstones) weighing 30-to-40 tons. Only the construction of the fortified sites can be considered relatively old, the result of an increase of intertribal conflicts caused by a large population

competing for available resources. That could also be the reason that certain people fled and set out to discover new uninhabited territories toward the northwest, in Micronesia and the eastern Pacific. It is known, however, that these voyages were mostly deliberately planned, because they took care to embark in double canoes, not only to survive on the open sea but on the unknown lands as well. Thus were pigs, dogs, chickens and useful plants, cultivated over the centuries in Southeastern Asia and then in the western Pacific, introduced into the archipelagos of eastern Polynesia.

According to what is now known, these exiles colonized central Polynesia first: the Society Islands, according to oral tradition, then the Marquesas Islands, according to archaeological research. It is in this archipelago that the most ancient levels of occupation were discovered, dating to 300 A.D. The elements of the material culture discovered are comparable to those of the Samoan Islands: simple quadrangular or triangular adzes, ornaments, and even pottery shards, the only ones to be found in eastern Polynesia. Nonetheless, some elements have no equivalent in Samoa or Tonga, which sug-

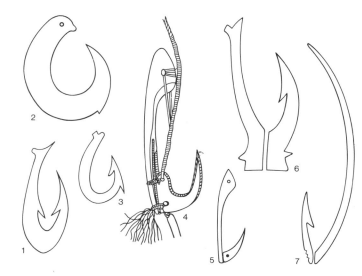

Different types of Polynesian fish hooks:
1, 2, 3. Simple blades
4, 5. Blades with a spoon for catching trout
6, 7. Compound blades

Paepae of the Marquesas Islands (island of Ua Pou). *These high lithic platforms are characteristic of the archipelago. On top, they supported an open and cobbled space and a small structure made of perishable materials. Their importance varied with their function as simple dwellings, chief's hut, or for a socio-religious purpose.* Ph. J. Garanger.

gests a time of evolution, a chronological hiatus, between the departure from western Polynesia and the first colonization of the Marqueses Islands. Perhaps more ancient sites on the Society Islands remain to be discovered.

No archaeological research has yet been conducted on the atolls of the Cook Islands to the north, the passage between western and central Polynesia. This ancient material culture continued to evolve in central Polynesia before spreading, between A.D. 600 and 700, to the Hawaiian Islands, then to New Zealand circa 800. Certain new kinds of adzes and fish hooks had by then appeared, posing troublesome questions of origin. These diverse forms, in mother-of-pearl or bone, are unknown in the southwest Pacific (except the most recent levels of the Polynesian islets isolated at the border of Micronesia and Melanesia), but are found, with all of their typological variations, more to the west and north, and as far away as Japan.

It is the same for the numerous kinds of hafted adzes (by a frontal and laterofrontal binding) and diverse cross-sections, unknown in western Polynesia and in Melanesia, but all present in eastern Asia. One could also cite the bone harpoon heads in the Marquesas Islands and in New Zealand, identical to those of the north Pacific.

The typological similarities are too numerous to be simply coincidental. They are probably the result of new supply techniques that reached eastern Polynesia, without passing by the southwest Pacific, and without having to assume new waves of migrations, such as formerly imagined to explain the peopling of the Pacific. Today it is thought that this peopling was the result of slow modification and the progressive extension of multiple networks of interisland relationships. This system provided a way in which ideas and techniques could be spread from island to island (by the archipelagos situated to the north of the equator) and be adopted very far from their origin.

Unity and Diversity in Eastern Polynesia

A small and relatively recent population, as well as the great distances that separate the center of eastern Polynesia from its extremities, explain a more homogenous cultural unity than is found in the southwest Pacific, and at the same time certain regional evolutions. The representations of the gods and ancestors, for example, the crude wooden statuary of the Hawaiian Islands, or the grimacing gods made of baskets and covered with colored flowers, are hardly comparable to the Maoric representations, very finely chiseled in wood. In the Society Islands, anthropomorphic figures are in roughly hewn stone, those spirits of ambiguous power, the ti'i. In the Marqueses Islands, these tiki are, in contrast, more carefully etched whether large statues in stone, low relief, or lithic monuments. At Easter Island, representations of ancestors became the stone giants that still astonish the world.

This diversity, starting from one ancient theme, is still seen in the arrangements of religious and profane sites. In New Zealand, the place dedicated to the cult of the ancestors remains apart from public places. In the Marquesas Islands, domestic public and religious structures are found side by side, all constructed on imposing lithic platforms. In the Society Islands, the monumental *marae* were erected around

Vestiges of a marae in Tahiti. *Ruins of these socioreligious monuments are still numerous in the mountainous interior regions of the Society Islands, abandoned after European settlement. Studying their architectural diversity and spatial arrangement provides insight into early social organization and its evolution. We see here the ruins of the* ahu, *a stone platform of three levels and about 10 feet (3 meters) high.*

the 15th century. They contain a court, perhaps enclosed by a wall, and a lithic platform, the *ahu* at one of the ends. On this platform the gods and ancestors, invited to join the living, come to sit among them. The site is a forbidden place, the property of the chieftain who raised it, symbolizing his lineage and displaying his hierarchical rank. Secular gatherings are held elsewhere, on a public site. The *heiau* of the Hawaiian Islands are somewhat similar, although of a more complex architecture. They are probably the result of a social stratification, more marked in the Society Islands than elsewhere. On Easter Island, public and religious gatherings are held in vast courts adjoining the *ahu*, the stone platform where statues of the ancestors, the *moai*, are erected.

These regional conventions quite often reflect the social structure. They were, however, largely determined, in New Zealand and Easter Island, by a necessary adaptation to nontropical environments, previously unknown by the Poly-nesians. The sailors of central Polynesia who reached New Zealand around the eighth century A.D. discovered a world very different from their homelands. They were incapable of cultivating the plants that they had brought with them, except for the sweet potato in the north, and, with difficulty, the yam and taro. They had to learn to utilize the local resources, not only to feed themselves but to equip and protect themselves from bad weather. They also discovered a large, unknown bird, the *moa* (genus *dinarnis*), an appreciable meat source, whose edible eggs also served as bowls. Its bones were useful for, among other things, the fabrication of fish hooks (because mother-of-pearl was not available). The *moa* was hunted so intensely that it disappeared early. Nevertheless the immensity of the land and the diversity of its resources allowed the Maoris to adapt successfully to this nontropical environment. It was once the same on Easter Island, small and isolated at the edge of southeast Polynesia.

Easter Island: *one of the unfinished* moai *in the quarry of the volcano Rano Raraku. The activity of the sculptors suddenly ceased with the social upheaval that shook the island at the start of the 1700s. Nearly 300 statues remain in various stages of completion, 70 erected on the slope of the volcano. Most of these stone giants would have been destined for transportation to different island locales to be erected on the* ahu. Ph. C. Lenars.

Polynological studies (of fossil pollen) have revealed that it was forested when the ancestors of the Easter Islanders discovered it, the "mystery" of the transportation of the *moai*, cut into the tuff of the Rano Raraku volcano, and their erection on the large *ahu* throughout the island, (achieved by using logs as rollers and levers). But this wood was consumed faster than nature could replace it in the porous soil and the cool and windy climate. By the 16th century, only some scraggy shrubs remained. The effects of the "small glacial age" aggravated the decline as did overpopulation: Dietary resources became scarce, yet it was no longer possible to build canoes to flee the island. By the 18th century, social disorder on a considerable scale put an end to one of the most astonishing Polynesian cultures.

Suggested Reading

Aikens, Melvin and Higuchi, Takayasu. *Prehistory of Japan.* New York and London: Academic Press, 1982.

Bellwood, P. *Man's Conquest of the Pacific: The Prehistory of Southeast Asia and Oceania.* Auckland: William Collins, 1978.

Howells, W. *The Pacific Islanders.* London: Weidenfeld & Nicolson, 1973.

Jennings, J., ed. *The Prehistory of Polynesia.* Cambridge and London: Harvard University Press, 1979.

Sahlins, Marshall. *Islands of History.* Chicago: Chicago University Press, 1987.

White, P. and O'Connell, J. F. *A Prehistory of Australia, New Guinea and Sahul.* North Ryde, New South Wales: Academic Press Australia, 1982.

Easter Island: Ahu *Nau Nau in the Anakena Bay, after restoration. The* ahu *are the lithic platforms erected along the sea and all facing in one direction. There are about 300 all around the island. As many as 20 of the* moai *were raised up there in order to represent ancestors. Transported from Rano Raraku, the finishing touches—symbolic carvings, painting, fixing a mobile eye—were done in place. Many were topped, as shown here, by a heavy red tuff. All of the* moai *were reversed on their pedestals during the internal wars of the 18th century.* Ph. J. Garanger.

CHAPTER ELEVEN

Françoise Treinen-Claustre

RECENT PREHISTORY OF AFRICA

Triangular arrowhead *with a concave base, from the Sudanese Sahara. Length, 1.75 inches (4.5 centimeters).* Paris, Museum of Man. Ph. J. Oster, Museum of Man.

The recent prehistory of Africa cannot be discussed without mentioning certain climatic and geographic conditions that presided over the birth, the flowering and the decline of the Neolithic and Post-Neolithic civilizations.

Geographic and Climatic Determinants

The habitual division between Saharan and Subsaharan Africa emphasizes the importance of the Sahara, an environment at first favorable and then hostile to human life. Less than 10,000 years ago, this was not the desert of sand and stones, one of the most desolate in the world, that we know today. An intense life thrived there. Between 7000 and 2000 B.C., a vast humid phase explains the development of climatic zones of the Mediterranean or Submediterranean, Sahelian and tropical, before the arid Saharan belt expanded, in the second millennium, beginning a process of accelerated desertification. The range of this Humid-Holocene, a climatic optimum, allowed large lakes and fish-filled rivers with verdant shores to form in the heart of the Sahara, steppes rich in grasses and wooded savannahs, inhabited by an abundant and varied fauna of small and large mammals. In such an environment black and white populations were able to settle permanently, to raise herds while continuing to hunt and fish, to practice an embryonic agriculture and to engage in the development of ceramics and a tool kit in polished stone. The inventions common to the Neolithic, defined according to socio-economic and technical criteria, were made here as elsewhere on the continent.

During the last four millennia, the progressive drying up of the Sahara exiled its inhabitants and set off significant migrations toward the south. Its vast expanses became petrified, dehumanized. It is crossed by humans, but no one settles there.

Another example of geographic and climatic determinism is the barrier of the great equatorial forest south of the Sahara that also cuts Africa in two. Hot, humid, impenetrable, this

151

forest zone—to which are linked some endemic illnesses dangerous to people (malaria) and to animals (tripanosomiasis)—has been a serious handicap to breeding and agriculture, at least before iron metallurgy was widespread. That is why there is a chronological interval in the advance of Neolithic civilizations to the south of the northern tenth parallel.

The final ecological determinant is the Kalahari Desert in southern Africa, where the harshness of the environment has maintained the Bushmen at the level of hunter-gatherers, although they have been in contact with breeders and agriculturalists. Living in small groups, dwelling in huts made of branches, they hunt with the bow and dig up roots to survive by using in a calculated manner the resources of their environment. They are the descendants of the marvelous artistic authors of the carvings and paintings of southern Africa.

The Nile Before the Pharaohs

The stereotype of an Egyptian center, the primary and unique source of cultural diffusion across Africa, from east to west, from north to south, is waning. It is nevertheless evident that the Nile valley, well irrigated by its river, was a pinnacle of civilization as early as the Neolithic and Predynastic times, before the union of Upper and Lower Egypt created a state under the authority of a pharaoh about 3000 B.C.

The excavations in the Faiyum, today a simple depression but once an ancient lake, and of Merimde in the Delta, revealed the first agriculturist-breeders of the fifth millennium, inhabiting flimsy huts of palm and matting, grouped or aligned in rows along a twisting road. Numerous hearths and grain silos have been found: buried jars, or pits lined with basketry and coated by clay. The dead were buried inside the villages, interred in a fetal position and wrapped in fabrics.

The lithic tools of these Egyptian Neolithics (in flint, jasper, limestone and volcanic rock) are varied, including millstones, polished and flaked axes, clubs, hoes, the frames of denticulate sickles and beautiful arrow heads with concave bases and bifacial retouches. Truncated and spherical vases are smoothed or polished ceramic, monochrome in red or in black. The bone industry (awls, spatulas, harpoons, pins) is advanced.

Some more southerly deposits in Sudan have revealed the existence in the fourth millennium of different Neolithic and sub-Neolithic cultures. The Khartoum culture, established on the left bank of the Blue Nile, shunned agriculture and breeding. No trace of grains is found, but remains of fish, hippopotami, buffaloes, antelopes, wart hogs, crocodiles and tortoises abound, the refuse of semisedentary fisher-hunters inhabiting wattled huts. They developed a Mesolithic-type microlithic industry in quartz (segments of circles, small blades, augers and trapezes), an abundance of barbed harpoons in bone, and a ceramic with characteristic wave decorations—the "wavy line" which has often wrongly been traced east-to-west toward the Sahara. Also found were stone rings, net weights, bone awls and needles, as well as some pearls in ostrich egg shells. Another Sudanese culture, derived from that of the Khartoum, is the Shaheinab culture, called often the "civilization of the gouges or hollow chisels" because of the large number of these tools found with clubs, axes, drawing-knives, scrapers, harpoons and fish hooks. The pygmy goat and dog were domesticated.

In the margin of this classic picture of the Neolithic, some recent discoveries urge us to place the appearance of ceramics and the domestication of oxen at an earlier date, from the seventh millennium (at Tagra, to the south of Khartoum; at Nabta Playa, in the southern Egyptian desert). A greater age for ceramics is more easily acceptable than for breeding, which it is not necessary to date, like agriculture, beyond the end of the sixth millennium.

The Badarian, Amratian, Gerzean (from the famous sites Badari, El Amrah, Gerzeh), to mention just a few cultures grouped under the Naqada, form a brilliant regional culture in Upper and Lower Egypt in Predynastic eras, contemporary with or later than the Neolithic cultures. Progress and innovation was marked, and the cutting of flint reached its apogee. Industries in bone, skins, basketry, and textiles also ad-

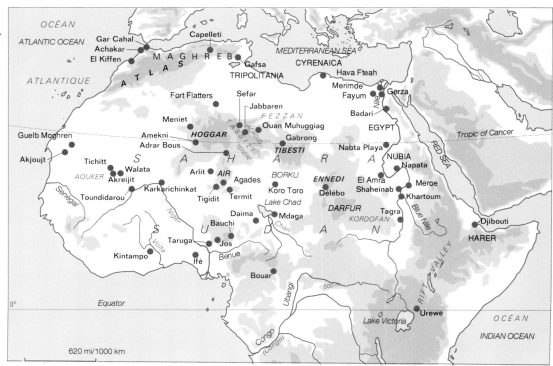

Africa north of the Equator

vanced. Ceramics, well known by the numerous offering bases discovered in the deep tombs of the vast necropolises, became increasingly refined and sophisticated, with painted polychrome decorations of geometric motifs, boats, plants and animals. The taste for adornment and personal items developed, if one judges by the multitude of pins, bracelets, necklaces, palettes for makeup and stone pearls excavated. Figurines, anthropomorphic and geomorphic, in ivory, sandstone and terra-cotta, testify to an art in full development. Copper was worked by hammering, and gold and silver were first used. Other technological improvements include better irrigation systems and rectangular housing with clay or raw brick walls, converging toward a rapid social evolution that leads to the historic eras.

The Neolithic Cultures of the Maghreb and the Sahara

The Saharan Neolithic is known through the profusion of arrow heads, polished axes, millstones, pottery and many other objects (ornaments, tools or weapons in bone), gathered sometimes by chance on prehistoric surface deposits. Certainly, with the Neolithic appears a new archaeological wealth of personal objects, corresponding to the improving technology particularly evident in this part of Africa. However the Neolithic evolution is not limited to this rich arsenal. Other components, even if they are more difficult to determine here than in the Near East or in Europe, are essential. Although the activities of hunting, gathering and fishing will continue to be essential, breeding and agriculture, leading to the settlement process or led by it, slowly develop.

Although the linkage in time and in space of the diverse components of the Neolithic is rather complex, some general lines are evident. The long duration and the great age of the Neolithic around the Saharan massifs are no longer in question. For about 20 years the number of tests of radiometric age has unleashed a kind of "war of dates." Through such datings, claims are made for such or such a development in such or such a place. Numerous ^{14}C dates, between the fifth and eighth millennia B.C., have been obtained for sites with ceramics at Hoggar (Amekni, In Hanakaten), Air (Mount Bagzanes), Ennedi (Delebo) and Tibesti (Gabrong). Thus the greater age of the Neolithic civilizations of the Nile Valley compared to those of the central Sahara has been disproven and the latter has become seen as an early focus of Neolithic industry and a center of ceramic invention, independent of the cultures of the Mediterranean and the Nile. The pastoral vocation of the Neolithic population has been established and a preagricultural economy even prevailed in certain regions. It is equally likely that the fisher-hunters, proto-agriculturalists and breeders, before living in large permanent and well-structured villages, had begun to settle, explaining the grouping of more or less temporary constructions in perishable materials or the plans of underground shelters.

Another important point consists in recognizing the variety of cultural features in North Africa and the Sahara. Three principal avenues of the Neolithic process corresponding to the Sahara-Sudanese Neolithic, the Neolithic of the Mediterranean and Atlantic littoral, and the Neolithic of the Capsian tradition have been distinguished.

The Sahara-Sudanese Neolithic, whose name reflects not a strict unity but a cultural relationship between the Sahara and the regions situated along its southern edge, began as early as the eighth millennium, covering vast period of time and revealing numerous regional variations. It is characterized by a rich and abundant ceramic industry, next to a less-developed lithic one. The bone industry comprises polishing tools, awls and, in a more recent phase, harpoons and fish hooks. Large vessels with simple forms, spherical, hemi-

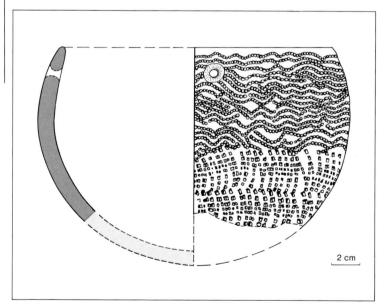

2 cm

2 cm

(Left) **Reconstruction of the decoration of a vase** of the ancient Neolithic period of Tibesti (Tirenna). This flame motif was common and obtained by using a comb.

(Above) **Reconstruction of a spheroid vase** of the ancient period of Tibesti (Gabrong). It is adorned with a wave decoration (wavy lines).

spheric, or cylindrical in shape are completely decorated with variable impressions of combs, awls or stamps, of hollow plant stems, braided coils, or pricks from fish spears. One of the most common is a motif of flames, obtained by a pivoting impression of a comb.

Amekni is the type site of the ancient phase of the Saharan-Sudanese Neolithic of the fifth and sixth millennia. Settled on a granite ridge, a small community had erected huts between blocks of stone. Men hunted horse, buffalo, wart hogs and gazelles on the surrounding savannahs; they captured perches and catfish of the *wadi* in dikes or by constructing dams. Millet was perhaps cultivated in the valley, dotted with olive trees, nettle trees and other fruit trees. In the encampment, women ground edible grains from colocynth between the granite millstones. A peaceful site, lacking only oxen and sheep.

The Tenere who occupied the Tenere of Tafessasset extending as far as Tassili and Barkou, developed a brilliant culture in the Middle Neolithic in the fourth and third millennia. Many refinements are evident in this society of cattle breeders, including polished tools, pestles, millstones, necked axes. These accomplished stonecutters used jasper to fashion fine elongated arrowheads, hacking knives, foliated pieces, very flat disks and some knives that recall Predynastic Egypt. They were also excellent sculptors of animals who fashioned statuettes of bovids, gazelles, ram heads and other animals in granite, basalt, sandstone and gneiss.

The Dahr Tichitt has been named as the last Neolithic "paradise." Toward the end of the third millennium, as the desert took hold, the region of Aouker in southeast Mauritania was favored by relative humidity and, until the middle of the first millennium was a place of refuge for shepherds retreating from the north. All along the arc of cliffs of Tichitt-Walata, extend the ruins of more than 100 fortified Neolithic villages. Along the pools of water on the plain or on the edge of the plateau that the breeders of sheep, goats, and cattle were established, as are the antelope hunters and fishers, and very probably millet cultivators.

The Tichitt-Walata culture is characterized by its numerous dry stone constructions that testify to a permanent

(Right) **View of one of the fortified villages** *established along the cliff of T'chitt-Walata (Mauritania). Dating to the end of the Neolithic, these constructions in dry stone were placed into a network of plazas, streets and enclosures in a true urban center.* Ph. Renaudeau-Hoa-Qui.

(Above) **Millstone and grinder in quartzite** *from the Adrar region in the Algerian Sahara. Length of the millstone, 12.5 inches (32 centimeters); length of the grinder, 6 inches (15 centimeters).* Paris, Museum of Man. Ph. J. Oster, Museum of Man.

settlement, the first display of architecture and proto-urbanism. Villages, encircled by defensive walls, enclosed plazas, networks of streets and courts. The main element was the enclosure or court where one lives, keeps water, wood and seeds. The village of Akreijit, particularly well studied, has 128 such spaces over five acres (two hectares) structured with pillars, circles of stones and hearths.

The Neolithic of the Atlantic and Mediterranean littoral of the Maghreb is marked by exterior influences of civilizations that had developed in the western basin of the Mediterranean as early as the sixth and fifth millennia. Thus the presence of the corded ceramic that is characteristic of the Ancient Mediterranean Neolithic is explained in small caves along the Moroccan coast, like those of Achakar and Gar Cahal. Obsidian, which is found in several deposits on the Tunisian and Algerian coasts, is imported from the Lipari and Pantelleria Islands. A south Iberian influence very probably affected the remarkable ceramic group from the tomb of El Kiffen (near Casablanca). In general, the material culture of the Mediterranean Neolithic did not display the same bril-

liance as that of the Sahara, but the economy of the littoral populations thrived.

The Capsian Neolithic tradition, formed in Capsian, a culture of the Epipaleolithic identified in the region of Gafsa in Tunisia, appeared later than the Sahara-Sudanese or the Mediterranean Neolithic. The Neolithic descendants of the Capsians occupied eastern Algeria, southern Tunisia, northern Libya, the Saharan Atlas and the northern Sahara. They are Mediterraneans of a white race, in contrast to the first negroid occupants of the Sahara. Their civilization has well-noted characteristics. While ceramics are not abundant (vessels with conical bottoms, decorated only under the rim), the lithic industry is exceptional: flint blades (polished from contact with graminae or cereals), fine small blades, drills, small scrapers, microburins and especially microliths and innumerable points in a variety of forms. In the immediate region of Fort Flatters, 3,300 points have been found.

Another characteristic was the use of ostrich egg shells, transformed into containers, finely carved and decorated by geometric or animal motifs. The bone industry was diversi-

fied, and objects of ornamentation in stone, bone or shell abound. The last demonstration of the Neolithic people of the Capsian tradition is found in the cave art of the Atlas, whose representations of bovines, rams and sheep led by the shepherds, confirm the practice of the domestication of animals.

The Cattle Herders

The appearance of domestic animals in Africa progressed from the north toward the south of the continent. In Egypt cattle and sheep are known as early as the fifth millennium B.C. The Mediterranean fringe of Libya and Algeria bred small livestock (*Ovis longipes*) at this early date; also in Cyrenaica, Libya, (Haua Fteah cave) and in the Aures (Capelleti cave) in Algeria. The ox (*Bos ibericus*) appears as well. Sites of the Saharan massif of Acacus (Ouan Muhuggiag, Ouan Telocat) furnish dates from the sixth and fifth millennia for the domestication of oxen. It is uncertain if the animal (which also exists in Southeast Asia), was introduced by emigrants coming from Greece or Crete by a maritime route or was native. The case of the sheep is more simple, because there exists no local root stock for ovines.

In the fourth millennium, the Sahara is a clear attraction for shepherds, who found good pasturage in the well-watered massifs. The deposits between 4000 and 3000 B.C. are numerous (Meniet, Adrar Bous, Arlit, Sefar, Sabbaren). Starting around 2500 B.C., a second migration of breeders as far as the equatorial forest corresponds to a dispersion of game herds toward the south as the increasingly arid Sahara becomes a desert.

Between 2500 B.C. and the start of the modern era, the domestication of cattle and/or sheep and goats is attested to in the Subsaharan zone up to the edge of the large forest and on the plateaus of eastern Africa. Mali, at Karkarichinkat

(2000 to 1500 B.C.), in Mauritania, at Tichitt (1500 B.C.), central Ghana, at Kintampo (1500 B.C.), on the banks of Lake Chad, at Mdaga and at Daima (500 B.C.), and far to the east, in the highlands of Kenya and the Rift Valley (1000 B.C.). Pastoralism appears there in an environment with features of what some authors call the "Late Stone Age." Hunting and fishing populations passed slowly to an economy of production. Microliths are found side by side with polished axes, ceramic or stone containers, millstones and arrowheads.

In the rest of Africa, it is only at the start of the first centuries A.D., or a little before, that livestock will penetrate the lands situated between the Equator and the Cape. Present rather early around Lake Victoria, livestock will arrive in Zambia only in the fifth century A.D., with iron, and to the south of Rhodesia only toward the year 1000.

The domestication of animals is sometimes difficult to prove because of the absence of ancient bone remains, or those badly preserved. In the Sahara, the information furnished by cave art largely compensates for this deficiency. Thousands of paintings and engravings, made between the Nile and the Atlantic, depict oxen in abundance. Their predomination together with sheep, goats and some wild fauna, is so marked that a "bovine period" has been distinguished in the evolution of wall art; it covers a large part of the Neolithic and reaches its apogee in the fourth and third millennia, during the pastoral phase of the Middle Neolithic. No doubt human beings dominated bovines then. One is struck by the frequency of representations of enormous herds of domestic oxen with magnificent ploychrome coats complicated design, advancing with dignity under the guidance of their guardians, sometimes carrying richly dressed women. Certain details, such as the artificial deformation of the horns, and the bearing of jugulars testify as well to the existence of breeding methods, because they are customarily linked to those. These marvelous compositions provide us with fascinating information on the physical types, the dress of the "Bovineans" and their daily life. The population is not uniform; we see depicted Ethiopians, Hamites, dark, slender, bearded, strongly resembling the Peuls of today. Other types are juxtaposed: blacks, whites and Mediterraneans. The figures may be naked, but they are frequently dressed in loin cloths or in tunics without sleeves, with one shoulder bare; headdresses sport horns and feathers. They are equipped with throwing sticks and lances, but especially with the bow, arrows held in the hand or carried in a quiver. The women are often elegant, with their hair formed into a crest or voluminous braids, long dresses and flowing skirts, and aprons made from goat or gazelle skins. They wear bracelets, necklaces, pectorals and other ornamentations.

Work and leisure are revealed in numerous realistic scenes. In front of circular huts, near which are seated women and children, calves are in a line, attached to a cord, while adult beasts are gathered behind. One man is in the process of milking a cow, another plays with a child. In the interior spaces, where pottery and goatskins are depicted, figures

Herd of oxen. *This wall painting of Sefar, in Tassili, is from the Middle Neolithic. The presence of realistic details (many oxen, huts, millstones, jewelry, etc.) provides important information about the human and animal environment of this "Bovine" epoch.* Ph. Boizot/Explorer.

sleep or eat. A woman grinds grain with a mortar or mills it on a stone. Hunters pursue game with the help of their dog, tied to the line characteristically coiled. It is necessary to mention scenes of dancing, mating, conversation to these examples, which could be infinitely multiplied. Only the religious or magical aspect of the bovine art is hard to find.

The Mystery of the Chariots

At the end of the Neolithic era, the age of the "horse" succeeds the "bovine" age in northern and western Africa, throughout the first millennium B.C. This is the epoch of the "equidaean" cave paintings and engravings, which represent horse breeders, chariot drivers or horsemen, and is the consequence of the introduction of the horse to the Sahara, and, a technological event directly linked to it: the use of the wheel and the construction of the chariots.

The horse is clearly not indigenous to Africa; its European or Asian origin is probable. Known in Egypt as early as the 16th century B.C., it seems to diffuse gradually through the eastern Libyans, from Cyrenaica towards the south (Fezzan, Saharan massifs) and the west (Tripolitania, Maghreb). This first domestic horse is the ancestor of the Barbary Horse, of heavy gait, but a good mount.

The distribution of paintings and carvings of chariots, harnessed or led by a coachman, or unharnessed, covers an immense area from the Atlantic to the Nile, from the Atlas to the Sudanese savannahs. More than 600 figures have been recorded, which have never ceased to intrigue archaeologists. Some have imagined "trans-Saharan" chariot routes, some axis of northeast-southeast penetration, obtained by linking the sites and following the zones of concentration. Two paths appear, one from Fezzan to the loop of the Niger past Tassili, the other, from the Saharan Atlas to the south of Mauritania. These axis routes are now very controversial, because the location of the figures of chariots is in part attributable to the presence of an adequate rocky base; however, that these chariots existed and were used for prehistoric peoples, proven by recent experiments, becomes the point of interest.

The Saharan chariots are generally designed for two horses, with two wheels, not necessarily made out of metal; four-wheeled vehicles are rarer. The harnessing remains simple: no shoulder collar or hoist strap, loose reins, yokes or crossbars for stabilizing the shaft. A platform made of lashed leather carries the rider. Certain chariots are represented "in a flying gallop," with the four legs of the horses shown off of the ground, a position frequently encountered on the paintings of Hoggar, Tassili and Acacus. Other carvings are more schematic.

The Equidaeans, chariot riders or horsemen, are often shown armed with javelins and lances, and carry a round shield. Dressed in a short tunic, their features are unclear. During the late phase of the "horse" age, the bitrangular anthropomorphic figurines are stylized, with squared shoulders and thin forms.

The function of the chariots has often been speculated upon. Too light at 65 pounds (30 kilos) to serve as a means of commercial transportation, they have been called sporting vehicles or vehicles of war. Certainly, Herodotus mentioned the Garamantes of Fezzan, or Equidaeans pursuing the Ethiopians with their four-wheeled chariots, but this mortial use must have been limited. Another explanation has been proposed that chariots were prestigious devices, belonging to the warrior castes to dominate the inferior populations.

The use of the chariot was abandoned at the start of our era. It is at this moment that the camel or, more correctly, the dromedary, an animal better adapted to the desert conditions than the horse, appeared in North Africa. Multiplying rather rapidly, it would play a determining role in the establishment of trans-Saharan liaisons and commercial relations, and serve as a precious aide in wars. With its appearance downs the "camelid" era, marked as well by the emergence of iron metallurgy. In the wall art of the Berber horsemen, camel drivers stylized with the lance or short spear are represented. Arriving from Asia, the dromedary was introduced into Egypt after the Persian conquest in the seventh century B.C., then expands toward Cyrenaica and Maghreb, Nubia and central and southern Sahara.

The Origins of African Agriculture

Agriculture here is noted by the transition from simple gathering of plants to the deliberate preparation of the soil to grow crops from tubers or seeds. This change was certainly not abrupt, and the progress of the agricultural econ-

omy, in several parts of Africa, must have been slow and staggered. This is why the term proto-agriculture is so often used in relation to the economy of the Neolithic Saharan and Subsaharan, requiring preliminary steps in order to proceed to a true agricultural evolution.

The evidence of the existence of agriculture is diverse: identification of cereal pollens, the gathering of seeds, the imprints of seeds in pottery clay and the presence of milling materials and agricultural tools. The direct proof of the domestication of plants is unfortunately very rare in certain regions, because of the poor preservation of seeds and fossilized pollens. For this reason indirect proof should be accepted with caution. The millstone could have served to grind wild seeds, digging sticks to destroy uncultivated plant roots. Axes and hoes in polished, flaked stone, outside of a clear archaeological context, are often the only meager sign of a struggling agriculture, sometimes late and even dating to the Iron Age. This is the case with the beautiful polished axes in hematite, with Uelian features from northern Zaire, hoes from Guinea and lithic tools from other cultures of the Late Stone Age in the forested lands of Central Africa (Cameroon, Gabon, Congo). It is no longer accepted that ceramics are born from the alimentary modifications related to agriculture and are proof of its existence. The Saharan cave representations are not helpful here, because none of the scenes depicted are truly agricultural. Botanists are thus of considerable assistance in clarifying the problem of the origin of domesticated plants.

Despite the difficulty in finding traces of plants formerly cultivated, their identification has been established in their respective area of domestication, even if their date of appearance sometimes remains uncertain or unclear and it has been proven that the African continent was the birthplace of some agriculture and horticultural developments. The most ancient cultivated plants, wheat and barley, originally from Southeast Asia, came from the agricultural center of the Near East. Dependent upon winter rains of a Mediterranean climatic regime, they are found in North Africa, in the Nile Valley, where irrigation systems were significant, and in Ethiopia, where they have been maintained because of the altitude and climate. In the tropical zone they were unable to adapt to summer rains, and it is there that indigenous wild seeds were domesticated. The Sahelian zone formed a primitive agricultural center for the first cultivations of millet, the most important grain in Africa.

Sorghum, or thick millet, also called Guinea wheat, was cultivated as early as the third millennium, between the desert and the savannah, from the Nile to Lake Chad. In the Sudan, it appeared as early as 4000 B.C. Its dispersion was vast, at first toward the west, later, during the first millennium A.D., toward the south, at the time of the expansion of the Bantu agriculturists, for whom the cultivation of sorghum was traditional.

Tufted millet (*Pennisetum*), or small millet, or pearl millet, was domesticated from the Atlantic to the west of the Nile. It would have been domesticated in the fifth millennium at Hoggar, because at Amekni, two pollen seeds have been identified, which by their size would relate them to a cultivated *Pennisetum*, and at Meniet two other cereal pollens have been found. This slim evidence of the existence of a truly ancient agriculture in the central Sahara needs to be confirmed. The cultivation of tufted millet however, is definitely

(Left) **Chariot in a "flying gallop."** Wall painting of Illizi (Wadi Djerat, Tabakat-n-Rali). This description was suggested by the manner of representing the extended legs of the horses. These very numerous depictions of the "equidaean" era (first millennium B.C.) highlight the importance of the introduction of the horse (of European or Asiatic origin) and that of the chariot. Ph. Thomas/Explorer.

(Above) **Dromedaries, horsemen and warriors** with weapons. Painting from Sefar, in Tassili, belonging to the "Camelid era." The dromedary was introduced first in Egypt after the Persian conquest, then penetrated into the Sahara. Its presence aided, in particular, the diffusion of the metallurgy of iron throughout Africa. Ph. F. de Keroualin.

present at the end of the second millennium at Tichitt, in Mauritania, where impressions of *Pennisetum* seeds in pottery have been found. The extension of this grain reaches the Equator only at the end of the first millennium A.D. while the Pygmies of the great forest will remain hunter-gatherers even until the 20th century.

Grass, especially cultivated in East Africa, was domesticated in Ethiopia and in the north of Uganda. Fonio, another variety of millet, appears in the savannahs of West Africa, but we possess no archaeological data concerning no more than for teff, a local plant whose cultivation is limited to Ethiopia. There exists as well a specifically African rice, different from the Asian rice introduced later by the Arabs and Europeans. Its cultivation may be ancient in the Nile Delta, but for this grain we lack any archaeological information.

Horticulture and arboriculture were born at the edge of the forest in the arboreal savannahs of Nigeria and Ghana, which was the site of the first indigenous cultivation of certain roots, such as yams, and certain trees, such as the varieties of palm oil trees. The local cultivation of yams, tubers with great nutritive value, was very important and could date back several millennia. Palm oil, rich in protein and vitamins, apparently known in Ghana toward the middle of the second millennium B.C., will become one of the alimentary bases of several lands of humid, tropical Africa. In the southwestern part of Ethiopia, the Abyssinian banana will be cultivated for the consumption of its root. A certain number of vegetables (okra, varieties of spinach, gourds, melons) and leguminous plants (certain varieties of beans and peas) are of African origin and have been domesticated as well, but their ages are not certain. Plantain, manioc, corn were imported from Asia or America.

The First African Metallurgy

The chrono-cultural order of the ages of metal is clearly defined where the succession of the Copper, Bronze and Iron Ages is steady. This is not the case in Africa. Protohistoric Africa is regarded as an obscure period. The existence of an ancient Copper Age is attested to in certain regions, but the appearance of iron often precedes copper and copper and bronze alloys.

The use of copper is first known in the Nile Valley, as early as the Predynastic period; that of bronze is developed there in the historic era. In North Africa, in the second millennium B.C., traces of a Copper and a Bronze Age are perceptible, notably in the western part of Maghreb, where the cultural influences from southwest Europe are most easily discernible: the importation of objects in copper (points, flat axes, daggers), the introduction of bell-shaped beaker pottery from the Iberic Chalcolithic, and the plausible appearance of a metallurgy of bronze, whose presence is suggested by the daggers and the halberds in images carved on the rocks of the High Atlas of Morocco.

In the western Sahara, the metallurgy of copper precedes that of iron. In effect, a Chalcolithic existed in Mauritania during the first millennium B.C., in the area of Akjoujt, which is rich in copper ore. The copper-bearing deposits of Guelb Moghrein were exploited from the eighth to the third centuries B.C. for the production of axes, points lance heads, awls and other small objects.

Another center of copper metallurgy has been discovered in Niger, in the region of Agadez. It seems this is the oldest center of metal use in the Subsahara—non-Nile Africa—dating to the start of the second millennium B.C. The numerous remains of furnaces, discovered near the cliff of Tigidit, prove the smelting of metal. This copper industry is divided into two phases: Copper I (around 2000 to 800 B.C.), corresponding to a premetallurgy using natural copper, and Copper II (around 800 B.C. to the beginning of the Christian era), a veritable metallurgy processing different types of ore. In the Niger, as in Mauritania, the same kind of low furnace was used. Objects of copper (very flat arrowheads, spatulas, pins, burins) were fabricated by hammering the hot metal. The forgers were probably traveling artisans.

Western Africa also knew an early iron industry. Iron was worked in the Niger, in the massif of Termit, as early as the seventh century B.C., and in the region of Agadez in the fifth century B.C. However, it is in Niger, on the plateau of Jos, that this metallurgy was particularly developed, from the middle of the first millennium B.C., without being preceded by a copper industry. The excavations of Taruga have provided remains of furnaces associated with terra-cotta figures, which characterize the famous "Nok culture " and form the evidence of a remarkable ancient sculptural art in Africa, similar to that later in Ife and Benin. A deep stylistic unity is characteristic of this group of human heads, where naturalism and schematization are combined. The technique of perforating triangular eyes, nostrils and ears is typical.

The quality of these works of art should not make us forget that Nok was an important center of iron production, whose antiquity and geographical situation pose the general problem of the origin and the diffusion of iron in Africa. There works were imported by the Assyrians in Egypt, from where it expanded outward, back down the Nile, into the Kingdom of Meroe, one of the primitive centers of the iron industry between 400 and 200 B.C. It was used by the Phoenicians in the colonies of the Mediterranean coast.

It is at the beginning of the Nile corridor and the Mediterranean basin that the advocates of diffusionist theories believe that iron conquered the remainder of the continent. For certain others, Kushite metallurgists, following the rulers of the Kingdom of Meroe, would have transmitted to Kordofan, Darfour and Chad the iron, which would have then progressed toward western Africa, across the Nile-Chadian savannah. This metal could have traveled as well along the White Nile to enter central or eastern Africa. Other archaeologists favor the Trans-Saharan movement of cultural diffusion from northwest Africa toward the Niger and claim the Berber origin for iron working in Africa. Finally, for some authors, there exists independent centers of African iron production; Nok would be one of these autonomous centers. Taking a strong stand for one of the three theses mentioned is nonproductive, each region providing a different answer to the problem of the emergence of the iron industry. For example, the metallurgy of the Bauchi plateau, in Nigeria, seems to owe nothing to Meroe. On the other hand, the culture of the Iron Age of Koro-Toro, in northern Chad, which reaches its peak between the third and eighth centuries A.D., displays Egyptian-Nubian affinities through its beautiful red and black painted pottery.

In the middle southern region of Africa, the most ancient manifestations of an Iron Age are encountered in the north and west region of Lake Victoria, in Uganda. The Bantu population, possessing the secrets of metallurgy, would have been moved to the east, leaving southern Cameroon and middle Benoue, their homelands, to establish the culture of Urewe during the last three centuries B.C. The knowledge would then have been transmitted during the first part of the

(Left) **Speaking figure** *with a halbard to his right and a dagger above his head. This engraving from Gogour (High Atlas, Morocco), dates to the Bronze Age. Rendered by J. Malhomme.* Extracted: Bulletin of Moroccan Archaeology, T.III, 1958–59, p. 386.

Chap 11, p. 160–61, #2

Nok art. *Female terra-cotta head (500 B.C. to 200 A.D.).*
This very beautiful figurine, which evokes the much later art of Benin or Ife, is an example of the Nok culture, an important center of iron production but also a center of sculpture, remarkable for its balance between naturalism and stylization. Jos, Nigeria, National Museum. Ph. Held-Artephot.

first millennium A.D., at first in Tanzania and Kenya, then in Zambia, Mozambique and Zimbabwe. The characteristic ceramics of the Urewe culture included containers with umbilical bases or "dimple-based" pottery and is similar to another kind of fluted pottery ("channeled ware"), both widely distributed. With these ceramics are found the remains of furnaces, sometimes tall, decorated brick kilns, like those in Rwanda. Ore was plentiful and forging techniques were simple. Iron was extracted by the "catalan" method or smelted at low temperatures.

The rapid expansion of the varied cultures and the rapid diffusion of the metallurgy of iron during the first millennium-A.D., covering an extended territory south of the Equator, are often compared to the expansion of the Bantu. In addition to the techniques of metal working these people brought a knowledge of ceramics to groups of hunter-gatherers who had remained at the technological level of the Stone Age. To iron working were also added gold and copper metallurgy, which had a particular importance in the northern and southern areas of Zambezi.

Toward the end of the first millennium and during the first half of the second millennium A.D., the north coast of Africa entered history and belongs to the successive Mediterranean civilizations. The east coast was opened to various external influences: Arabs, Indians, Indonesians, etc., before the European colonizers arrived. Tropical Africa maintained strong contact with the Islamic world. However, the interior of the continent witnessed the expansion of local cultures and the birth of African kingdoms and states. For example, the art of the Sao civilization, on the Chadian plain, is one of the most original, amazing and significant in Africa, expressed in a rich statuary of clay and bronze.

Megalithism and Funerary Monuments

Megalith building appears in Africa in very diverse forms, including dolmens, menhirs and stela, stone circles and funerary monuments. Its appearance is later than in Europe, but its area of distribution was vast. The African megalithic civilizations develop in North Africa, in the whole of the Sahara, Senegambia, Mali, the Central African Republic and in Ethiopia, to name only some of the most prominent.

In North Africa, dolmens, hypogea and burial mounds are numerous. The eastern Maghreb is rich in megalithic burials and hypogea, whose Mediterranean origin is clear. The dolmens of northern Tunisia and eastern Algeria, dating as far as back as the second millennium B.C. have chambers set into low burial mounds, bordered by a circle of stones, or inserted into a base with steps. Some large megalithic monuments in Morocco and central Tunisia, much more recent, show a great complexity, including porticos, multiple chambers and ceremonial rooms. The hypogea of the Bronze Age, comparable to the burials in Sicily, are dug into the cliffs and rocks of the littoral, particularly to the east of the Maghreb. Small and square, they sometimes contain a primitive corridor.

The North African burial mounds, widely distributed, seem native and represent several kinds present throughout the Sahara: the "redjem," the "chouche" and the "bazinas." The redjem are conical or sub-conical burial mounds formed by a simple piling up of stone, covering individual or collective graves. The chouchet type corresponds to a low, cylin-

(Above) **Vase painted red and black** *Koro-toro civilization (northern Chad). Representative of the Iron Age (circa 500 B.C.), this civilization reached its apogee between the third and eighth centuries A.D. The shapes and colors of its painted pottery recall that of Egypto-Nubian art.* Ph. F. Treinen-Claustre.

(Right) **Sao art**. *Horseman of terracotta. The figurines of the Sao, established in the plain of Chad, maintain a purely African tradition, which seems to have escaped any outside influence. Height 12 inches (31 centimeters).* Private collection. Ph. Held-Artephot.

drical cake-shaped grave containing a small quadrangular or circular central chamber, with room for the deposition of a body in an often contracted position. The bazinas are burial mound monuments with steps.

The Saharan dry stone funeral monuments made of are particularly varied and numerous. Often grouped in vast necropolises, they occur on the flanks of the mountains where there are rocky plateaus. The name of "Preislamic tombs" given to such burial sites reveals the imprecision of their dating. They are located in a wide chronological range, from the Neolithic to modern times, some range in age from the protohistoric to the Iron Age. In the Fezzan, they were used as tombs of the Garamantes war chiefs, of the Equidaean epoch.

Certain characteristic structures of Hoggar, Tassili or Tibesti merit attention: burial mounds, surrounded by dressed slabs erected on a perimeter; burial mounds hollowed out in a crater with a central shaft; immense flagstones in the shape of crescents, elongated by antennae, open to the east; monuments composed of elliptical or circular wall, linked to a central burial mound by a corridor, in the shape of a "keyhole"; finally, large bazinas, in various degrees, with diverse layouts, including alleys, niches and altars.

West Africa is a landscape of shaped stones. The group of 180 monoliths of Tundidaro, in Mali, is a good example. Other sites are known in Mauritania, the Niger, Togo and Senegal. The Senegambian megalithic group is the most important: more than 16,000 monuments in an area of 11,500 square miles (30,000 square kilometers). Three main types of monuments, dating from the second century B.C. to the sixth century A.D., have been studied: the circle of monoliths, the tumulus rock formed from a mound full of laterite blocks, the circle stones forming a circular wall of laterite blocks. An exterior frontal structure completes the circle that forms the superstructure of collective graves.

In the Central African Republic, the megalithic civilization is concentrated in the northwest, in the Bouar region. It is represented by stone boxes, formed form three slabs placed

Stone circle in Senegal (c. 10th to 11th centuries A.D.). Three kinds of funerary monuments that dominate in the west of Africa have been documented: the circle of monoliths, the stone tumulus and the stone circle, erected with lateritic blocks.

on edge, a low wall of dry stones and a stone slab. These vaults often aligned, are found in the oval-shaped tumulus topped by standing stones reaching 13 feet (4 meters) in height. Called *tajunu* ("standing stones") by the local populations they date to the first millennium A.D.

The three basic shapes of megalithic building, dolmens, tumulus and stelas, are found in Ethiopia and Djibouti. The dolmens, large blocks, are grouped in necropolises in the mountains above Harar. They are individual burial sites built during the second millennium B.C. The stela, less ancient, are numbered in the thousands. They may have a phallic appearance or be etched in relief. The tumulus are numerous in Ethiopia and the area near Djibouti, where some original shapes have been noted.

Aerial view of the ruins of Zimbabwe, capital of the Mononotapa empire, at the end of the first millennium A.D. Ph. Gester-Rapho.

Suggested Reading

Clark, J. D. *The Prehistory of Africa.* New York and London: Thames and Hudson, 1970.

Oliver, R. and Fagan, Brian M. *Africa in the Iron Age.* Cambridge: Cambridge University Press, 1975.

Phillipson, D. W. *The Later Prehistory of Eastern and Southern Africa.* London: Heinemann, 1977.

CHAPTER TWELVE

Jean Gascó

PROTOHISTORY OF EUROPE

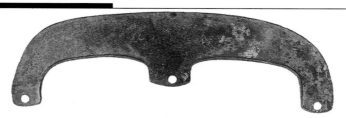

Bronze tools, *produced by the dynastic civilization of Mesopotamia at the end of the third millennium. Adzes, flat hatchets and fenestrated hatchets were made, first in the local areas of Anatolia or the Iranian plateau. With Egypt, the Indus Valley, Asia Minor and the Near East, Mesopotamia is one of the hearts of metallurgy of copper and bronze. Ph. Briard.*

During the second millennium B.C., the European people adopt bronze, an alloy more resistant than copper, which they still worked. Tin will create the wealth of the regions of Bohemia, Cornwall and Galicia. Commercial relations between peoples are being consolidated, amber from the Baltic Sea, so prized by the artisans of the Aegean world, competes against poor-quality material of eastern glass; trinkets or bronze weapons begin to circulate. The last Copper Age groups, Bell Beaker and Corded Ware makers skillfully exploit this change. At first, from 1900 to 1500 B.C., metal objects are unequally divided among the various segments of society, but the commerce and desire for bronze objects will contribute to their diffusion in the course of a middle phase, from 1500 to 1100 B.C., of metallurgy. During the final Bronze period, significant villages without their own workshops are rare. Such economic expansion engenders, in different rhythms according to the regions, a general change of lifestyle, the consequences of which already suggest the organization of historic societies.

The Model Unetice

Toward the end of the third millennium, ingot-targnes of copper produced in Asia Minor reach outer Europe. The blacksmiths of Bohemia-Moravia copy them and expand their use from the north to Transylvania. The tin from Bohemia permitted the Unetice civilization, named after a necropolis near Prague, to produce a series of bronze objects: Pins for clothing, daggers carved with geometric motifs, flat axes, halberds, etc. are found in dwellings or the burial site of Unetician tribes. The first "smelter's caches" are also seen. The caches enclose both finished and rough-hewn objects, and ingots. Often local wares are found next to imported goods, with scraps from objects that were refounded. During the centuries, the practice of burying such hoards is seen more and more in Europe.

Trade and exchange of all sorts profited the peoples of Bavaria and Saxony. The former had become specialists in the production of bar ingots and ornaments and conical *tutulus* for clothes; the latter controlled the sale of weapons from Unetice. A rich aristocracy formed in Saxony; although their power was rather short-lived, monumental tombs affirm their temporal might. Lesser lords were buried in funerary houses of wooden beams, with roofs made of planks and thatch. Sometimes the death of a chief also demanded the sacrifice of a servant or a relative, as at Leubingen. Funeral rites were conducted in the Campaniform tradition with individual tombs, the bodies in contracted positions. Burials in jars in the eastern fashion (in Bohemia) and the incineration of children were rare. Unetice pieces are imitated as far as southern Europe, then regional workshops developed their own styles. From the upper course of the Soane, from Doubs to the low Rhone Valley, the Rhodanian civilization maintains, at the start of the second millennium, the circulation of alpine objects in exchange for Mediterranean products. Beautiful daggers with geometric decorations, various axes, ornamentation always subject to the taste of fashion, will reach the central Massif and Aquitaine. Multicolor shells from the south, in turn, will advance as far as Bohemia.

Necklaces made from these rare shells, among which are the famous columbelles, appear to have symbolized distinction and social power. During the Middle Bronze, their diffusion will diminish considerably. The canoes and river rafts, the first chariots with wooden wheels allow transports hazarding days. Valleys and alpine passes connect the western world with Piedmont and Lombardy. The culture of Polada rules from villages established on the bank of alpine lakes and rivers, the gates of the Adriatic. Its blacksmiths were inspired by the continental metallurgy to produce torques with whorls and various pins, then daggers and axes. In borrowing their container shapes from the people of southern Italy, the potters of Polada affirm their Mediterranean affinities. They make an elegant pottery whose popularity will last for several centuries in the western Mediterranean.

The Princes of the Atlantic

The lands fronting the Atlantic and the North Sea became another center of civilization. Gold, copper and stanniferous lodes assured the wealth of the Atlantic developments. They discovered early the secret of molten glass, turned blue by copper salts. Gold from Ireland and southern England was exported over the continent; *lunulas*, hammered crescents, were worn on the chest, attached by small chains or hooks. In Normandy, Poitou and as far as Languedoc, torques with helicoidal forms and hooks of great beauty were formed. The brilliant civilization of Wessex was in the center of this trend. Its princes are known to us by vast tumuli, circular trenches enclosing their burial sites. They also erected or embellished large structures, formed from posts placed in concentric circles (Woodhenge) or menhirs, as in Avebury or Stonehenge. These monuments (and their accompanying rituals) were probably born in the Neolithic period, serving as astronomical temples where priests and sorcerers officiated. These elite appear to have come from German lands on the North Sea. They imposed their practices, particularly burials on local groups, but they did not allow them to share their riches. In Brittany they formed a society very like that in Wessex. The most powerful were buried in tombs in the Nordic style, but these houses of the dead, made of birch,

Protohistory of Europe

thatch and ferns, did not survive in the megalithic traditions of Breton. In Armorica, the tumulus covered stone vaults, for individual (not collective) burials. The rich funerary personal goods involved in these burials sometimes were contained in oak boxes. This culture perfected flint arrowheads, amber pendants, pins, axes, metal daggers in skin or leather sheaths. The bronze blade handles are sometimes studded; one from Kernonen-en-Plouvorn, pricked by 5,000 minute gold points is comparable to the masterpieces from Normanton in Great Britain.

Throughout the second millennium these funerary customs become progressively adapted by the less wealthy populations. In Armorica, in the tholos and megalithic chambers, metal became rarer and less sumptuous while pottery offerings became more and more numerous. In Great Britain, tumuli were reused, with the remains cremated and simply buried in the mounds.

Barbarians from the Land of Amber

The Scandinavian lands, poor in ore but rich in blocks of amber on the Jutland coasts, adopted bronze metallurgy later. Daggers from the Unetice had reached that area around 1600 B.C., but they gave way to remarkable copies flaked in flint. It is only around 1400 B.C. that the tumuli from these lands reveal a brilliant Bronze Age civilization. Exceptional preservation conditions—clay soils and ferric salts, a woodland climate and acidity—prevent the decay of precious funerary artifacts. The tumulus protects the stone vaults and oak coffins, obtained by hollowing out half trunks of trees. Some of these coffins have handles. Shrouds made of the skins of bovines and the naturally mummified bodies of the deceased were preserved. The costumes of

brown wool also remained intact; the jackets of young women have three-quarter sleeves and fibulas formed from two pins attached the clothing. The funerary headdresses are wide-brimmed hats for the women, who had long hair. The men wore skull caps of wool, or funnel-shaped caps. Belts are decorated with tubular bronze pearls, seen frequently in Europe. Combs, a few carved in bone, are sometimes attached. The tomb of Strhoj (east of Jutland) has yielded the remains of a young woman, interred during the summer, as is indicated by a wreath of yarrow. She wore a woolen jacket belted with a bronze disk, decorated with spirals.

The Tumulus Grave Culture

In the middle of the second millennium, the barbarians of continental Europe affirm the unity of their culture by

(Left) **From the beginning of the Middle Bronze**, in Valais, Switzerland (at Weimingen ZH "Hardwald"), five tumuli have yielded burial sites and signs of cremation. The bodies of women were adorned with pierced pins with large heads, at least two bracelets and sometimes bronze leggings. Men wore a clothespin, bracelets and either a dagger or, more rarely, a sword. Amber or glass beads, twisted golden cords and terra-cotta completed the tomb's contents. Zurich, National Swiss Museum. Ph. From the Museum.

(Above) **Bronze pins** of a great variety of shapes, from the tenth and ninth centuries B.C.: pins with rolled heads and a ring, headed pins decorated with small bits of shining metal, pins with vasiform heads, etc. The largest here measures 1.2 inches (3 centimeters) in diameter. The pieces were sometimes cast in a single mold or forged. Carving finishes these pieces, used to fasten clothing. (Provenance: Thielle-Wavre NE, Hauteriver-Champreveyres NE, Auvernier NE, Concise VD, Font FR, Estavayer FR). Ph. J.J. Luder, Cantonal Museum of Archaeology, Neuchâtel.

adopting identical funerary rites. However, the Tumulus grave culture remained diverse with numerous regional groups; each peasant people conserved its customs. While these populations appear to have assimilated the social changes of the preceding centuries, they fully developed new techniques as well. Bronze was commonly used. Production was already specialized, and the workshops produced series of objects, using stone molds. In the Danubian region, some lesser chiefs were buried as warriors, with traditional battle axes and large shields with menacing spurs. Those from Bavaria, subject to Hungarian influences, display swords with heavy hilts. On the Rhine and in the Wurtemburg region, bracelets and leggings with spirals ornament men and women. In northern Germany, Nordic influences are found in coffins made from wooden trunks, split and hollowed out. Everywhere in Europe the tumuli become necropolises, containing hundreds of tombs. In Alsace, the forest of Haguenau houses 500 of such tombs containing weapons, bracelets and spiral leggings, of which 200 tumuli date to the Middle Bronze Age. The peasants of these regions, it is believed, bred pigs and the animal was considered a symbol of wealth and power: In the forest of Haguenau, a princess rests for eternity, her head lying on the body of a pig, used as a mortuary pillow. From northwestern France, the civilization of the Tumulus originated practices that spread out toward the west (Normandy and Charente) and the south of France: The technique of incised ceramics, in geometric reliefs, is one example.

The peoples of the Atlantic and Mediterranean regions barely participated in this continental movement, sometimes qualified as "Proto-Celtic." In Great Britain, the descendants of the princes of Wessex adapted the rite of cremation and even introduced it into Holland and Belgium. On the Atlantic shores, and particularly in the Médoc, metallic pieces were the work of large shops, often established at the mouths of rivers. In pennisular Italy, copper and tin from the hills of Tuscany were also exploited; the peoples of the Middle Bronze Age in the Appenines, and the culture of the Terramare in the north, pursued their own developments.

The Urn Field Culture

Between 1200 and circa 700 B.C., within the groups of the Tumulus Grave culture, cremation, until then rare, spread widely. The diffusion of ceramic styles went hand in hand with the practices of this new rite. The origin of this phenomenon has long been placed in Silesia (Lausitz culture), but various groups of southern Germany did, in fact, propagate this custom in western Europe. "The Urn Field Culture" seems to have been diffused gradually, sometimes over great distances, as far as Spain and northern Italy.

During the Final Bronze Age, the fields of urns are necropolises formed by graves, tombs or tumuli sometimes circled by stones. An urn contained the ashes of the dead, which had been burned on a funeral pyre generally separate from the burial site. Some offerings were placed in the urn or next to it—weapons and ornaments, but also receptacles and pieces of meat. This ritual underwent regional variation, depending on the resistance of local cultures and the eras. During this period, no doubt, some population migrations took, but they have been overestimated for a long time. These were less invasions than an intertwining of cultures, which led to true upheavals. In the same era, the Mediterranean civilizations suffered disastrous traumas: the Dorian people, who mastered iron, put an end to the Mycenae; the glorious Troy, collapsed before the Achaeans; the Hittite Empire fell; and the Sea Peoples troubled Pharaonic Egypt.

The Rivalry of the Blacksmiths

The maritime world, from the Atlantic to the North Sea, remained in the grip of this agitation and experienced a slower evolution. The British Urn Field culture belonged to

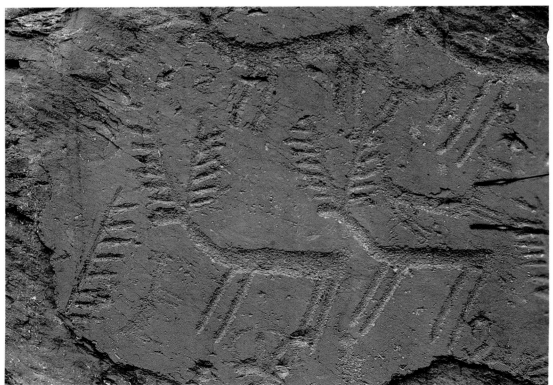

(Left) **The engravings of the Camonica Valley**, in the Italian Alps, depict the activities and objects of daily life of the populations of the valley since 2500 B.C. The representations of the Middle Bronze Age include numerous deer, whose importance surpasses that of the horned bulls, seemingly marking a new cult. In the Celtic world, the deer-god would be venerated during the last half of the first century. Ph. Scala.

(Right) **The "Protoceltic" tumulus of Pitten in Austria**, from the Middle Bronze Age, circa 1500 to 1200 B.C., contains the tombs of minor dignitaries. The tumulus, introduced by the Chalcolithic peoples, was adapted by some groups during the Bronze Age, becoming the most widespread funerary custom. The bodies are laid out at the back of the tomb. Toward the end of the period, cairns are constructed, but cremation rites became generalized. Ph. Lessing, Magnum.

the tradition of the Middle Bronze Age groups. The wares of the Atlantic workshops supplied trading centers at the borders some distance away. From Ireland and Scotland came riveted cauldrons and trumpets in bronze. From the Cantabric lands, socketed hatchets with terminal rings reached England and Scandinavia, others appearing toward the southeast, as far as Sardinia. The most beautiful products, and the most abundant, are diffused around 750 B.C. An important center in Brittany produced, in mass, sleeved axes. Several Atlantic workshops, perhaps starting with prototypes coming from the low Loire Valley, also made swords with carp tongue ends in. On the commercial routes of the continent, the French river valleys draw these products together with those of the forges of the northwest, in the Alps. In the central west of France, the Venat group combines the influence of the continental Urn field culture with those of the southern region and the indigenous inventions during the Final Bronze Age, reaching its height toward the middle of the eighth century.

In Scandinavia new customs appear. The helmeted Norse warrior is henceforth armed with a massive sword and a lance and carries a shield. At Vixö, in Zealand, these helmets have raptor beaks, horns made of sheet iron and plumed crests. The wealth of these warriors is evident in their tombs: Jewelry, and toilet objects are abundant, including razors with forged handles engraved with designs of ships with their sails fully unfurled. The Scandinavians made offerings to the gods of the waters, casting arms and jewelry into the sea, with votive objects and solar barks. Slivers of gold were thrown into the marshes, to the sound of large trumpets with circular horns, called lurs, adorned with pendants.

The New Symbols

The society of the second millennium still bears the stamp of the Neolithic tradition. In the southern Alps one found carved representations of daily and cultic life. The Valley des Merveilles at Mount Bego depicts a bull cult, with numerous carved bovine heads. A "tribal chief," with horned symbols, was perhaps a priest; other figures brandish lightning or kneel. In Lombardy, the engravings of the Camonica Valley depict horned stag/men. Mortuarty cultic practices develop and symbolic offerings represent more complex rites than those in former traditions. New artifacts symbolize these new times: solar disks, bronze cones and bird figures. The birds of Dupljaja in Banat, Yugoslavia, with elongated necks, formed bodies with a votive chariot with two wheels, date to 1400 to 1200 B.C. This chariot contains a human figure

whose long robe and neck and back ornaments are comparable to other statuettes in terra-cotta from the Danubean world. These last ones were inspired by Mycenae. In central and southern Europe, birds are equally represented on certain bronze leggings, helmets or jewelry. They appear on the side frames of small cultic chariots, surmounted by bronze cauldrons. The symbol of protector birds appears more and more. The solar figures, more often equally widespread, appear on the engravings of the Camonica Valley, or under the form of a round piece of leather, on the heads of pins, or sometimes in the form of golden disks, mounted on certain pieces of jewelry. An exceptional discovery was made in the Danish peat bog of Trundholm (Seeland Islands). This was a heavy disk, plated with gold, mounted on a chariot with six wheels, pulled by an elegant horse.

The gold cones in repoussée sheet are also amazing emblems of this complete Bronze Age. They are dated to the eighth century B.C. Their forms evoke fiery flames. These symbolic objects from the religious customs of the Bronze Age are known from Poitou to the Palatinate.

Work and Daily Life

The farmer's life in the second millennium was still organized around the cultivation of wheat and barley, leguminous plants sometimes also important, as in northern Italy. Thus the swing plough was employed. At Mount Bego it is depicted with one or two pairs of oxen. The fields, represented in geometric enclosures on the carved stones of Capo di Ponte, are furrowed and seeded. Barrows were also utilized. These augmenting techniques permit some more important gatherings. The harvest, with bronze sickles, becomes generalized in all regions. Breeding is standardized as well. Stalls for domesticated animals in medium mountains appears in the Final Bronze Age; by then the migration during the summer toward the high mountainous pastures was already habitual. The herds of oxen, pigs, sheep and goats play an important economic role. The horse, from then on domesticated, is still rare. It was used for pulling wagons with plank wheels linked to crosspieces in dovetails (Wasserburg-Buchau, High Schwabia). However, in Europe, it was often still an animal of ceremony, harnessed, on the engravings of the Camonica Valley, with chariots comparable to those of Mycenae. Hunting also contributed to this economy, as did the gathering of fruits and berries.

(Below left) **The chariot of Trundholm** *Between the 13th and 14th centuries B.C., the chariot was broken intentionally and then thrown, as an offering, into the peat bog of the Island of Seeland (Denmark). The chariot (24 inches/60 centimeters) has six wheels. It is pulled by a horse, whose head is finely carved, trailing a hollow bronze disc. The disc, plated by a sheet of gold, is richly decorated, representing the sun. This cultic chariot has other European counterparts, where the solar symbol is produced on ceramics or on bronze pieces that hold an important place in the religious conceptions of the Bronze Age civilizations.* National Museum of Copenhagen. Ph. from the Museum.

(Below) **A cone in a thin sheet of finely embossed bronze** *from Schiffestadt (Palatinate) is dated to the eighth century B.C. Known from three examples in Europe (from Avanton, near Poitiers, and from Etzelsdorf, near Nuremburg) these enticing objects have been considered cultic emblems, representing the flame of a blazing fire. Their full symbolic meaning and their use remain unknown.* Pflatz, Historical Museum. Ph. from the Museum.

Organized Villages

The large villages of the Bronze Age were often established on the axis of well-traveled routes. The most ancient had, in Bohemia, rectangular 100 to 200 feet houses (30 to 60 meters) of wood, in part dug into the soil. A rough coat extracted from neighboring pits protected the walls, as was done in the plains of Europe for hundreds of years. The fortifications of these villages are often imposing, like those of Pritlicky in the Danubian region or those of certain Alpine sites.

Under the water of the lakes, the architectural wood has been well preserved. The floors were remarkably well laid out. At Baldegg (Bleichi), the houses were aligned according to a preconceived plan: a circular wall with a funnel-shaped entry protected them. On Lake Ledro a hamlet on a small mountain lasted nearly 600 years: the first fir tree piles placed in the chalk were buried under the accumulated debris.

The peat bog of Fiave (Trente) shows, as well, some wooden houses with piles, pegged and set extensions, sometimes 43 feet (13 meters) long. An isolated village on a small island was founded there around 1400 B.C. It is mounted on foundations, as in Switzerland and in southern Germany. In temperate Europe, the villages of the end of the Bronze Age often have important protective mechanisms. Such is the case in Burgundy, where some camps protected by imposing ramparts have often been reconstructed over Neolithic fortifications. At Myard (Vitteaux), a frame of wooden trunks preceded the strong stone construction established there.

Montlingerberg (Saint-Gall) possesses a rampart of 13,000 cubic yards (10,000 cubic meters) of clay, blocked in by crossed trunks. At Flaue (Sissach, near Bale) or at Wittnauerhorn (Argovia [Jura balois]), houses were built on strong slopes, attached to narrow terraces. The villages and hamlets of the low plains involved in agriculture are more open. It appears that settlements set on high ground, such as certain refuge grottoes, assured the temporarily endangered society (grotto of Planches à Arbois in Jura). The villages often have regular plans. At East Cortaillod, eight streets lying perpendicular to the lake define the placing of aligned rectangular houses at the lake. A fence is near the earthen walls of the village. In Saxony, Biskupin belongs to the end of the Lausitz culture: established on a boggy peninsula of almost four acres (1.5 hectares). It is protected by important defenses, with a rampart and a breakwater of 35,000 posts. The plan, regulated throughout, contains some quarters and parallel alleys. Small houses are grouped, approximately 23 by 30 feet (seven by nine meters), with two rooms and attics. These rectangular houses numbering 38, are known as early as the 12th century B.C. in the village of Wasserburg Buchau (Wurtemburg). In Lovcicky, in Moravia, there are similar structures. On this last site, they border a house-farm, a true prototype of the European buildings of the Iron Age. This construction covered 1600 square feet (140 square meters) and its three halls were used to separate the housing from the stable.

Around 800 B.C., Wasserburg was rebuilt; three house farms were erected around one location, the site fortified at its foundation by a wooden fence, which encircle an oval surface 360 by 500 feet (110 by 150 meters).

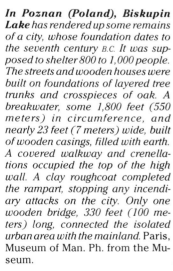

In Poznan (Poland), Biskupin Lake has rendered up some remains of a city, whose foundation dates to the seventh century B.C. It was supposed to shelter 800 to 1,000 people. The streets and wooden houses were built on foundations of layered tree trunks and crosspieces of oak. A breakwater, some 1,800 feet (550 meters) in circumference, and nearly 23 feet (7 meters) wide, built of wooden casings, filled with earth. A covered walkway and crenellations occupied the top of the high wall. A clay roughcoat completed the rampart, stopping any incendiary attacks on the city. Only one wooden bridge, 330 feet (100 meters) long, connected the isolated urban area with the mainland. Paris, Museum of Man. Ph. from the Museum.

The Hallstatt Culture

The metallurgy of iron appeared for the first time in Europe during the ninth century (Greece) and developed slowly. It was present in peninsular Italy, starting in 800 B.C., in France circa 700 B.C. The early phase of the Iron Age (or First Iron Age) was epitomized by the Hallstatt culture, the name taken from the site of a necropolis of 3,000 graves in the rock salt lands of Austria. It was, in fact, a cultural complex, with numerous regional adaptations. This civilization extended from Bosnia to the west of France and from southern Germany to Catalonia. Hallstatt is the junction of two large provinces, one eastern, which carried traces of the Steppes people (Illyrian, Scythians and Thracio-Cimmarians); the other, in the west, was influenced by the first Greek and Etruscan colonies.

Certain of these peoples were the ancestors of the Celts, who appear as an identifiable nation during the first half of the fifth century. This period corresponds to the second phase of the Iron Age, called the "La Tene Period." At the edge of Lake Neuchâtel, La Tene was the center of production and the commerce of bronze and iron objects.

During the first Iron Age, the great migrations of armed people had not yet commenced, despite the sudden settlements of Hallstatt cultures in Belgium, eastern France and as far as the Iberian peninsula. The warrior chiefs who seem to have dominated the society adopted iron weapons, such as daggers with embellished handles, with extensions, and long swords called "knights." They rode horses from that time on, in the Cimmerian style. Bridles and bits appear in certain tombs. However, the economy of the Hallstatt communities seems to have been centered more on commerce than on conflict or conquest. As before, blacksmith products (now in iron), jewelry and glass pieces circulate in Europe, accompanied by commercial livestock, hunting products and raw materials. The distances covered by certain merchandise are at times surprising. The first vases of Phoenician glass arrived in southern Germany. The tumulus of Hochmichele, in Bavaria, has yielded up fragments of silk from China. The most important, however, were the tin items of the Greek world and salt, which was gathered in the salterns in southeast England and on the French Atlantic shores. The wealth of the Hallstatt community came from rock salt, which they extracted from neighboring mines. The mine was responsible for the wicker baskets and the wooden sleighs, which were dragged into the mines as they were worked with the help of porous materials or bronze picks in the light of torches made of resinous woods. Several people lost their lives there, buried by cave-ins.

In certain regions, the indigenous cultures which followed the Urn Field culture of the Bronze Age, took on the cultural traits of continental Europe with less enthusiasm. Such was the case in Champagne and Languedoc. The Mailhac culture, in the Mediterranean area, furnishes a good and clear example of indigenous populations who assured their survival by drawing on their own resources and by adapting to the innovations of the times. On the shores of the western Mediterranean, the Italic civilizations, amongst which were those of Villanova, followed similar paths.

The Time of Fortresses

The people of the Iron Age, during the sixth and fifth centuries B.C., occupied by preference the zones of plateaus or hills bordering the great plains of Europe. Some hamlets in Bohemia were groups of three-to-five large rectangular wooden farmhouses. Sometimes, in Central Europe, these farms used cave granaries, with deeply excavated areas, of about 33 feet (10 meters) square. On occasion they also sheltered artisans who worked in metals or fashioned pottery. Heuneburg (Württemburg), a hamlet of this type, located to the west of a fortress, has been deemed a true town. Like the other small Hallstatt towns, Heuneburg dominated the region from a natural spur located over a valley beside the Danube. The high wall that encircled the seven and a half acres (three hectares) of the site was clearly influenced by Mediterranean architecture. It used sun-dried bricks of earth, poorly adapted to the rigors of the climate, and ramparts with jutting bastions. The quarters and the houses were aligned along narrow alleys, showing a planned organization, perhaps inspired by the first towns of antiquity. Toward the southwest, the industrial quarter housed the metallurgists and their workshops. The rivalries and violent tensions that existed in the ancient Celtic world caused between 600 and 450 B.C., the fortress to be besieged three times and generally set on fire. The high wall had to be reinforced at seven intervals. The military chiefs of the citadel directly controlled the activities of everyone. These men directed work and kept the laborers building and supplying the fortress. At Ruben, in northwest Bohemia, some transportation of stones was conducted over 12 miles (20 kilometers). At Zav, to the south of Prague, the ramparts were formed out of masses of blocks. The residences of the chieftains were situated at the base of the walls. In later eras, the aristocratic dwellings of Heuneberg had four rooms in a building 80 feet by 36 feet (25 meters by 11 meters) surrounded by a fence. A great market, a bit larger still, was under the protection of a master of the cultic and market gatherings.

The Powerful Before Death

The princes of the fortresses based their authority on the control of commerce and the artisan class. The wealth of their tombs added to their legends as well. In Styria, in southeastern Austria, the five princely tombs of Kleinklein dominate nearly 1,500 small tumuli from their mounds. This necropolis developed at the foot of Burgstallkogel, a fortress occupied from the seventh to the sixth century B.C. The burials of the chiefs and their relatives involved considerable personal property. Chamber number six of Hochmichele in Bad-Wurtemberg received the bodies of a warrior and a woman, interred under a four-wheeled chariot with harnesses. The funerary chamber was stocked with silk, fabrics, wool and skins. Some bronze containers, weapons and jewelry, of which a collar of 2,700 pearls, intended for the woman, constituted the ornamentations of the dead. The large mound of Hohmichele, with a diameter of 260 feet (80 meters) covered a formerly looted burial site. In France, the most famous of the princely tombs was discovered at the foot of the small town of Mount Lassois, in Bourgogne. The tomb of Vix was a tumulus of stone 130 feet (40 meters) in diameter and 20 feet (six meters) high, sheltering a chamber full of some of the richest grave goods ever discovered. The princess lay on a dismantled ceremonial chariot, with wheels wrapped in fabric. Among the sumptuous jewelry was a diadem or collar of gold, which was attributed to a Greco-Scythian or Iberian goldsmith. Vases, silver cups, a wine pitcher and some bronze Etruscan bowls, as well as Attic cups with black figures, were placed in offering next to the famous crater of 1,160 quarts (1,100 liters) made from one single piece of cold-beaten bronze. It demonstrates the complex relations between the Celtic peoples and the Etruscan or Greek peddlers in the last quarter of the fifth century B.C. The bonds between the various Celtic tribes were also very strong. For several centuries the southern German communities exploited their products, moving them east to France, to the north and into the Parisian Basin. Thus, at the end of the first Iron Age, the great mound of Lizeray (Indre) was raised as a tomb providing a burial in a wooded ditch, lined with slabs much like those found in Germany. It held the remains of a rich warrior, with hair entwined with golden nails and adorned by luxurious possessions. Some Hallstattian influences are found as well in the last phases of the Nordic Bronze Age. During the course of the second Iron Age, these influences would be seen in the rise of the practice of cremation; The cemetery of Borholan held more than 2,500 graves showing signs of cremation.

The Mediterraneans in Barbaric Europe

During the ninth and eighth centuries B.C., the Mezzogiorno and the Tyrrhenian region experienced population growth. In northern Italy, notably in the region of Bologna, some villages contained growing populations (Villanova civilization). The Latium offers good examples of towns organized into quarters and dominating smaller villages. Certain sites are fortified. Some ramparts of thick blocks fit together as at Elceto (near Alumiere), a true acropolis. Tarquinia and Cerveterithus grouped together several thousand inhabitants. The necropolises are widespread and the oldest maintain an egalatarian character. The variations in wealth are evident in these cemeteries later. The noble class based its power on the control of local mineral

A cauldron from the Gunderstrup marsh (Jutland, Denmark). It is composed of metal plates, attached to a cup; the decorations were hammered and gilded. The busts, with arms raised or folded, and the composition of warriors and animals are of a very figurative style. It weighs nearly 20 pounds (9 kilograms). This masterpiece, dated to almost the start of the Christian era, seems to be from Thrace (Bulgaria-Romania). National Museum of Copenhagen. Ph. from the Museum.

resources and the salt marshes located at the mouth of the Tiber as well as on commercial endeavors with distant groups. The wealthiest acquired Phoenician or Egyptian vases, and one among them even employed a Greek artist, as early as the end of the eighth century at Pithekoussai. The artist signed a crater with geometric decorations; his name is one of the first epigraphic pieces of evidence in the Euboean Greek language known in the West.

The tombs of the Villanovan culture contained cremated remains. In Tuscany, the funerary urns are surmounted by a crested helmet in terra-cotta; in Latium, the urns take the form of round huts with roofs of cross logs, ending in the figures of birds or humans. In Venice and Haute-Carniole (Kram in ancient Slovenia), during the seventh and sixth centuries B.C., other populations developed, as in the eastern European zone of Hallstatt, the art of the cauldron: bronze cauldrons, the plaques of umbo or the bronze lids are decorated by orientalizing frieze figures.

As early as the foundation of the Phoenician town of Massalia (Marseilles), around 600 B.C., and the ports in Adria and Spina, in the Po plain, exchanges between the eastern world and the Hallstatt were reinforced. The zones then fell under the occupation or influence of the Greeks, Etruscans and Carthaginians, who slowly modified the local societies. These initiatives in the Mediterranean colonies had repercussions in the most diverse areas. They provide jewels and vessels, but they also offer new products, such as wine or coral as finery. They also have a ceramic industry, based on the invention of the potter's wheel, a technique adopted by the indigenous potters of Bourgogne and Bohemia as early as the fifth century. The eastern styles appear as well in the decorations—vegetal and animal motifs, scenes of chariot races, banquets or boxing that adorned Etruscan bronze vessels. Other artists of the sixth century discover monumental statuary. They used it at Hirschlanden, in a sandstone statue of a Halstattian prince, whose style renewed the anthropomorphic representations of certain tomb stones from Wârttemburg in the seventh century.

On the routes linking the barbaric world of the Alpine north with the Mediterranean, there is a rippling effect that

A bowl discovered at Vix (Côte d'Or) comes from a large sepulchral tumulus of a young woman, dated to around 500 B.C. This enormous bronze vase, nearly 450 pounds (208 kilograms) in weight and 5.4 feet (1.64 meters) high, has a capacity of nearly 1,200 quarts (liters). It was made in Peloponnesus or a Greek colony of southern Italy (Tarente region). Large, scrolled handles frame busts of gorgons. The cistern, in a single piece, carefully hammered, is topped by a neck decorated by a frieze of 23 subjects, applied by rivets: hoplites, soldiers, armed and wearing cuirasses and Corinthian helmets. Chariots precede them, each one drawn by a team of four horses. The bowl was closed by a lid pierced with holes arranged in petals, and a female statuette affixed to its center. In the richly decorated tomb, a silver cup, decorated by a navel of gold and enveloped by plaiting, rested on the vase. Museum of Châtillon-sur-Seine. Ph. Giraudon.

reaches stronger locales. Shipments leaving the rivers for land routes were watched; the local chiefs often demanded tolls for safe passage. The small town of Pegue (Drome) was narrowly linked until the middle of the fifth century to traffic in the area of Massalia. The local painted ceramics began to imitate Ionian models. In Bourgogne, the fortress of Vix adopted the luxurious polychrome pottery; this small town served as an important relay for the traffic of Atlantic tin, which was transported toward the southern Alps in return for Etruscan or Greek personal goods. Some Mediterranean products reached even farther—as far as Wârttemburg and the Metalliferes Mountains. Thus, coral was used in jewelry and other ornaments in Europe as early as the end of the sixth century, in association with amber from the Baltic. The wine that was transported, often still in goatskins and mixed with

aromatic resins, is exported even farther. Numerous containers (amphora) kept it until it is prepared (in cauldrons) or consumed, becoming from that time on a part of the personal needs of the wealthy. Some utensils for wine serving were buried with princes.

In the Mediterranean zones the civil architecture was influenced by the art of the eastern builders. At Bessan, near the Agde, the houses with apses from the Monediere are, at present, the most ancient buildings of Greek influence known between 550 and 500 B.C. on the soil of Gaul. The stone constructions supplanted architecture in wood in the Midi. In the sixth century the houses were designed with a square or rectangular plan. The arrangement of the towns appears planned in the fifth and fourth centuries as well. These small towns, economic and political centers, were entrenched behind ramparts with quadrangular towers.

Hallstattian regions still maintain certain cultural strata. Thus, the most Nordic lands are the seats of the long-enduring Atlantic Bronze Age vestiges. On the shores of the Mediterranean, on the other hand, Greek and Etruscan colonies announced the progressive development of local societies.

The Celts, Armed Farmers

The first Iron Age civilization is for the most part, Celtic. It is in the Tumulus grave culture of the Middle Bronze Age from Bourgogne to Bohemia that the Celtic nation probably took root. Subsequently, numerous other ethnic groups, during the various phases of the Urn Field culture of the Final Bronze Age, had contributed to its formation. It is from these bases that the Celtic civilization will emerge in the fifth century B.C., and its development will cover the whole second Iron Age (the La Tene Period).

Between 480 and 250 B.C., the Celtic world intensified its contacts with Greek and Etruscan cities. Italy attracted numerous merchants from temperate Europe and the first mercenaries. In the north, Etruscan metal vases and Greek ceramics from the east and the west were occasionally de-

(Above) **The Celtic helmet** *preserved at Soissons is of a simple shape, which lasted until the first century B.C. It is furnished with a curved cap, and a short visor in front; the back covering the neck is slightly shaped. Straps passed through the holes of the helmet, securing it on the head. Other examples of helmets from La Tene II or III bear plumes and decoration, but the most widely used helmets correspond to this example.* Municipal Museum of Soissons. Ph. Lauros-Giraudon.

(Right) **The large Gallic residence** *of Verberie (Oise) was discovered during the great drought of 1976 in France, thanks to aerial photography. The house is 72 feet (22 meters) long, and 41 feet (12.5 meters) wide. The building was constructed in posts and cob, with a hard-packed floor; its roof would have been thatch. It contains two rooms. The layout of this Gallic house was possibly the prototype of a large number of small Gallic-Roman regional towns.* Ph. R. Agache.

posited in Latenian graves, from Champagne to Bohemia. Military leaders were buried with their helmets, lances or javelins, and swords at their sides. Sometimes the bodies were adorned with simple gold jewelry. Two-wheeled war chariots, accompanied certain of the dead. The tombs containing chariots were sometimes encircled by a trench or covered with a mound. In the cemeteries of the Marne, the tombs are placed in "familial" groups; some indicate the existence of classes of laborers, artisans-metallurgists, or farmers, but differences in wealth in these tombs are barely discernible. The German necropolises provide a glimpse of a different world. To the south of Salzburg, the tomb of Waldalgesheim contained sumptuous gold jewelry and a bronze seal made in the Tarente region.

Celtic art was permeated by eastern influences. The geometric decorations of the barbarians were abandoned in favor of plant and animal motifs. Thus, the treasure of Basse Yurtz, in eastern France contains two stamnos and two cups, decorated with coral and enamels. Ducks and mythical animals depicted on these containers are of Greco-Scythian inspiration. One style incorporated the palm leaf and lotus flower, carved by the artisans with the aid of a compass. Trees of life are surrounded by animals or monsters (the most successful of which are the dragon on Gallic coins of the first century). Toward the end of the fourth century, this naturalistic art will tend toward abstraction and geometrism; the winding curves of the plant motifs will slowly become complex and ambiguous, and the style of the Celtic artists will be freed of the influences of its original inspiration.

The End of the Barbarians

The societies of southern Europe enter first into history. As early as the sixth century B.C., Greek, Etruscan and Iberic writings promote relations between the peoples of the western Mediterranean (western and Nordic Europe will only discover writing later, and the coin becomes another unifier. As early as the end of the sixth century, massaliot coins increase commercial exchange while in Celtic lands the stateres of Philip II of Macedonia give way in the west to local currencies during the third century.

In this era, increased production and needs lead to inegalitarian and hierarchical societies. The populations increase, without the powerful chiefdoms achieving unity. The barbarian lands are, in fact, isolated, even when they maintain relations and ancestral cultural bonds. The Roman colonies will later benefit from this situation, as much by armed conquest as by the insidious material culture that they will impose, thus both laying and renewing the foundation of "European" civilization.

Suggested Reading

Coles, J. M., and Harding, A. F. *The Bronze Age in Europe: An Introduction to the Prehistory of Europe.* London: Methuen, 1979.

Herity, M., and Eogan, G. *Ireland in Prehistory.* London: Methuen.

The portico of Roquepertuse (Bouches-du-Rhône) from an indigenous sanctuary, strongly inspired by the Celtic culture. It was situated in a small natural semicircle on a hill where religious gatherings took place. The building was comprised of a portico with three pillars. Skulls were placed in niches in the limestone blocks, whose surface still carries traces of white, black and red paint. Only a few festoons (garlands), wolf teeth and the image of a horse remain visible. The monument is dated to the second to third centuries A.D. It was destroyed by the Romans. Marseille, Borely Museum. Ph. Lauros-Giraudon.

CHAPTER THIRTEEN
Jean Vaquer

RELIVING PREHISTORY

Potter's furnace *from the late Bronze Age from Sevrier (Haute-Savoie, France). A replica was made and used successfully by P. Andrieux.* Ph. Center for Documentation of Alpine Prehistory.

Experimental archaeology is becoming an important branch of a discipline that wants to move past the stage of simple collection and description of archaeological facts and to seek to understand their significance. The interpretation of archaeological facts is a delicate exercise for which the archaeologist has recourse to various processes: logical deduction; ethnographic or historic comparison; experimentation, or more correctly, simulation. While the collection of the ethnographic or historic data is essential, the insights gained from experiments or reconstruction are complementary. The re-creation of objects, techniques, habitats or monuments can be very suggestive if certain conditions, as defined by the British archaeologist John Coles, are met: the use of adequate materials and techniques, precise description of experimental data (kind of material; accurate measurements of duration, speed, temperature, pressure, etc.); repetition of experiments to ascertain correctly the limits of the tested objects; and a clear indication of choices that have been made and alternative solutions that have been abandoned. These experiments cannot have the value of proof, but form working hypotheses, more or less justified.

Making Stone Tools

The reproduction of flaked stones represents some of the first attempts at experimental archaeology.

The first insights into lithic technology did not come from the early European specialists, who often used direct percussion, but from ethnologists, who had the opportunity to observe Aboriginal flakers. Among them, one of the most famous is the Indian Ishi, the last survivor of the Yahi people, who taught two anthropologists from the University of California at Berkeley the techniques of flaking with the *blade punch* and retouching by pressure. Scientific flaking experiments began in 1950 and aimed at the rediscovery of cutting techniques that allowed one to obtain as many standardized products as possible. One of the best known methods is the Levallois method, whose different stages and variants have been defined and explained on various occasions by experimenters in the prehistoric such as F. Bordes, J. Tixier and J. Pelegrin. This flaking technique, characteristic of the Lower

177

and Middle Paleolithic, aimed at the production of fragments, points or blades of the Levallois type, whose predetermined shapes were obtained from a prepared core. The preparation consists of the thinning of the lower face to outline a peripheral striking platform and removing the cortex of the upper face by centripetal removals, so as to produce a weakly convex surface.

All of the steps in this preparation follow a logical order that it is possible to determine by examining the final products and discarded fragments of even the most complex examples such as Levallois points fashioned by the Nubian method. The production of a series of blades and small bladelettes, which characterize numerous industries of the Upper Paleolithic and more recent periods, has been attempted by numerous specialists such as L. Coutier, F. Bordes, Donald Crabtree, and J. Tixier. Although the technique can be adapted, the core must be precisely prepared by bifacial retouches to produce a crest. The crest will permit the cutting of the first blade by creating ribs that will serve as guides for the following blades. The cutting itself is done by direct percussion with a mineral, animal or vegetal hammer. One large piece is obtained from the core by indirect percussion, using a punch, most often a cervid horn. Obtaining small regular blades with perfectly parallel edges from the cannelated core is difficult, but can be achieved using the techniques of cutting by pectoral pressure with the help of a support. The method, finely tuned by the American archaeologist Donald Crabtree, for cutting obsidian, was applied then to flints whose properties would be improved by heating. The experimental reproduction of prehistoric tools is not especially difficult, except for a few types that require great dexterity and intensive training by the experimenters: large Solutrean foliated points, Folsom points, Egyptian knives with oblique retouches and daggers or hatchets of the Danish Chalcolithic.

The Use of Artifacts

For a long time, the function of prehistoric tools was tentatively determined by the analogies that they seemed to have with modern tools or with tools recently used by the primitive populations of Australia, America or Africa. The function of prehistoric tools can today be determined more correctly thanks to microscopic analysis of the traces of use, a recent discipline largely based on experimentation.

The first research concerned with glosss visible to the naked eye on the cutting edges of sickles was conducted by E. C. Curwen, but the true pioneer of microwear analysis is S. A. Semenov, who discovered traces of visible wear with a microscope on experimental tools used in various tasks. The study of microwear, or the polishing caused by use, and striae observable with the metallographic microscope (magnification of 200 or 400) was undertaken by Larry Keeley and has had considerable success in the characterization of functions and the materials used. More than 400 experiments have been performed by P. Vaughn to refine this method of analysis, which takes into account the different material (flint, obsidian) from which the tool was made, its possible functions (cutting, sawing, scraping, drilling, etc.) and the materials (bone, wood, antler, plants, etc.) used to fashion the tool. Using this method, one can compare the effects of use on wood, skins and plants, as well as the movement of the tool, depending upon whether the striaes are parallel or

Cutting obsidian blades by pectoral pressure with the help of a support. Experiment by J. Tixier. Ph. J. L. Princelle.

Rupestrian designs from the Bronze Age
1. *Two men brandishing a hatchet on a boat (Bohuslan, Sweden)* Drawing by E. Sprockhoff
2. *Design of a horse and chariot above a boat (Bohuslan, Sweden)* Drawing by E. Sprockhoff
3. *Representation of a boat with a solar wheel (Bohuslan, Sweden)* Drawing by L. Baltzer
4. *Boat carrying two men (Evje-Tune)* Drawing by J. Bing
5. *Three men with raised arms on a boat (Skjeberg, Ostfold, Norway)* Drawing by G. Gessing

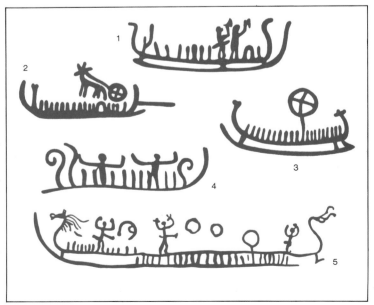

perpendicular to the edge. The analysis of prehistoric series has revealed traces of use equally well on retouched and unretouched flints; often several functions can be attributed to the same tool.

A similar correspondence, can be determined between certain tool types and functions: flint scrapers, for example, very often show wear from dry skins. Experiments have shown that phytoliths of plants can be trapped in the cutting edge of flint. Their observation requires the use of an electron microscope, with scanning magnification in the range of 1000 to 10,000x. These minuscule silicious concretions appear in a great variety of shapes and dimensions, according to their function in the tissues of a single plant, but distinctions are especially marked from species to species. Research conducted by P. Anderson-Gerfaud has identified a number of these phytoliths. The application of the method to certain polished sickles from the Near East has paradoxically shown that these tools were not used primarily to harvest grain but to cut other plants used for basketry or thatching.

Reconstructing Boats and Attempts at Navigation

Much archaeological evidence shows that prehistoric travel and transport was conducted principally via waterways and the techniques of navigation are extremely old: The straits of the Wallace zone, between Indonesia and Australia, were crossed at least 30,000 years ago. Obsidian from the island of Melos was exported to Peloponnesia as early as the eighth millennium B.C. As direct evidence of these ancient navigations is lacking, we can only speculate about the kinds of crafts possible in the Paleolithic (rafts made of wood or reeds, small boats of skins or bark, dugout canoes?). In Europe, the most ancient remains of boats that have reached us are single- hull dugout canoes: large hollowed out oak trees, found in the alluvial deposits of rivers, estuaries or lakes. The most ancient of them date to the Mesolithic (dugout canoes from Noyen-Est to Noyen-sur-Seine, Seine-et-Marne) but their use has continued until very recent times. Although there is much prehistoric and ethnographic research concerning the methods used to build these dugout canoes, only a few experiments have been done in Denmark, which have shown that these small boats can only be used in calm water. Small prehistoric boats capable of navigation in the open sea are of two types: the skin boats like the *umiak* and boats made from lashed planks, dating from the Bronze Age (ruins of North Ferriby, Yorkshire, England). Taking into account varying data—from the remains found at Dalgety in Scotland, cave etchings and decorated blades from the Bronze Age Scandinavians, texts concerning the coracles from the Highlands of Great Britain or the curraghs of Ireland—a reconstruction of a skin boat of the Bronze Age was attempted by O. Johnson in Norway. The keel ribs, braces and gunwales were cut from 24 young elders and one linden tree. The covering of the wooden structure was made with eight cow skins, sewn with waxed thread. A prominent keel was placed at the exterior and fixed at the ends to avoid tearing the skin covering. This boat, which measured 23 feet (6.8 meters) long, weighing only 400 pounds (180 kilograms) could carry one ton of cargo and sail at the speed of 2.8 knots with six paddlers. No experiment has been attempted with wooden replicas but reconstructions on a reduced scale have been accomplished at the National Museum of the British Navy. Outside of Europe, reconstructions of boats and voyages have been attempted, notably in Polynesia, to test the ability of double canoes to navigate freely. The *Hôkule'a*, built by B. R. Finney, with two masts and 11 tons of cargo capacity made a trouble-free round-trip voyage of 6,700 miles (10,800 kilometers) between 1975 and 1976. The most extraordinary maritime archaeological experiments are those directed by Thor Heyerdahl in trans-Pacific navigation on a balsa-type raft of pre-Columbian design, the *Kon-Tiki*; a trans-Atlantic navigation on a raft of Egyptian papyri, the *Ra II*; and navigation from Iraq to Djibouti on a reed raft of Sumerian design, the *Tigris*. Although undertaken to prove ill-documented theories, Heyerdahl's experiments have the immense merit of demonstrating the remarkable aptitudes of several kinds of prehistoric or protohistoric ships of the Old and New World.

Prehistoric Hearths

For nearly 400,000 years, fire played a crucial role in the evolution of humanity. In prehistoric habitats, hearths are often the most prominent feature. A great variety exists in the arrangement of the component elements. The experimental study of heating structures used for cooking still offers a vast field for investigation. The remarkable stone-bordered hearths of the Magdalenian site of Pincevent have been rebuilt with the goal of analyzing the method of stone fracture. Before the invention of pottery, cooking in boiled water could be accomplished by plunging heated stones in skin containers or in bark; this method was successfully tested by various researchers. According to some Scots and Irish accounts of the 16th century, a more unusual method would have consisted of boiling the meat in sheep skins, suspended above an open fire, but the experiments conducted by M. Ryder have been inconclusive. The attempts at boiling meat in animal stomachs, by the same researcher, have scarcely been convincing, although this process is described among the Scythians by Herodotus, and among certain North American Indians. In several Irish deposits of the Bronze Age, hollowed out troughs have been found in the bogs, lined so that they could be filled with clean water, associated with heated stones and hearths. These structures appear to correspond to a traditional method of cooking deer meat, known by the name of "fulacht fiadha." A successful experiment of boiling meat by plunging hot stones into the trough for nearly four hours was done by O'Kelly. Stewing food in pots over pits filled with pebbles and heated was common through time and around the world. The hearths of this type were sometimes very large (in Polynesia), so that at times these structures were the objects of divergent interpretations. Several hundred round or rectangular examples have been excavated in Neolithic deposits of Saint-Michel-du-Touch or Villeneuve-Tolosane in the Garonne Valley (France), where they were sometimes thought to be huts. In fact, it could be demonstrated that these structures were very efficient ovens. Four experimental structures were constructed by A. Aspinall, P. Philipps and J. Vaquer. Thermocouples revealed that the stones heated in wood fires easily reached 1300° F (700° C) and measurements of magnetism with a magnometer have revealed values comparable to those of prehistoric structures. There was also similarity in the appearance of the burned stones, reddened and fragmented. Concerning the

use of hot hearth stones, two methods have been distinguished: grilling the food, over the stones uncovered, or covering them with earth. In the first case, a temperature 572° F (300° C) was maintained for about three hours, and, in the second case, the pebbles remained hot for more than five hours. Cooking experiments with meat and fish have been completely successful.

The Rebuilding of Prehistoric Habitats

Outside of waterlogged environments, the remains of prehistoric habitats are scarce. Most often their impression in the earth is limited to a few post holes or foundation trenches, sometimes near pits and other archaeological evidence. These elements are generally difficult to interpret, giving rise to the practical decision to try to reconstruct the various habitats that have vanished. Despite the uncertainties inherent in such a process, these replicas help archaeologists and others understand the methods of construction and appreciate the size and the investment of labor that these buildings demanded.

In western Europe, the Paleolithic habitats in the open air are most frequently represented by heating structures, surrounded by debris and rough pieces of stone broken off from the ancient walls. It is from the information gathered in extremely precise excavations that the rebuilding of Magdalenian tents of Pincevent (Seine-et-Marne) has been accomplished on the site of their discovery. These replicas (like those done at the Beaune Archaeological shelter after the

Experimental reconstruction of prehistoric oven with heated stones. The temperature is increased by the help of thermocouples. Ph. J. Vaquer.

Experimental baking of modeled pottery in the Neolithic style in a cistern with an open hearth. Ph. and experiment by G. B. Arnal.

digs of Marsangy [Yonne]) form remarkable illustrations of an encampment of deer hunters from the Upper Paleolithic Period. The elongated houses of the Danubian Neolithic are known on many numerous European sites, which have revealed the standardized plans comprising five rows of massive post holes marking the location of the walls and pillars that supported the roof and the internal partitions. These simple houses have been rebuilt in numerous sites: Museum of Asparn an der Zaya in Austria; the Beaune Archaeological shelter; and the Cuiry-les-Chaudardes site in France. The reconstruction of a Lacustrian village on piles at Unteruhidigen on Lake Constance in Germany is somewhat questionable, in that most of the Neolithic establishments were, in fact, situated on the shore in periods where the level of the lakes was lower than today. In southern England, the experimental farm at Butser includes several constructions, of which the most remarkable is a vast round house of the Iron Age. This replica is based on the very precise plan from the excavation of deposits of Pimperne in Dorset and measures 42 feet (13 meters) in diameter; its height could be

correctly determined by the imprints of the oblique posts that reinforced the roofing. The major technical problem was the construction of the roof which was resolved by making wood rings, over which were fixed batten strips (wattle work) daub and thatch. At Chassemy in the Aisne, an experimental archaeological center contains several Gallic-type buildings, including vast square house, built according to the observations from excavations at the site of Villeneuve-Saint-Germain (Aisne). The experimental center of Lejre, near Copenhagen, Denmark, contains an Iron Age village, rebuilt in the shelter of a palisade. The rebuilt houses have been constructed with appropriate materials and techniques, and their resistance to time and weather have been particularly well studied. One of the houses was even burned in order to analyze in detail the process of destruction and the archaeological traces of such an event. The protohistoric group built at Beskupin, Poland, is without doubt the most extraordinary. Thanks to the exceptional preservative conditions in the marshy terrain, the wooden architecture of this village of the first Iron Age can be studied in its minutest details over a vast excava-

Reconstruction of a Magdalenian deer hunter's tent, based on the evidence of a paleo-ethno-graphic excavation of the Pincevent site, the Grande Paroisse, (Seine-et-Marne, France). Ph. G. Gaucher.

tion site, which has been open for 50 years. The reconstructions erected on the site are impressive. The rampart in log cribs filled with earth, measures three meters wide and six meters high, rebuilt with a fortified gate. The rows of adjoining houses, made of logs, reveal the eminently sophisticated character of these wooden structures and the high degree of social and economic organization required for the building of such a village.

Agricultural Experiments

Numerous experiments have been conducted in order to understand ancient agricultural techniques and the development of cultivation outside of the main centers of domestication. The development of such experiments on large enough plots of land and with significant duration has required the creation of true prehistoric forms, such as those of Lejre in Denmark, started by H. O. Hansen, or that of Butser in England, started by P. J. Reynolds. In temperate Europe the first fields were opened at the heart of an immense leafy forest, as many polynological analyses of peat bogs reveal. Other than fire, the axe was the principal tool of clearing woods. Some handled-axe replicas have been made according to examples found in the lacustrian environment. Stone blades, which must be used with very acute cutting angles by making rude first cuts, permit the cutting down of a tree of 8 inches (20 cm) in 15 minutes. However, they are three times less efficient than bronze and five times less efficient than steel blades. Cultivation on cleared land for several types of ancient grains, such as wheat spelt has revealed some surprising yields in

the first year (nearly three fourths of a ton per acre, or 1.7 tons per hectare), but a very rapid decline is evident at the end of three years. The plowing of cleared parcels was first accomplished with digging sticks, spades or furrowing sticks, then with swing ploughs. A kind of swing plough, propelled by humans, dating to the Old Neolithic, has been found at Satrup Moar in Germany, comprised of a long stick whose spatulate end is perforated near the handle. Some attempts have been made with a copy, which made furrows of ½ to 2 inches (one-to-five centimeters) deep. Swing ploughs from the Bronze and Iron Ages were found in peat bogs, like that of Dostrup, Denmark, and replicas have been made, using also the data from numerous rupestrian engravings of northern Europe. Some paired oxen have been especially trained for the experiments of Hansen. With a yoke fixed behind the head by a collar (buckles at the horns), they developed an average traction force of 330 to 450 pounds (150 to 200 kilograms). The swing plough was thus practical only in light soils. Wooden ploughshares wear rapidly and one needs six of them to plow an acre (or half hectare). The use of crossed plowing permitted understanding the ancient patterns seen on several sites, as did the method of formation of the small earthen "Celtic" levies (1500 and 500 B.C.), which encircled the fields, that aerial archaeology has revealed in England and Holland. For the harvests, copies of flint or bronze sickles have been made, notably by A. Steensberg. The storage of seeds destined for later consumption was a major problem for the first agricultural communities. To avoid loss to bacterial agents, insects or rodents, the most frequently adopted solution was the use of subterranean silos, which represent one of the most numerous and widespread types of archaeological structures. Numerous experimental silos were built by P. J. Reynolds, who was able to demonstrate scientifically their efficiency. It is absolutely imperative that these pits be dry and watertight, thus their location on hills and their shape, narrowing at the top. Devices for recording temperatures, humidity and carbon gas allowed understanding of the mechanism permitting seeds to reach a state of dormancy. When the pit is well waterproofed, the seeds continue to breath until the atmosphere is anaerobic. If the temperature

Experimental Gallic farm at Chassemy *(Aisne, France) during construction, based on the findings in an excavation of the Villeneuve-Saint-Germain (Aisne). Ph. A. Coudart.*

Bronze Age swing plow
1. *Cross-shaped swing plow found at Hvorslev (Viborg, Denmark)*
2. *Arch-shaped swing plow found at Dostrup (Alborg, Denmark)*
3. *Detail of a swing plow*
4. *Rupestrian drawing of agricultural labor (Bohuslan, Sweden). Ph. Drawing by J. Jansen.*

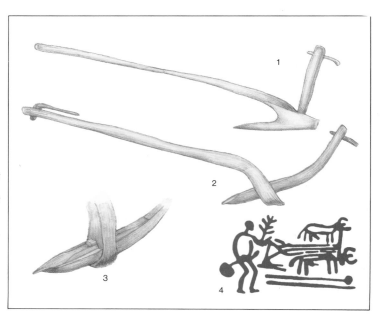

is then sufficiently low, the activity of the micro-organisms and molds is inhibited.

Raising Megalithic Blocks

The prehistoric megalithic monuments of the Old and New World fascinate archaeologists and engineers alike, who have pondered their construction. The shaping, transportation and erection of several ton-blocks by Stone Age tribes are challenges of the first order. Legendary explanations resorting to giants, mythic beings, or supernatural forces still find their adherents. When the problem is examined more closely, however, one sees that even the most massive megalith of the European Neolithic (the large broken menhir of Locmariaquer, Morbihan) and the statues of Easter Island only very rarely exceed 100 tons, which places them far behind certain Egyptian monuments. The great obelisk of Aswan weighs 1,168 tons and the two Colossi of Memnon each weigh 1,000 tons. The techniques of extraction, transportation and erection used by the Egyptians have been studied through the many ruins, pictographic representations and some texts. Simple techniques, such hammering the hard stones, the use of wooden wedges, elevation by levers, wedges or even inclined ramps, and the transportation on sleds or on wooden rollers, in most cases adequately responded to the technological problems posed. The efficiency of these activities has sometimes been the object of experiments. The erection of a statue on Easter Island, with its head attached, was accomplished by Heyerdahl, using levers and a sloping stone ramp so that the monolith swings onto its *ahu*, the platform. In England, a block of the same weight (three tons) as the blue stones of Stonehenge, was hauled on a sled with or without rollers by a team consisting of 24 to 32 people, directed by R. Atkinson. A similar experiment conducted by Jean-Pierre Mohen is one of the most significant: a block of 32 tons, equivalent to one of the slabs of the necropolis of Bougon (Deux-Sèvres), was hauled over a moveable system of wooden rollers. The 50-member hauling team succeeded in dragging the block more than 130 feet (40 meters) while other groups assisted with the movement of the rails and rollers. With the help of large levers, the same block was raised up to a yard (meter) in height. Besides the technical achievement, this experience revealed the importance of demographic, economic, psychological and political factors in the Neolithic societies that built the megaliths. By its multiple social implications this experiment offers a remarkable illustration of the rich contributions made by the experimental process of archaeology.

Reliving Prehistory

Although the recreation of technical feats remains the domain of experimental archaeological research, there are numerous other ways to recapture the experience of prehistoric life. To taste, after 2,500 years, a soup identical to the

Experimental Iron Age farm at Butser, Hampshire (Great Britain), started by P. Reynolds. Ph. A. Coudart.

one found in the stomach of a man from the peat bogs of Denmark, Sir Mortimer Wheeler and Glyn Daniels concocted a base of barley and linseed groats, with numerous other plant seeds. The mixture had a formidable taste! The attempt to call forth the sounds emitted by the horn of the Bronze Age of northern Europe proved fatal to R. Ball, an Irish archaeologist of the 19th century, who ruptured a cerebral vessel while trying to blow into one of these enormous bronze horns, whose hoarse sound can be heard several miles/kilometers away. The crafts of the artisan potters, metal casters, welders, and weavers have been recaptured by numerous archaeologists. Other researchers have transformed themselves for a time into a prehistoric people, taking subsistence only from the wild environment. Other attempts to relive the past have been made, notably in the United States by E. Callahan at the Pamunkey River in 1974–1975 where two successive teams survived by hunting, gathering and fishing, and by respecting scrupulously the techniques of the Middle Woodland age. In Holland, in the polder (land reclaimed from the sea) of Flevo, an experiment in Neolithic life was carried out by H. de Haas and a well-trained team. Although not without scientific interest, these limited-duration trials cannot entirely recapture the reality of the past. They simply permit us to record the practical response of modern people in an unusual environment, without yet revealing the cultural depths, forever lost, of these prehistoric societies.

Suggested Reading

Coles, J. M. *Archaeology by Experiment.* London: Hutchinson, 1973.

———. *Experimental Archaeology.* London: Academic Press, 1979.

Hansen, H. O. *The Prehistoric Village at Leijre.* Leijre (Netherlands): Historical-Archaeological Research Centre, 1977.

Heyerdahl, T. *The Kon-Tiki Expedition.* London: Allen and Unwin, 1950.

Keeley, L. H. *Experimental Determination of Stone Tool Uses.* Chicago: University of Chicago Press, 1980.

Reynolds, P. J. *Iron Age Farm: The Butser Experiment.* London: British Museum Publications, Ltd., 1979.

Transporting a 32-ton block of stone over logs, with the help of 200 people at Bougon (Deux-Sèvres). Ph. and experiment by J. P. Mohen.

Cave engravings from Tanum
(Sweden). Bronze Age (1500 B.C.).
Ph. Candelier-Brumaire-Artephot.

Chronology (C 14)	WESTERN EUROPE	CENTRAL AND EASTERN EUROPE	NORTH AFRICA SAHARA WESTERN AFRICA	CENTRAL, EAST AND SOUTH AFRICA	SOUTHWEST ASIA	CENTRAL ASIA INDIA
1000	Middle Ages		Iron in the Chad Basin			
	Antiquity	Rome	Iron in Niger, Nigeria, Great Lakes	Iron in Kenya, Uganda, Tanzania, Zambia, Rhodesia	Rome	
0	Iron Age	Iron Age		First farmers in equatorial forests	Empire of Alexander	Mauryan Empire (India) Scythians of the Steppes
−1500 −1000		Greece			Persian Empire Phoenicians	Iron in India Development of pastoralism
	Bronze Age	Bronze Age	Copper in Niger	Development of agriculture in East Africa		
−2800 −2000	Campaniforms	Mycenae	Tichitt	Carthage	Hittites Assyrians	Bactrian towns Harappan civilization (towns in India)
	Chalcolithic	Corded Ware Cultures	Neolithic	Pharaonic Empires	Akkad Sumer	Writing
−3800 −3000		Domestication of horses	Tenere			
	Walled villages	Central European Chalcolithic		Art of the Hunter-Gatherers in East Africa	Bronze Age	
−5000 −4000	First Megaliths					
	Ancient Neolithic (Agriculture, breeding, pottery)	Danubian Neolithic	Neolithic Mediterranean and Egyptian		Chalcolithic	Neolithic in Iran Caucasus, Turkoman Irrigation
−6000 −5000			Neolithic Saharan and Sudanese		Copper metallurgy Irrigation	
−6000	Tardenois	Agriculture, breeding (goats, cattle, pigs) in Greece in Eastern Mediterranean			Neolithic ceramics (sheep and goat husbandry)	Preceramic in Iran Afghanistan and Baluchistan
−7000	Sauveterrian		Ceramics		Neolithic Preceramic B (Agriculture: wheat, barley)	
−8000		Biface cultures des pointes à dos		Wiltonian	Neolithic Preceramic A	
−9000	Azilian		Caspian Neolithic			
		Late Gravettian complexes of the plains Mezin, Kostenki		Magosian	Natufian	Khandivli
10 000	Late Gravettian	Black Sea		Lupemban	Kaberian	
	Magdalenian					
	Solutrean	Epigravettian	Iberomaurusian		Atlitian	
20 000	Epigravettian		Sibilian			
	Gravettian	Pavlonian			Aurignacian	
30 000	Aurignacian (First artistic developments)	Aurignacian				
	Chatelperronian	Szeletian	Aterian	Stillbayan	Emiran	Angaran Culture
40 000						
					Amudian	
50 000						
	Mousterian (First tombs)	Mousterian	Mousterian	Fauresmithian	Jabrudian	
80 000				Mousteroid	Mousterian	Late Soan
100 000	Micoquian		Micoquian	Sangoan		
	Upper Acheulian	Upper Acheulian				Acheulian
200 000						Soan
300 000	Tayacian		Acheulian	Acheulian	Acheulian	
	Middle Acheulian	Middle Acheulian				
500 000	Clactonian					Pre-Soan
	Lower Acheulian	Lower Acheulian				
1 000 000	Pebble Cultures	Pebble Cultures	Lower Acheulian			
			Pebble cultures	Lower Acheulian	Pebble Cultures	
2 000 000				Oldowan		?
3 000 000				First humans First carved tools		

FAR EAST (CHINA, JAPAN, SOUTHEAST ASIA)	OCEANIA (GREAT AUSTRALIA) Tasmania	Australia	New Guinea	OCEANIA WESTERN PACIFIC	EASTERN PACIFIC	SOUTH AMERICA	MESO-AMERICA	NORTH AMERICA Eastern United States	Plains and Prairies	West Southwest Great Basin	Northwest Coast Interior Plateau	ARCTIC Alaska	Western	Chronology C 14	Sidereal Calendar scale
	Hunter-Gatherers			Horticulture and cultivation (without ceramics)		Empires / Moche Culture	Classic Maya civilization	Mississippian	Plains Village Tradition	maize cultivation (Southwest)	Northwest Coast Tradition	Eskimo Tradition	Eskimo Tradition	0	
...ron Age in China ...hou Period							urbanization	Diffusion of crops						−1 000	−1 500
...ronze Age ...China (Shang)						Chavin Culture (Peru)	Olmec civilization	Woodland Tradition	Woodland Tradition			Arctic Microblade Tradition	Arctic Microblade Tradition	−2 000	−2 800
Chinese Neolithic of ...ongshan		Small tools	Ceramics	Ceramics		Cities on Pacific Coast / Domestication of the llama	Formative / First known ceramics	Woodland Tradition			Northwest Coast Tradition			−3 000	−3 800
						First known ceramics	First known ceramics / Start of maize cultivation		Archaic Plains Tradition						
Chinese Neolithic of ...angshao			Horticulture			Cultivation of beans, squash and maize				Desert Tradition	Old Cordilleran Tradition	Northwest Microblade Tradition		−4 000	−5 000
Rice Culture? / Millet culture / Pig breeding						Horizon of foliated points	Horizon of pedunculated points		Big Game Hunting Tradition Paleo-Indian					−5 000	−6 000
North Chinese Neolithic	Pleistocene toolkit					Archaic		Archaic Tradition						−6 000	
Hunter-Gatherers ...China (Ancient Jomon)						Horizon of Lerma points				Paleo-Indian	Old Cordilleran Tradition		−7 000	
Hoabinnian ...Southeast Asia			Pre-horticulture								Paleo-Indian	−8 000	
						horizon à pointes "en queue de poisson"	Horizon of Folsom points	Big Game Hunting Tradition	Paleo-Indian					−9 000	
							Horizon of Clovis points	Paleo-Indian	Pre-projectile phase	Paleo-Indian				10 000	
Pre-Jomon Ceramic (Japan)	Marine regression					Horizon of Pre-projectile phase	Pre-projectile phase	Paleo-Indians			Pre-projectile phase	Pre-projectile phase	Pre-projectile phase	20 000	
	Pleistocene toolkit scrapers, dispersed pebbles, thick flakes, slight retouching							Pre-projectile phase						30 000	
Sen-Doki														40 000	
	SAHUL						?							50 000	
Culture of ...Igandong														80 000	
Ordos Culture														100 000	
...en Culture														200 000	
						First settlement								300 000	
Padjitanian														500 000	
														1 000 000	
Dispersed pebbles														2 000 000	

Principal prehistoric civilizations on five continents.

To represent the oldest phases of human history in this table, mankind's early origins have been greatly compressed (below column 4), due to the ancient origin and duration of this evolutionary process.

INDEX

Italic page numbers indicate illustrations.

A

Abbeville, 42, 46
Aborigines, 77–78, 137
Abri du Facteur, 49
Absolute chronology, 29
Abu Hureyra, 81
Acacus, 73, 82, 156, 158
Achaeans, 168
Achakar, 155
Achaemenids Empire, 106
Achenheim, 42
Acheulian civilization, 40–45, *44, 46*
Acorns,.117
Adena culture, 117, 119
Adrar Bous, 157
Adria, 174
Adzes, *137*, 147–148
Aegean, 9–10
Aegyptopithecus, 33
Aerial archaeology, 13
Aerial photography, *13*
Afghanistan, 83
Afontova Gora, 57
Africa, 151–164
  Acheulian civilization, 41
  agriculture, 158–160
  appearance of humans in, 9
  art, 72–74
  Aterian culture, 58
  cattle herders, 156–158
  chariots, 158
  evolution of primates, 31–36
  geographic and climatic determinants, 151–152
  Homo erectus, 40
  megalithism, 162–164
  Meghreb and Sahara Neolithic cultures, 153–156
  metallurgy, 160–162
  pottery, 82
  pre-dynastic Egypt, 152–153
Agadez, 160
Agriculture, 79–88
  Asia, 80–82
  Bronze Age Europe, 170
  Central and South America, 134–135
  China, 85–86
  Eastern Woodlands culture, 117
  Europe, 83–84, 86–88
  experimental archaeology and, 182–183
  India, 82–83
  Mesopotamia, 98–99
  Middle East, 81–82
  Neolithic Africa, 158–160
  Oceania, 140, 145
  pottery and, 82
  rise of civilization and, 10
  Southwest North America, 117
  Soviet Union (USSR), 84–85
Ahaggar, 82
Ahu, 149–150
Ai Bunar, 91
Ain Hanech, 40
Air, 82
Akjoujt, 160
Akkadian Empire, 101
Akmak Complex, 118
Akreijit, 155
Alaca Hüyük, 19, 106
Alacaluf Indians, 126
Alarnek, *120*
Alaska, 117–118
Albarracin region, 69
Alexander the Great, 100
Algeria, 40–41, 88, 155–156, 162
Ali Kosh, 82–83
Alloys, 100
Alpaca, 129–130
Alps, 71
Alsace, 168
Altamira Cave, *62*, 63
Altithermal, 111
Altonian, 111
Altyn Tepe, *84*, 105
"Alyampitin" points, 127
Amaranth, 134–135
Amber, 165, 167
Ambrona, 42, 46
Amekni, 153–154, 159
America—*See Central and South America; North America*
Amino acids, racemization of (dating method), 29
Amotape phase, 132
Amratian culture, 152

Amri, 104
Amur River, 74
Anaktuvuk Pass, 118
Anancus osiris, 40
Anasazi culture, 117
Anatolia, 74, 81–82
Anau, 95
Ancestor cults, 90, 149
Anderson-Gerfaud, P., 179
Andes, 128–129
Angles-sur-l'Anglin, *61*, 66
Animals, domestication of—*See Domestication of animals*
Anjira, 83
Ankara, 74
Anse-Amour, 119
Ansevich region, 71
Antelope, 68, 73, 152
Anthracology, 16, *16*
Anthropoids, 33
Aogashima Islands, 146
Aouker, 154
Apollo II, 73
Aq Kupruk, 83
Aquitaine, 54
Arago Cave, 29, *30*, 40
Arambourg, Camille, 40
Archaeology, experimental—*See Experimental archaeology*
Archaeomagnetism, 24
Archaic period, 117
Architecture—*See Dwellings; Temples; Villages*
Arctic, 119, 121
Arctic Microlithic tradition, 118–119, 121
Arcy-sur-Cure, 48
Ardeche, 66
Arene Candide, 84
Argentina, 76, 127, 131, 135
Argil sickle, 98
Aridos, 42
Arizona, 77,.117
Arlit, 157
Armadillos, 76
Armorica, 167
Arnhem, 77–78
Arrowheads
  Fell's Cave, *127*
  North America, *113*
  Sudan, *151*
Arsenic, 100
Art, 19–20, 61–78
  Africa, 72–74, 158
  Alaska, 118
  Altamira Cave, *62*
  Angles-sur l'Anglia, *61*
  Australian Aborigines, 77–78
  Bédeilhac Grotto, *67*
  Bronze Age Europe, 169–170
  Camonica Valley, *168*
  Cap-Blanc, *64*
  Caspian Neolithic, 156
  cave, of France and Spain, 64, 66–68
  Celtic, 176
  Central and South America, 130–132
  Chalcolithic, 96
  climatic changes and, 68–69
  conservation of sites, 78
  Djanet, *74*
  Dorset culture, 121
  El Castillo Cave, *66*
  Fetcani Glen shelter, *76*
  of great spaces, 74–77
  Iron Age Europe, 174
  La Marche Grotto, *68*
  Lascaux, *62*
  Merveilles, Vallée des, *78*
  in mountains, 70–71
  nature and, 62–63
  Niaux, *63*
  Nok culture, 160–161, *160–161*
  predynastic Egypt, 153
  Saharan cultures, 157–158
  Saint-Michel-d'Arudy, *67*
  Sao culture, *162*
  Sefar, *72*
  Sireuil, *71*
  Spanish Levantine shelters, 69–70
  Tassili, *156–157*
  techniques, 63–64
  Vitlycke, *70*
Asia, 41–42, 80–82—*See also Polynesia*
Asparn an der Zaya, Museum of, 181
Aspinall, A., 180
Assyrians, 161
Athabascan Indians, 119
Atkinson, R., 183
Atlanthropus, 40–41
Atlatl, 114
Aurignacian culture, 56–57, 64, 66
Aurochs, 69
Australia
  appearance of humans in, 10
  art, 77–78
  glacial period, 138–139
  settling of, 112, 137
Australopithecus, 9, 31, 34, 36–40

Australopithecus afarensis, 9, 34, 36, 38
Australopithecus africanus, 34, 36
Australopithecus boisei, 34
Australopithecus robustus, 34, 36
Austria, 172
Austronesian language, 140, 146
Autochthonism, 18
Avebury, 166
Avocado, 135
Axe, 45
Azilian culture, 57

B

Badarian culture, 152
Bad-Wurtemberg, 172
Bagzanes, Mount, 153
Baikal, Lake, 74, 85
Baja California, 132
Baldegg, 171
Ball, R., 184
Baltic, 167
Baluchistan, 83, 104
Bamboo, 145
Banana, 140, 145, 160
Banat, 169
Bania Buena, 134
Banpo site, *85*, 86, 104
Bantus, 159, 161–162
Barbary Horse, 158
Bardon, Abbé, 58
Bargas, 66
Baringo Lake, 32
Barley, 81, 84, 159, 170
Barnenez, Cairn of, 90
Basketry, 115
Basse Yurtz, 176
Bauchi plateau, 161
Bavaria, 165–166, 168, 172
Bazinas burial mounds, 162–163
Beans, 134–135, 160
Beaune Archaeological shelter, 180–181
Bédeilhac Grotto, 67, *67*
Bego, Mount, 63, 71, 169–170
Beidha, 81
Belgium, 168, 172
Bell Beaker culture, 165
Belle Isle Strait, 119
Beluga, 121
Benin, 160
Benoue, 161
Beothuc tribe, 119
Berbers, 158, 161
Beringia, 112
Bering Sea, 118, 121
Bering Strait, 109, 112, 122
Berries, 117
Beskupin, 181
Bessan, 175
Beta radiation, 26
Bhopal, 74
Biface, 45, *127*
Big Game Hunting tradition, 114, 117, 119
"Big Men," 95
Bilzingsleben, 40, 42
Birds, 76–77, 121, 169–170
Birmania, 42
Birnik culture, 118
Biskupin Lake, 171, *171*
Bison, 68–69, 114–116
Bison, great horned, *113*
Blacksmiths, 168–169
Blade punch, *177*
Blattspitzen, 54
Blot, Le, 49
Bluefish Cave, 114
Blue Nile, 152
Boars, 69
Boats, 179
Bodo, 32
Boghazköy, 106
Bogs, 87
Bohemia, 165, 172
Bolivia, 77
Bone industry, 45, 153, 155–156
Bongras, 81
Boomerang, 140
Boqueirao da Pedra Furada, *125*
Bordes, François, 11, 54, 177–178
Borholan, 173
Borkou, 154
Bos ibericus, 156
Bouar region, 163–164
Bouclier, 119
Boule, Marcellin, 52, 58
Bouqras, 82
Bourdeilles, 48–49
Bourgogne, 175
Bouriet, 50
Bouyssonia, Abbé, 58
Bovines, 69
Bows, 116, 118
Bray-les-Mareuil, *13*
Brazil, 127, 133–135
  appearance of humans in, 10
  cave art, 74–76, 130–131
  Paleolithic remains, 124–125

Breadfruit, 140, 145
Breuil, Abbé, 11, 50, 57, 69, 73–74
Brézillon, M., 107
British Columbia, 114–115
Brittany, 89–90, 166–167, 169
Brno, 55
Bronze Age
  Africa, 160, 162
  China, 105
  Europe, 165–171
  Mesopotamia, 100
  Scandinavia, 167
Buck, Peter, 140
Buffalo, 152
Buffalo, water, 145
Bulgaria, 83, 88, 91–92
Bull cults, 71, 169
Burgstallkogel, 172
Burgundy, 171
Burial customs—*See also Megalithism*
  Adena and Hopewell cultures, 117
  Africa, 162–164
  Bronze Age Europe, *167*
  Celtic, 176
  Chalcolithic, 96
  Great Plains, 116
  Iron Age Europe, 172–173
  Neandertal man, 58, 60
  North America, 115
  Oceania, 139
  predynastic Egypt, 152
  Saxony, 165
  Tumulus Grave culture, 167–168
  Western Subarctic, 119
Burial Mound period, 117
Burial sites
  social factors gleaned from, 19
  Upper Paleolithic, 58
Burins, 119
Burma, 86
Burren, *89*
Bushmen, 72
Butser experimental farm, 181–182, *183*
Bylany, 18, 84
Bylot Island, *120*, 121

C

Cagny-la-Garenne, 42
Cagny-l'Epinette, *46*
Calaforno, 90
California, 77, 113–116
California Valley tradition, 116
Callahan, E., 184
Camelids, 126, 130
Cameroon, 159, 161
Camonica Valley, 63, 71, 78, 169–170
Campaniform tradition, 166
Canals, 98
Canaques, 143
Can Hasan, 95–96
Cantabria, 66, 68
Canyon de Chelly, 77
Cap-Blanc, Le, *64*, 66
Cape Krusenstern, 118
Capelleti Cave, 156
Capibaras, 75–76
Capo di Ponte, 170
Capsian, 58
Carbon-14, 25–27, 114, 153
Carbonates, 16
Caribou, 112–114, 116, 121–122
Carnac, 89–90
Cartographic analyses, 13
Casablanca, 40
Cascade points, 114
Caspian Neolithic tradition, 155–156
Castille, 67
Catal-Hüyük, 62, *80*, 81–82
Catalan method, 162
Catarrhinians, 33
Cattle, 73, 156–158
Cavaillon, Jean, 38
Caves—*See specific cave*
Cavillon Cave, 60
Cayonu, 82
Celts, 172, 175–176
Central African Republic, 162–164
Central and South America, 10, 123–136
  agriculture, 134–135
  alpaca and llama, 129–130
  art, 130–132
  conquest of Andean highlands, 128–129
  fishing, 132
  hunting, 126–127, 132–134
  Pleistocene, 125–127
  settling of, 123–125
  villages, 135–136
  weapons and tools, 127–128
Central Asia, 105
Ceramics
  agriculture and, 82
  America, 107
  California, 116
  Chalcolithic, 96
  China, 86
  Danubian Neolithic, *83*